Can Africa Claim the 21ˢᵗ Century?

Can Africa Claim the 21ˢᵗ Century?

The World Bank
Washington, D.C.

Copyright © 2000 The International Bank for Reconstruction
and Development / The World Bank
1818 H Street, N.W.
Washington, D.C. 20433, U.S.A.

The World Bank holds the copyright on this report on behalf of all the institutions that contributed to its development—the African
Development Bank, African Economic Research Consortium, Global Coalition for Africa, United Nations Economic Commission for
Africa, and World Bank. Although the collaborating institutions endorse the main messages of the report, it does not necessarily reflect the
official views of these institutions or of their boards of directors or affiliated institutions.

ISBN: 0-8213-4495-1
Cover designed by Drew Fasick
Photo credits for cover: World Bank Photo Library

Library of Congress Cataloging-in-Publication (CIP) Data has been requested.

To order:
The World Bank
P.O Box 960
Herndon, VA 20172-0960 USA
Tel: 703 661-1580 or 1-800-645-7247
Fax: 703 661-1501
E-mail: books@worldbank.org
Web: www.worldbank.org/publications

Text printed on paper that conforms to the American National Standard
for Permanence of Paper for Printed Library Materials, Z39.48-1984

Contents

Figures

Tables

Foreword

Our central message is: Yes, Africa can claim the new century

THIS REPORT IS THE PRODUCT OF A COLLABORATIVE EFFORT THAT began in October 1998, when representatives of several institutions—including the African Development Bank, African Economic Research Consortium, Global Coalition for Africa, United Nations Economic Commission for Africa, and World Bank—met to initiate a study on Sub-Saharan Africa's prospects for economic and social development in the 21st century.

The question of whether Sub-Saharan Africa (Africa) can claim the 21st century is complex and provocative. This report does not pretend to address all the issues facing Africa or to offer definitive solutions to all the challenges in the region's future. Our central message is: Yes, Africa can claim the new century. But this is a qualified yes, conditional on Africa's ability—aided by its development partners—to overcome the development traps that kept it confined to a vicious cycle of underdevelopment, conflict, and untold human suffering for most of the 20th century.

The new century provides unique opportunities for Africa, and three emerging positive factors. The first is increasing political participation in Africa, opening the way to greater accountability and a new development discourse. Second, the end of the Cold War can help change Africa from a strategic and ideological battleground to a new business address for trade and development. Third, globalization and information and communications technology offer enormous opportunities for Africa to leapfrog stages of development.

This report proposes strategies for ushering in self-reinforcing processes of economic, political, and social development. Progress is crucial on four fronts:

- Improving governance and resolving conflict.
- Investing in people.
- Increasing competitiveness and diversifying economies.
- Reducing aid dependence and strengthening partnerships.

Africa is a diverse region. Some countries are caught in poverty and conflict—and where nation-building is failing, the prospects are cloudy.

Other countries, having implemented significant macroeconomic reforms, are ready to move forward with more comprehensive programs. Yet others are still grappling with basic reforms. There is no simple formula, but in facing enormous challenges, countries can draw on many positive examples. All countries, however, must commit to a coherent and comprehensive vision of development and nation-building.

Any "business plan" for putting in place this vision of development should be conceived, owned, and implemented by accountable governments, anchored in broad national consensus and supported by Africa's development partners. Claiming the future involves enormous challenges—not least of which is resolving the problems of the past. Much of Africa's recent economic history can be seen as a process of marginalization—first of people, then of governments. Reversing this process requires better accountability, balanced by economic empowerment of civic society—including women and the poor—and firms relative to governments, and of aid recipients relative to donors. Without this shift in power and accountability, it will be difficult to offer the incentives Africa needs to accelerate development and break free of poverty.

All countries must commit to a coherent and comprehensive vision of development and nation-building

Members of the Steering Committee

Ali A.G. Ali, United Nations Economic Commission for Africa
Tesfaye Dinka, Global Coalition for Africa
Ibrahim Ahmed Elbadawi, World Bank
Augustin Fosu, African Economic Research Consortium
Alan Gelb, World Bank
Kupukile Mlambo, African Development Bank

Acknowledgments

THIS REPORT IS THE JOINT PRODUCT OF FIVE COLLABORATING institutions, represented by a Steering Committee coordinated by Alan Gelb (World Bank) and composed of Ali A.G. Ali (United Nations Economic Commission for Africa), Tesfaye Dinka (Global Coalition for Africa), Ibrahim Ahmed Elbadawi (World Bank), Augustin Fosu (African Economic Research Consortium), and Kupukile Mlambo (African Development Bank). Under the supervision of the Steering Committee, the report was put together by a team headed by Alan Gelb and composed of Ali A.G. Ali, Tesfaye Dinka, Ibrahim Elbadawi, Charles Soludo, and Gene Tidrick. Ibrahim Elbadawi, assisted by John Randa and Charles Soludo, coordinated the project and acted as a secretary to the Steering Committee. Further support to the Steering Committee was provided by its associate members: Paul Collier, Guy Darlan, Beno Ndulu, Tchetche N'guessan (who also represented Centre Ivoirien de Recherches Economiques et Sociales), Waheed Oshikoya, Ademola Oyejide, Delphine Rwegasira, Neeta Sirur, Charles Soludo, and Gene Tidrick. Lishan Adam, Melvin Ayogu, Hans Binswanger, Nicholas Burnett, Michael Chege, Lionel Demery, Carol Lancaster, Brian Levy, Aileen Marshall, Robert Townsend, and Tshikala Bulalu Tsibaka contributed to the chapters.

Robert Calderisi, Christopher Delgado, Stephen Gelb, Gerry Helleiner, Benno Ndulu, Stephen O'Connel, Dani Rodrik, Elwaleed Taha, and Kerfalla Yansane provided detailed reviews of the manuscript. Meta de Coquereaumont, Paul Holtz, Molly Lohman, and Bruce Ross-Larson, of Communications Development Incorporated, edited the report and oversaw its layout and production. The report was laid out by Alan Thompson. Alex Bangirana, Nancy Lammers, and Randi Park, of the World Bank's Office of the Publisher, coordinated the cover design and printing.

As inputs to the chapters, 15 background papers were prepared and presented at a July 1999 research workshop in Abidjan, Côte d'Ivoire, hosted by the African Development Bank. The papers were written by Lishan Adam, Ali A.G. Ali, Ernest Aryeetey, Jean-Paul Azam, Hans Binswanger, Nicholas Burnett, Michael Chege, Paul Collier, Lionel Demery, Lual Deng, Stephen Devereux, Augustin Fosu, Alan Gelb,

Martin Greeley, Afeikhena Jerome, Carol Lancaster, Brian Levy, Taye Mengistae, Kupukile Mlambo, Njuguna Ndung'u, Waheed Oshikoya, Ademola Oyejide, Catherine Pattillo, Lemma Senbet, Robert Townsend, Tshikala Bulalu Tshibaka, and Howard White. Useful comments were provided by Shimeles Abebe, Regina O. Adutwum, Nick Amin, Alexander Amuah, Patrick Asea, Melvin Ayougu, M.J. Balogun, Tesfaye Dinka, Josue Dione, Abdul-Ganiyu Garba, Abdalla Hamdock, Jeffrey Herbst, Gerard Kambou, Louis Austin Kasekende, Kamran Kousari, Patience Bongiwe Kunene, Tundu Antiphas Lissu, Hailu Mekonnen, Sipho S. Moyo, Keith Muhakanizi, Harris Mule, Andrew K. Mullei, Tchetche N'guessan, Delphin Rwegasira, Affiong Southey, John Strauss, Gabre Michael Woldu, and Kelly Zidana.

The first draft of the report was discussed in December 1999 at two workshops hosted by the African Economic Research Consortium in Nairobi, Kenya. The first workshop solicited views from African stakeholders (practitioners and policymakers); the second gathered comments from researchers. Useful discussions and able moderation at the meetings were contributed by Oladipupo O. Adamolekun, Degefe Befekado, Abdallah Bujra, Micha Cheserem, Getachew Demeke, Kammogne Fokam, Rachel Gesami, Alan Hisrch, Mwangi Kimenyi, Nguyuru Lipumba, Nehemia Ng'eno, Germano Mwabu, Dominique Njinkeu, Benson Obonyo, Abena Oduro, Hezron Nyangito, Brian de Silva, and Albert Tavodjre. Sections of the report were also discussed in Addis Ababa, Ethiopia, at seminars with the United Nations Economic Commission for Africa and the Organization of African Unity, and in Johannesburg, South Africa, as part of a conference organized by the Trade and Industrial Policy Secretariat. The final dissemination of the report occurred at the May 2000 annual meeting of the African Development Bank in Addis Ababa.

Catherine Gwin, Kim Jaycox, Massoud Karshenas, Nicholas Minot, Machiko Nissanke, Howard Pack, Jim Tybout, Adrian Wood, and William Zartman led discussions at an Africa seminar series—organized by Shantanaya Devarajan and Ibrahim Elbadawi—in support of the project during its early stages. Other colleagues in the collaborating institutions contributed to these discussions and provided input. Many other colleagues, not mentioned here, have made valuable contributions and given support and encouragement.

Claudia Carter, assisted by Jocelyn A. Schwartz and Choye Yee, provided logistical support and assisted with the management of the project. John Randa and Satya Yalamanchili provided research support.

The Steering Committee would also like to acknowledge the generous support of the Swiss and Dutch governments, and of the Canadian International Development Agency, which translated the study into French.

The responsibility for this report remains with the Steering Committee of this project. Although the collaborating institutions endorse the main messages of the report, it does not necessarily reflect the official views of these institutions or of their boards of directors or affiliated institutions.

Summary

ESPITE GAINS IN THE SECOND HALF OF THE 1990s, Sub-Saharan Africa (Africa) enters the 21st century with many of the world's poorest countries. Average income per capita is lower than at the end of the 1960s. Incomes, assets, and access to essential services are unequally distributed. And the region contains a growing share of the world's absolute poor, who have little power to influence the allocation of resources.

Moreover, many development problems have become largely confined to Africa. They include lagging primary school enrollments, high child mortality, and endemic diseases—including malaria and HIV/AIDS—that impose costs on Africa at least twice those in any other developing region. One African in five lives in countries severely disrupted by conflict.

Making matters worse, Africa's place in the global economy has been eroded, with declining export shares in traditional primary products, little diversification into new lines of business, and massive capital flight and loss of skills to other regions. Now the region stands in danger of being excluded from the information revolution.

Many countries have made important economic reforms, improving macroeconomic management, liberalizing markets and trade, and widening the space for private sector activity. Where these reforms have been sustained—and underpinned by civil peace—they have raised growth and incomes and reduced poverty. Even as parts of the region are making headlines with wars and natural disasters, other parts are making headway with rising interest from domestic and foreign businesses and higher investment.

But the response has not been sufficient to overcome years of falling income or to reverse other adverse legacies from the long period of economic decline—including deteriorated capacity, weakened institutions,

Major changes are needed if Africans—and their children—are to claim the 21st century

and inadequate infrastructure. Major changes are needed if Africans—and their children—are to claim the 21ˢᵗ century. With the region's rapidly growing population, 5 percent annual growth is needed simply to keep the number of poor from rising. Halving severe poverty by 2015 will require annual growth of more than 7 percent, along with a more equitable distribution of income.

Moreover, Africa will not be able to sustain rapid growth without investing in its people. Many lack the health, education, and access to inputs needed to contribute to—and benefit from—high growth. Women are one of Africa's hidden growth reserves, providing most of the region's labor, but their productivity is hampered by widespread inequality in education and access. Thus gender equality can be a potent force for accelerated poverty reduction. And HIV/AIDS looms as a new menace, threatening to cut life expectancy by 20 years and undermine savings, growth, and the social fabric in many countries.

Africa thus faces an immense, multifaceted development challenge. But the new century offers a window of opportunity to reverse the marginalization of Africa's people—and of Africa's governments, relative to donors, in the development agenda. Political participation has increased sharply in the past decade, paving the way for more accountable government, and there is greater consensus on the need to move away from the failed models of the past. With the end of the Cold War, Africa is no longer an ideological and strategic battleground where "trusted allies" receive foreign assistance regardless of their record on governance and development. Globalization and new technology, especially information technology, offer great potential for Africa, historically a sparsely populated, isolated region. Though these factors also pose risks, including that of being left further behind, these are far outweighed by the potential benefits.

Making these benefits materialize will require a "business plan" conceived and owned by Africans, and supported by donors through coordinated, long-term partnerships. African countries differ widely, so there is no universal formula for success. But many countries face similar issues, and can draw on positive African examples of how to address them.

Improving governance and resolving conflict is perhaps the most basic requirement for faster development. Widespread civil conflicts impose enormous costs, including on neighboring countries. Contrary to popular belief, Africa's conflicts do not stem from ethnic diversity. Rather, in a pattern found around the world, conflicts are driven by poverty, underdevelopment, and lack of economic diversification, as well as by political

Improving governance and resolving conflict is perhaps the most basic requirement for faster development

2

systems that marginalize large parts of the population. But conflicts perpetuate poverty, creating a vicious circle that can be reversed only through special development efforts—including long-run peacebuilding and political reforms. With success in these areas, countries can grow rapidly, and flight capital can return.

Countries that have made the greatest gains in political participation are also those with better economic management. Again, this conforms to a global pattern that suggests multiethnic states can grow as fast as homogeneous ones—if they sustain participatory political systems. Many countries need to develop political models that facilitate consensus building and include marginalized groups.

Development programs need to be win-win, improving the management and distribution of economic resources and contributing to more effective states. Programs should empower citizens to hold governments accountable, enable governments to respond to new demands, and enforce compliance with the economic and political rules of the game. Development efforts are starting to move in this direction, with greater beneficiary involvement in the delivery of services and more emphasis on results. But far more needs to be done to strengthen Africa's institutions—including ensuring that representative institutions, such as parliaments, play their proper role in economic and budgetary oversight.

Investing in people is also essential for accelerated poverty reduction. Many countries are caught in a trap of high fertility and mortality, low education (especially of women—less than one-quarter of poor rural girls attend primary school), high dependency ratios, and low savings. In addition, greater political commitment is urgently needed to fight HIV/AIDS.

While the resources available for education and health are inadequate in some countries, many need to translate their existing commitment to human development into effective programs for delivering essential services and increasing gender equality. Africa has some of the world's strongest communities, yet services are usually provided through weak, centralized institutions that are seen as remote and ineffective by those they are supposed to serve. Deconcentrated service delivery through local communities, supported by capacity building at local levels and effective governance to ensure transparency and empower recipients, could have a major impact. With effective regional cooperation and donor support through coordinated, long-term partnerships—including for international public goods such as new vaccines—Africa could solve its human development crisis in one generation.

Investing in people is also essential for accelerated poverty reduction

3

Increasing competitiveness and diversifying economies must be a third area of focus if Africa is to claim the new century. Job creation is slow not because of labor market rigidities (though there are exceptions) but because of the high perceived risks and costs of doing business in Africa. These need to be lowered by locking in reforms and delivering business services more efficiently—with less corruption, better infrastructure and financial services, and increased access to the information economy. Africa trails the world on every dimension of these essentials. Lowering these barriers requires new approaches, including more participation by the private sector and by local communities, a more regional approach to overcome the problems posed by small African economies, and a central government shift to regulating and facilitating services rather than providing them.

Though Africa's agriculture has responded to limited reforms, it remains backward and undercapitalized, the result of centuries of extractive policies. Recapitalizing the sector will require maintaining and improving price incentives (including by encouraging competitive input markets), channeling more public spending and foreign aid to rural communities (including for local infrastructure), and tapping into the savings potential of farmers. These changes are also needed to create incentives to reverse severe environmental degradation. Public-private partnerships can make a contribution, including in agricultural research and extension, where a regional approach would also help. And wider access to OECD markets for agricultural products would make a big difference—at some $300 billion, subsidies to OECD agriculture are equal to Africa's GDP.

Since the late 1960s Africa's loss of world trade has cost it almost $70 billion a year, reflecting a failure to diversify into new, dynamic products as well as a falling market share for traditional goods. Africa's trade reforms have mostly been negotiated with donors as part of adjustment programs. Reforms still need to be embedded in a development strategy that is export oriented, anchored on competitive and stable real exchange rates, and enables exporters to access imported inputs at world prices. Governments need to increase consultations with business, working to develop world-class service standards. Here again a regional approach is vital, not only to encourage intra-African trade flows but perhaps more important, to provide a wider platform to encourage investment. And African countries need to work together to participate in the global negotiations that shape the world trading system. The capacity requirements for this are too great for small, poor countries.

Increasing competitiveness and diversifying economies must be a third area of focus if Africa is to claim the new century

Reducing aid dependence and strengthening partnerships will have to be a fourth component of Africa's development strategy. Africa is the world's most aid-dependent and indebted region. Concessional assistance is essential if Africa is to grow rapidly while also increasing consumption to reduce poverty. Excluding private inflows, the savings gap for a typical country is about 17 percent of GDP, and other regions show that private flows cannot be sustained at more than 5 percent of GDP without risk of crisis. But aid, particularly when delivered in a weak institutional environment by large numbers of donors with fragmented projects and requirements, can weaken institutional capacity and undermine accountability.

High debt and debt service add to the problem, deterring private investment and absorbing core budget resources, making governments ever more "cash poor" but "project rich," with a development agenda increasingly perceived as being shaped by donors. Lack of selectivity compounds the problem, channeling a lot of aid to countries with poor development policies. And with few exceptions, aid has largely been confined to national boundaries rather than used to stimulate regional and international public goods.

These problems are widely recognized, and a consensus has emerged that the primary goal of aid should be to reduce poverty. But paradoxically, aid transfers are declining just when many of the problems are being addressed. Africa enters the new century in the midst of intense debate on aid, including what could be a watershed change in its relationship with the World Bank and International Monetary Fund, as well as important changes in development cooperation with the European Union and an enhanced program of debt relief. New aid relationships are being implemented in a number of countries—relationships that emphasize a holistic, country-driven approach supported by donors on the basis of long-term partnerships, and with greater beneficiary participation and empowerment over the use of resources.

The change is in the right direction, but there is a long way to go. In a typical poor country aid transfers might equal 10 percent of GDP, yet the poorest fifth of the population disposes of only about 4 percent of GDP. It remains to be seen how well partnerships can resolve the tensions between the objectives of recipients and individual donors, and how far the behavior of donors will change to facilitate African ownership of its development agenda. It also remains to be seen how far partnerships can extend beyond assistance, to include enhanced opening of world markets to African products and services.

Reducing aid dependence and strengthening partnerships will have to be a fourth component of Africa's development strategy

CHAPTER 1

Can Africa Claim the 21st Century?

SUB-SAHARAN AFRICA (AFRICA) ENTERED THE 20TH CENTURY a poor, mostly colonialized region. As it enters the 21st, a lot has changed. Education has spread, and life expectancy has increased. Many countries have seen gains in civil liberties and political participation. Since the mid-1990s there have been signs that better economic management has started to pay off in many countries, with rising incomes and exports and, in some cases, decreases in severe poverty. Even as part of the region is making headlines with crises and conflicts, other countries are making headway with steady growth, rising investment, increasing exports, and growing private activity. Africa's countries are diverse in many ways, including history and culture, incomes, natural endowments, and human resources. And in considering Africa's potential, it is worth remembering that the region contains Botswana, one of the world's fastest-growing economies in recent decades.

Africa's diverse economies reveal opportunities—and challenges

The Challenge of African Development

STILL, AFRICA FACES ENORMOUS DEVELOPMENT CHALLENGES. Excluding South Africa, the region's average income per capita averaged just $315 in 1997 when converted at market exchange rates (table 1.1). When expressed in terms of purchasing power parity (PPP)—which takes into account the higher costs and prices in Africa—real income averaged one-third less than in South Asia, making Africa the poorest region in the world. The region's total income is not much more than Belgium's, and is divided among 48 countries with median GDP of just over $2 billion—about the output of a town of 60,000 in a rich country.

Unlike other developing regions, Africa's average output per capita in constant prices was lower at the end of the 1990s than 30 years before—and in some countries had fallen by more than 50 percent (figure 1.1). In real terms fiscal resources per capita were smaller for many countries than in the late 1960s. Africa's share of world trade has plummeted since the 1960s: it now accounts for less than 2 percent of world trade. Three decades ago, African countries were specialized in primary products and highly trade dependent. But Africa missed out on industrial expansion and now risks being excluded from the global information revolution. In contrast to other regions that have diversified, most countries in Africa are still

Africa's share of world trade has plummeted since the 1960s

Table 1.1 Population, Income, and Economic Indicators by Region

Indicator	Africa excluding South Africa	Africa	South Asia	East Asia	Latin America
Population					
Population (millions), 1997	575	612	1,281	1,751	494
Population growth (percent), 1997	2.9	2.9	1.8	1.2	1.6
Dependency ratio (workers age 15–64 per dependent)	1.1	1.1	1.4	2.0	1.7
Urban population share (percent), 1997	31.1	31.7	26.6	32.2	73.7
Urban population growth (percent), 1997	5.2	4.9	3.3	3.7	2.2
Income					
GNP per capita (dollars, at market exchange rates), 1997	315	510	380	970	3,940
PPP GNP per capita, 1997	1,045	1,460	1,590	3,170	6,730
Gini index, latest year available	45.9	46.5	31.2	40.6	51.0
Economy					
GDP per capita, 1970[a]	525	546	239	157	1,216
GDP per capita, 1997[a]	336	525	449	715	1,890
Investment per capita, 1970[a]	80	130	48	37	367
Investment per capita, 1997[a]	73	92	105	252	504
Exports per capita, 1970[a]	105	175	14	23	209
Exports per capita, 1997[a]	105	163	51	199	601
Savings/GDP (percent), 1970	18.1	20.7	17.2	22.3	27.1
Savings/GDP (percent), 1997	16.3	16.6	20.0	37.5	24.0
Exports/GDP (percent), 1970	36.4	32.1	5.9	14.6	17.2
Exports/GDP (percent), 1997	33.0	31.0	11.4	27.8	31.8
Genuine domestic savings/GDP (percent), 1997	2.8	3.4	7.1	29.7	12.1
Incremental output-capital ratio (percent), 1970–97	12	10	23	23	14

Note: PPP stands for purchasing power parity.
a. 1987 dollars.
Source: World Bank data.

Figure 1.1 Change in GDP Per Capita, 1970–97

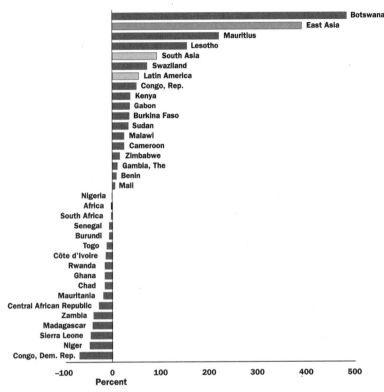

A few countries have gained, but many have lost

Note: Measured in constant local currency. Regional estimates are weighted by population.
Source: World Bank data.

largely primary exporters. They are also aid dependent and deeply indebted. Net transfers from foreign assistance average 9 percent of GDP for a typical poor country—equivalent to almost half of public spending and far higher than for typical countries in other regions. By the end of 1997 foreign debt represented a burden of more than 80 percent of GDP in net present value terms.

Africa is the only major region to see investment and savings per capita decline after 1970. Averaging about 13 percent of GDP in the 1990s, the savings rate of the typical African country has been the lowest in the world. Rapid population growth and environmental degradation compound the low savings. Estimates of genuine domestic savings (Hamilton and Clemens 1999), which capture the effects of resource depletion, are just 3 percent for Africa (see table 1.1). This is far below the genuine savings rates for other regions, though they too suffer from severe environmental degradation and resource overuse. And it is far below what is needed to sustain a major long-term boost in economic performance.

Africa's development challenges go deeper than low income, falling trade shares, low savings, and slow growth. They also include high inequality, uneven access to resources, social exclusion, and insecurity. Income inequality is as high as in Latin America, making Africa's poor the poorest of the poor. More than 40 percent of its 600 million people live below the internationally recognized poverty line of $1 a day, with incomes averaging just $0.65 a day in purchasing power parity terms. The number of poor people has grown relentlessly, causing Africa's share of the world's absolute poor to increase from 25 to 30 percent in the 1990s.

Because of high income inequality, Africa's poor are the poorest of the world's poor

Many people lack the capabilities—including health status, education, and access to basic infrastructure—needed to benefit from and contribute to economic growth. Health and life expectancy indicators are adverse, even taking into account low incomes: in many countries 200 of every 1,000 children die before the age of 5. Large parts of the population are locked in a dynastic form of poverty, progressively less able to escape because children lack the basic capabilities to participate in a productive economy—and so to contribute to growth. Despite recent gains, more than 250 million of Africa's people lack access to safe water. More than 200 million have no access to health services. In the only region where nutrition has not been improving, more than 2 million children a year die before their first birthday. More than 140 million youth are illiterate, and less than one-quarter of poor, rural females attend primary school. Disparities in social spending between poor African countries and rich industrial countries are massive. Education spending in poor African countries averages less than $50 a year—compared with more than $11,000 in France and the United States. Many Africans are excluded from basic services—and from the power to influence the allocation of resources.

Malaria typifies the tendency of many formerly global problems of basic development to have become mainly African. At the turn of the 20th century, Africa saw 223 deaths a year from malaria per 100,000 people, only slightly more than other developing regions. By 1970 the rate had fallen to 107 in Africa, compared with only 7 in other regions. But while the decline has continued elsewhere, the death rate has soared again in Africa to 165 per 100,000. Social upheaval and civil wars, a breakdown of health services in many countries, and growing resistance to anti-malarial drugs are to blame (*The Washington Post*, 20 October 1999).

Then there is the HIV/AIDS pandemic. With 70 percent of the world's cases in Africa, AIDS has already had an enormous impact on life expectancy in the countries most affected. It is projected to reduce life expectancy by up to 20 years from today's modest levels—more than erasing the gains since the 1950s. AIDS orphans already make up 11 percent of the population in the most afflicted countries. This could rise to more than 16 percent in the next 25 years, with disastrous implications for traditional social structures. The ultimate economic impact of AIDS, not yet fully known, promises to be devastating.

Without action, Africa's problems will only worsen

Unless action is taken, the scale of these problems will only increase. Population growth continues to be faster than in other regions, so primary school cohorts will continue to grow rather than shrink as in most parts of the world. For every potential worker between 15 and 64, Africa now has almost one dependent, almost all of them young (see table 1.1). Even with a progressive demographic transition, Africa's dependency rates will fall only gradually through the next century.

These aren't the only hurdles. The spread of conflict threatens economic and social progress. At least one African in five lives in a country severely disrupted by an ongoing war. Governance issues loom large in explaining the economic record of African countries. If present trends continue, few countries are likely to achieve the International Development Goals for 2015 endorsed by the international development community—goals covering poverty reduction, health, education, gender equality, and environmental preservation (OECD 1996). Indeed, economic performance will have to improve just to keep the number of absolute poor from increasing.

Africa Can Claim the Century—with Determined Leadership

In view of all this, what does "claiming the century" actually mean? Is it a credible objective for Africans—and for their children? Economists (and social scientists more broadly) are not known for their ability to predict short-term developments, let alone provide a vision of societies one hundred years into the future. A more modest approach would be to ask how, over the next few decades, Africa can reverse years of social and economic marginalization in an increasingly dynamic and competitive world, and so be well placed, after the early decades of the century, to take advantage of the rest.

As described below, simply preventing an increase in the number of absolute poor over the next 15 years will require annual growth rates in

11

excess of 5 percent, almost twice those of the dismal decades after 1973. And reaching the International Development Goal of halving the incidence of severe poverty by 2015 will require annual growth of 7 percent or more—and a better distribution of income. If Africa's terms of trade continue to deteriorate as they have for many countries since the late 1960s, the growth requirement for reducing poverty will be even higher.

Is the goal of reducing poverty impossible? Not at all. Africa is not doomed by its poverty or its poor development record. In the 1960s and early 1970s many prominent economists considered Asian countries, with their vast, poverty-stricken populations and limited resources, to be caught in a low-level development trap. It was inconceivable in the early 1960s that the Republic of Korea would emerge as an industrial power. The passing of time has shown how wrong such views were. The performance of other regions, the findings of cross-country studies, and the achievements of a number of African countries suggest that reversing the increase in poverty is possible.

Trends in Africa will need to change radically for a catchup process to materialize. This will require determined leadership within Africa. It will require better governance—developing stable and representative constitutional arrangements, implementing the rule of law, managing resources transparently, and delivering services effectively to communities and firms. It will require greater investment in Africa's people, as well as measures that encourage private investment in infrastructure and production. It will not happen without an increase in investment and efficiency. And it will require better support—and perhaps more support—from the international development community.

In facing these challenges, Africa has enormous unexploited potential—in resource-based sectors and in processing and manufacturing. It also has hidden growth reserves in its people—including the potential of its women, who now provide more than half of the region's labor but lack equal access to education and factors of production. African economies can perform far better. The region has great scope for more effective use of its resources—public and private, financial and human— and much scope for improving the delivery of the essential services needed to upgrade the capabilities and health of its people and increase their opportunities.

Even with better prioritization, the range of urgent challenges will strain Africa's limited capacity to make and implement policies and to nurture strong institutions. But the sheer number of challenges is not insurmount-

Africa has enormous unexploited potential and hidden growth reserves

able. Development processes are cumulative, with success in one area opening up opportunities in others. Like other developing regions, Africa can benefit from "virtuous circles" involving different aspects of development.

It will not be easy. Required is a major effort by Africans and their development partners to reverse the economic marginalization and exclusion of recent decades. That will take more than changing the allocation of resources. It will require greater economic empowerment and greater responsibility—a shift in the power of decisionmaking on allocating and managing resources so that excluded groups can take more responsibility and be held accountable for their use. Moreover, this deeper reform agenda will need to build on the democratization that has marked the region since the early 1990s—in a way that strengthens the formation of effective and representative states. Economic empowerment is critical for four groups:

Reform will need to build on the democratization that has marked the region since the early 1990s

- *Civil society.* For economic empowerment to keep pace with increased political participation, governments need to include civil society in ways that surmount the problems associated with Africa's highly multiethnic states. Instruments of accountability need to be institutionalized. This process—an essential part of the formation of states able to provide for sustainable development—is gathering momentum in some of the region's more advanced reformers.
- *The poor and the excluded.* Deep deprivation and systemic exclusion, including gender discrimination, require strategic and proactive remedies, often at the community level. If pervasive inequalities are not addressed—in incomes and in access to human development services and essential infrastructure—growth will not be sustainable and will not reduce poverty.
- *Producers.* Many African governments still have an uneasy relationship with business, which suffers under poor services and regulations that raise costs, contribute to perceptions of high risk, and discourage investment. An essential part of empowering civil society must be to involve producers—in agriculture and other sectors—to foster higher productivity and more effective competition in global markets. Without strong producers, it will be impossible to reverse past trends and shift from aid dependence to trade dependence.
- *Governments.* Building on the movement toward participatory government in the 1990s, African states need to be strengthened and given the power and accountability for development outcomes. This will

require a fundamental change from Africa's donors because Africa's governments are one of the excluded groups: with high aid dependence, in many countries development policy is seen as being the prerogative of donors rather than governments. Africa's interests also need to be articulated more effectively in global forums, especially those dealing with trade and investment.

The many positive examples of African development show how some countries are approaching common issues

Within Africa there has been increasing research, analysis, and rethinking on these issues. Consensus has emerged on the failures of past policies, though there is still debate on how best to move forward and a sense that the region still needs to find its place in the world economy. Africa has been experiencing its own Renaissance, in the true sense of a rebirth of thought on governance and development policies, particularly in the context of an increasingly globalized and competitive world. This is not surprising: some 70 percent of today's Africans were born after the end of colonialism, and that proportion is rising rapidly.

Donors have also been reevaluating their role, especially since the end of the Cold War reduced the imperative to fund loyal allies rather than support effective development states. Donors have entered the new century in the midst of a feverish debate on how to make aid more effective, including a watershed change in the Bretton Woods institutions—the World Bank and the International Monetary Fund, widely seen as the main external architects of Africa's economic policies.

This report selects a number of areas that seem important in answering the question of whether Africa can claim the 21st century. It brings together the implications of this recent body of work—particularly that emanating from Africa. It does not claim to be exhaustive. Nor does it attempt to lay out a blueprint for individual countries. But it draws on the many positive examples of African development to show how some countries are approaching common issues. African economies and subregions are diverse, and each will have to find its way to address the challenges of the 21st century.

How Fast Must Africa Grow to Reduce Poverty?

The International Development Goals for the 21st century—adopted by the global development community and endorsed by many developing country governments—set targets for poverty reduction, education, health, gender equality, and environmental sustainability for 2015

(OECD 1996). Here we concentrate on one goal: halving the incidence of absolute poverty, defined by the international poverty line of $1 a person per day, from current levels.

Growth is not sufficient for poverty reduction, but it is essential—no country has achieved a sustained improvement in the economic fortunes of its citizens without substantial, as well as broadly based, increases in income. Indeed, where growth has been sustained and has increased consumption, poverty in African countries has been reduced (chapter 3). How growth affects poverty also depends on how it is distributed. Especially with Africa's high income inequality, it is essential that growth be broadly based rather than narrow. But while cross-country evidence shows a wide range of variation between changes in income levels and distribution, it finds a neutral overall relationship between growth rates and inequality. So, income distribution is assumed here to be constant.

Growth is not sufficient for poverty reduction, but it is essential

The performance needed to halve the incidence of absolute poverty depends on the period in which it is to be achieved. Demery and Walton (1998) consider a period of 25 years, corresponding to the interval between the latest data available (for 1990) when the goals were formulated and 2015. This also produces a useful minimal criterion for Africa. The region's population is doubling every 25 years at current growth rates, so achieving this target would mean that the absolute number of absolute poor is neither increasing nor falling. To achieve this minimum goal, consumption per capita would need to rise by almost 2 percent a year. With a constant savings rate, GDP would need to grow by 4.7 percent a year. But savings rates are too low to sustain the investment needed for rapid growth. Adding in an increase in the savings rate of 10 percentage points spread over 25 years suggests a target GDP growth rate of 5 percent a year just to prevent an increase in the number of the poor. Only a few African countries, including Botswana, Mauritius, and Uganda, sustained such growth rates in the 1990s—and a recent evaluation suggests that few countries have the conditions and resources to sustain such growth in the long run (UNECA 1999).

But the growth hurdle to halving poverty by 2015 is now far higher because, on average, income and consumption levels did not rise in the 1990s. Including the projected increase in savings, the average GDP growth needed would be more than 7 percent a year. And if Africa's terms of trade continue to deteriorate, or if the savings provided by foreign assistance continue to fall, the growth requirement will be even greater.

Africa's growth goal is higher than those for other regions for several reasons. First, consumption per capita needs to rise rapidly because of low

*Savings must increase
while also allowing
consumption to rise fast
enough to reduce poverty*

incomes, large numbers of poor people, and a very high poverty gap. Second, Africa's population growth rate is the highest in the world. Unlike other regions—particularly East Asia, where the ratio of working-age population to dependents has risen sharply to around two to one—Africa's dependency ratio has remained close to one (see table 1.1). There are signs that Africa is embarking on a demographic transition, and some projections foresee a considerable decline in the dependency ratio in the middle of the 21st century. But today sharply lower fertility rates are limited to a small group of middle-income countries with far better reproductive health care, far higher contraceptive prevalence, and far higher health spending than the rest of the region (table 1.2).

A third factor raising the growth hurdle for Africa is the need to increase savings while also allowing consumption to rise fast enough to reduce poverty. Higher savings and investment are not sufficient for growth—the productivity of investment, as captured by the long-run incremental output-capital ratio, needs to double to place Africa on the same trajectory as fast-growing regions (see table 1.1). Africa can call on some hidden reserves. Countries can grow for a period with moderate investment rates when recovering from extremely depressed conditions, such as those caused by extended conflict. And reversing Africa's massive capital flight—estimated at almost 40 percent of private savings in the early 1990s (table 1.3)—could boost domestic savings.

Even so, in the long run investment rates would need to be sustained at around 30 percent for an extended period if growth is to make a major dent in poverty. Both agriculture and industry are severely decap-

Table 1.2 Indicators of a Demographic Transition in Africa by Income Group

Indicator	Lowest	Low	Middle	All
Fertility (percent), 1990	6.5	6.1	4.4	6.1
Fertility (percent), 1995	6.2	5.3	3.3	5.7
Infant mortality (per 1,000 live births), 1990	108	87	59	97
Infant mortality (per 1,000 live births), 1995	101	80	55	90
Maternal mortality (per 100,000)	1,015	606	277	822
Contraceptive prevalence (percent)	8	20	62	17
Health spending per capita (dollars), 1990–96	7.25	22.73	162.59	30.80
Public	3.19	9.58	71.99	11.22
Private	4.06	13.15	90.60	19.58

Note: Lowest-income countries are less than $300 per capita. Low-income countries are $300–765 per capita. Middle-income countries are more than $765 per capita.
Source: World Bank data.

italized. Estimates place levels of capital per worker at half those in South Asia (see table 1.3). Degraded infrastructure has emerged as a critical barrier to growth as other impediments have been relaxed by reforms (chapter 5). With costs up to three times world levels, transport now poses a potent obstacle to internal and external economic integration. Africa's economy is unusually sparse, with GDP per hectare one-sixth or less its value in other regions, so high transport costs are partly the result of geography. But in contrast to global transport costs, which have fallen continuously with deregulation and new technology, costs in Africa have risen because of poor road maintenance, regulatory barriers to competition, and, in some cases, long delays, heavy transit dues, and high taxes on vehicles and fuels. Power is another infrastructure barrier in countries that sustain growth, such as Uganda. Firms' investments in generators can consume more than one-third of their capital formation (Reinikka and Svensson 1998). Inadequate yet costly

Degraded infrastructure has emerged as a critical barrier to growth

Table 1.3 Human, Natural, and Physical Capital Indicators by Region

Indicator	Africa excluding South Africa	Africa	South Asia	East Asia	Latin America
Human capital					
Human development index, 1995	39.8	40.5	48.2	63.9	76.8
Life expectancy at birth (years), 1980	47.0	47.6	53.8	64.5	64.8
Life expectancy at birth (years), 1997	51.3	52.4	62.5	68.4	69.7
Infant mortality (per 1,000 live births), 1980	119.0	115.3	119.8	56.0	59.5
Infant mortality (per 1,000 live births), 1997	92.9	89.9	70.5	37.8	31.8
Under-5 mortality (per 1,000), 1995	—	157	116	53	47
Adult illiteracy (percent), 1980	57	57	58	30	18
Adult illiteracy (percent), 1997	46	43	51	17	13
Mean years of schooling , 1960	1.5	1.5	1.5	3.4	3.4
Mean years of schooling, 1990	2.4	2.4	3.4	6.2	5.2
Access to safe water (percent), 1996	45	47	81	77	75
Natural capital					
Land area per capita (hectares), 1970	8.03	7.85	0.67	1.42	7.09
Land area per capita (hectares), 1997	3.89	3.85	0.37	0.91	4.06
GDP per hectare (1987 dollars), 1970	65	70	357	111	172
GDP per hectare (1987 dollars), 1997	86	136	1,214	786	466
Average annual deforestation (percent), 1990–95	0.7	0.7	0.2	0.8	0.6
Physical capital					
Private capital stock per worker (dollars), 1990	1,069	—	2,425	9,711	17,424
Capital flight/private wealth (percent), 1990	39	—	3	6	10

Source: World Bank data; UNDP 1998; Wood and Mayer 1998; Collier and Gunning 1999.

telecommunications impede participation in the burgeoning information economy. The additional infrastructure investments needed to sustain rapid GDP growth have been estimated at about 5 percent of GDP over 10 years.

The growth target differs for countries depending on their initial conditions. For the poorest African countries, consumption per capita will need to rise faster to halve the incidence of poverty. These countries also have faster population growth and lower savings. With 60–80 percent of their people below the $1 a day mark, there is also less direct mileage from redistributive policies. Especially for the poorest countries, there needs to be an emphasis on removing regulatory and other barriers (including gender-based barriers) to productive activity (World Bank 1998c; Blackden and Bhanu 1999). Richer countries have more scope for addressing poverty with redistributive policies, including trade and fiscal reforms.

Especially for the poorest countries, there needs to be an emphasis on removing regulatory and other barriers to productive activity

Africa's Growth Crisis: A Retrospective

AT THE START OF THE 19TH CENTURY, AFRICA'S INCOME LEVEL stood at roughly one-third of Europe's. There then followed a long period of falling behind as industrialization, technology, and trade accelerated in the world's major centers (Maddison, cited in Bloom and Sachs 1998). African growth may have approximated that in Europe in the first half of the 20th century, and many countries performed well until the oil shock in 1973. But thereafter, Africa again fell behind, with most countries experiencing a steep economic decline that ended only with the recovery of the late 1990s.

Expectations and Outcomes

Africa's decline was not expected. During the decade that followed the independence of most African countries, Gunnar Myrdal wrote the three celebrated volumes of *Asian Drama*. This major work saw Asia, with its vast population and limited land resources, as doomed to stagnation. Meanwhile, Africa was poised to grow steadily along a path of relative prosperity. Indeed, in the 1960s many African countries were richer than their Asian counterparts, and their strong natural resource bases augured well for future trade, growth, and development.

In 1965, for example, incomes and exports per capita were higher in Ghana than in Korea. But projections proved to be far off the mark. Korea's exports per capita overtook Ghana's in 1972, and its income level surpassed Ghana's four years later. Between 1965 and 1995 Korea's exports increased by 400 times in current dollars. Meanwhile, Ghana's increased only by 4 times, and real earnings per capita fell to a fraction of their earlier value. The parallels are considerable between Africa today and Asia in the 1960s. Africa's economic and social indicators in 1995 were not much different from those of Korea in 1960 or Indonesia, Malaysia, and Thailand in 1975—although savings and school enrolment rates were somewhat lower (UNCTAD 1998). Many see Africa today as caught in a low-equilibrium development trap, just as Asia was viewed in the 1960s. Asia's experience shows that Africa's problems in accelerating development can be overcome. But why have African growth and development been so slow?

Asia's experience shows that Africa's challenges in accelerating development can be overcome

From Trade Dependence to Aid Dependence

Has Africa's low growth been due to a shortage of resources or to their ineffective use? Both. African investment rates, at about 18 percent of GDP, have been only slightly lower than those in East Asia and Latin America (22 percent). But when investment is measured in international prices that allow for Africa's higher costs, investment rates are a third lower in Africa than in other regions (Hoeffler 1999). Part of the reason for slow growth, then, is the fact that investment tends to be more costly in Africa than in other regions. For example, trucks in Southern and East Africa cost about twice as much as in Asia. These higher costs reflect outside factors as well as taxes and other policies.

But productivity differences also loom large in accounting for Africa's slow growth. Africa's investment productivity, as measured by the incremental output-capital ratio, was only half that in Asia in 1970–97 (see table 1.1). The deceleration of growth after 1973 from about 5 percent to barely 1 percent parallels the decline in investment productivity from 25 percent to 5 percent, even while investment levels in the earlier part of this period were at their highest (figure 1.2). As the return to borrowed funds fell short of the cost of borrowing, this phase saw a major increase in development assistance and a rise in external indebtedness. The growth recovery since 1994 has relied on productivity gains rather than an increase in investment.

Figure 1.2 Growth, Exports, Investment, and Investment Productivity in Africa, 1964–97

The erosion of Africa's world trade share between 1970 and 1993 represents a staggering annual income loss of $68 billion

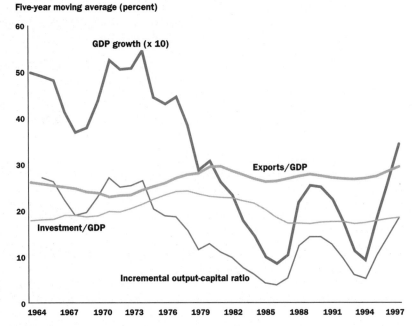

Five-year moving average (percent)

Source: World Bank data.

What role did trade play in this story? Strongly trade oriented in the 1960s, Africa was the only region to then experience a decline in real dollar exports per capita (see table 1.1). Paralleling its slow income growth, Africa's share of world trade fell from more than 3 percent in the 1950s to less than 2 percent in the mid-1990s (and to only 1.2 percent, excluding South Africa). The erosion of Africa's world trade share in current prices between 1970 and 1993 represents a staggering annual income loss of $68 billion—or 21 percent of regional GDP. Part of this loss reflected the erosion of the trade share for traditional products, as well as policies that discouraged private investment and diversification into products for which world demand was growing more rapidly (figure 1.3). Only in fuels did Africa emerge as a substantial new presence in world markets. Relative to GDP, exports changed only modestly (in current prices), benefiting from hikes in world oil prices. The more recent recovery stems from policy reforms, including exchange rate liberalization and realignment to reduce overvaluation (which cut GDP in dollar terms) and reductions in other disincentives to exporting.

Figure 1.3 Africa's Share in World Exports by Product, 1970–93

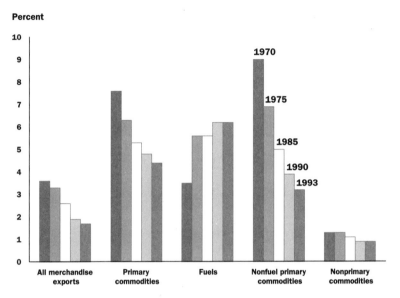

Percent

Source: United Nations, *Handbook of International Trade and Development Statistics,* various years.

For many countries, aid transfers have been offset by terms of trade losses

Worsening terms of trade were another source of loss for many African countries (figure 1.4). For African countries that are not oil exporters, and excluding South Africa, cumulative terms of trade losses in 1970–97 represented almost 120 percent of GDP, a massive and persistent drain of purchasing power. In addition to the depressing effect on income and growth, external factors, coupled with a failure to diversify exports and attract private capital in previous decades, lie behind the aid dependence of the 1990s. From modest levels before the oil shock, aid increased sharply to meet the crisis, so that the nonoil-exporting countries (excluding South Africa) received large transfers from grants and concessional loans. Cumulatively, these transfers amounted to 178 percent of GDP (table 1.4). But the increase after 1970–73 (125 percent of GDP) was little more than the terms of trade losses. In addition, by 1997 this group of countries had accumulated external debt equal to their GDP, raising their debt service obligations.

Terms of trade losses are not the whole picture, however. Africa's oil exporters have benefited from massive terms of trade gains (see table 1.4). But as with most oil exporters in other regions, the gains have not been used to place countries on a path of sustainable growth. Excessively positive shocks, as shown by a number of studies, can destabilize development as much as negative ones (Gelb 1988; Auty 1998).

Figure 1.4 Africa's Terms of Trade by Country Group, 1965–97

Excessively positive shocks can destabilize development as much as negative ones

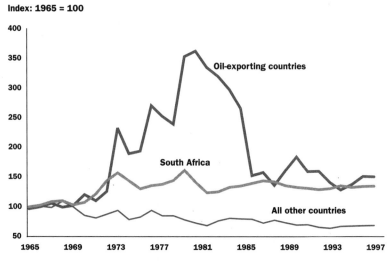

Index: 1965 = 100

Oil-exporting countries

South Africa

All other countries

Source: World Bank data.

Table 1.4 Cumulative Terms of Trade Effects and Financing Flows in Africa, 1970–97 (percentage of GDP)

Indicator	Oil-exporting countries	South Africa	All other countries
Terms of trade effect[a]	483	189	–119
Gross resource flows[b]	196	—	288
Net resource flows[c]	124	—	234
Net resource transfers[d]	5	—	176
Grants and concessional flows	27	—	178
Foreign direct investment	–5	—	–10
Nonconcessional and portfolio flows	–18	—	7
Change in net resource transfers from 1970–73 level	27	—	125
External debt, 1997	94	20	106
Present value of external debt, 1997[e]	91	19	83

— Not available.

a. Capacity to import less exports of goods and services, in 1965 constant local currency prices.

b. Long-term debt (excluding IMF), foreign direct investment (net), portfolio equity flows, and official grants (excluding technical cooperation).

c. Gross resource flows less principal repayments on long-term debt.

d. Net resource flows less interest payments on long-term debt and profit remittances on foreign direct investment.

e. Sum of short-term external debt and the discounted sum of debt service payments due on public, publicly guaranteed, and private nonguaranteed long-term external debt over the life of existing loans.

Source: World Bank data.

Explanations for Africa's Slow Growth

Africa's aid dependence entering the 21st century thus mirrors its lock-in to primary export dependence, its weakness in attracting private finance and reversing capital flight, and its failure to diversify. But there is more to the story. Many other countries, including those in East and South Asia, have experienced declining terms of trade but have been able to adjust to the losses, attract investment to new industries, upgrade skills, and diversify into more dynamic industrial and service product lines. Why did this not happen in Africa?

Explaining Africa's slow growth remains a major challenge

Explaining Africa's slow growth in the second half of the 20th century remains a major challenge to economists and other analysts. But even though the large and growing growth literature both inside and outside Africa does not provide a simple answer on how to accelerate development, it does suggest important lessons for the future (see Collier and Gunning 1998 and Azam, Fosu, and Ndung'u 1999).

The debate on Africa's slow growth has offered many explanations. Some factors—such as geography (tropical location, a low ratio of coastline to interior and the resulting high transport costs), small states, high ethnic diversity, unpredictable rainfall, and terms of trade shocks—are taken to represent "destiny," or exogenous factors beyond the control of African policymakers. Others, such as poor policies (including trade and exchange rate policies, nationalization, and other restraints on economic activity) can, in principle, be changed. A second dimension distinguishes such factors depending on whether they are primarily domestic or external.

These distinctions are only somewhat helpful, because over the long run it becomes hard to assess what is exogenous and what is endogenous. Policies respond to social, demographic, political, and structural factors, many of which also reflect the influence of income levels and trends over long periods. Policies and capacity can also moderate the effect of geography: the effect of being in a landlocked or tropical location depends partly on the efficiency of the transport sector and the health sector. Some factors that depress Africa's growth—such as widespread and persistent gender inequality in access to productive resources—reflect both current policies and longstanding traditional and social practices (box 1.1).

Geography, health, and demography. Bloom and Sachs (1998) offer estimates of the impact of various factors on Africa's growth. Geographic factors and the spatial distribution of its population lower Africa's potential growth by almost 1 percentage point relative to other regions. Africa's high dependency ratio lowers growth by another 0.6 percentage point. Low life expectancy (a proxy for a variety of health-related problems, including malaria) reduces growth by a massive 1.3 percentage points. A "catchup effect" due to Africa's low incomes partly compensates for these negative factors, adding almost 2 percentage points to Africa's growth potential. The remaining difference in Africa's growth rate, almost 1 percentage point, is explained by policies—a lack of openness to trade and weak government institutions and fiscal policies.

One interpretation of these results is that the potential advantages of Africa's low incomes for growth are more than offset by its unfriendly geography, its adverse public health, and its high dependency ratio. But poor health and high dependency are themselves influenced by income levels and public policies, as well as by the effectiveness of public service delivery, and so are not really exogenous. Even so, these findings are significant, especially for public policy.

Sparseness, ethnic diversity, and democracy. Low population density raises the costs of providing infrastructure services, disseminating information, and integrating production and markets. Low density is also associated

African women work far longer hours than African men

Box 1.1 Gender and Growth: Africa's Missed Potential

AFRICAN WOMEN WORK FAR LONGER HOURS THAN African men. On average, their workdays may be 50 percent longer, and their work is closely integrated with household production systems. Women are especially prominent in agriculture, particularly in processing food crops, and in providing water and firewood, although men predominate in agriculture in much of the Sahel. Income earned by women is more likely to be used productively—for children's food, clothing, and education.

But due to customary and legal restrictions, women in Africa have less access to productive assets, including land, and to such complementary factors of production as credit, fertilizer, and education. Women farmers receive only 1 percent of total credit to agriculture. Women are less likely to control the product of their labor than men, reducing their incentives to pursue productive, income-earning opportunities. And between 1960 and 1990 average schooling for African women increased by only 1.2 years, the lowest

gain of any region. Some cross-country studies suggest that if African women were given equal access to education and productive factors, growth rates could be as much as 0.8 percentage points higher. In addition, patterns of capital formation tend to be biased against investments, such as wells and fuel-efficient stoves, with the potential to unlock more female time for high-productivity activities and education.

Thus Africa is losing out on the productive potential of more than half its effective workforce. So, measures to increase gender equality in Africa, in addition to their social and distributional implications, have considerable potential to accelerate growth. What is standing in the way? Longstanding traditions and power. Women's political participation is still low—only 6 percent in national legislatures and 2 percent in cabinets. Half the national cabinets have no women.

Source: Blackden and Bhanu 1999.

with higher ethnic diversity, which several studies find associated with lower growth. A common perception is that higher ethnic diversity reduces growth by raising the risk of conflict. But new research suggests that Africa's extensive ethnic conflict is explained by its poverty rather than by its diversity (chapter 2). An alternative explanation is that diversity increases the difficulties of cooperation, both in commerce and in policy formulation. Collier (1999), however, finds that diversity reduces growth by 3 percentage points in undemocratic countries but has no effect in democracies. One implication for Africa is that efforts to nurture durable democratic systems will pay off in better economic management.

Efforts to nurture durable democratic systems will pay off in better economic management

External shocks and social conflict. The small size of Africa's nations and their high export concentration in a limited range of primary commodities leave them exposed to terms of trade shocks that have often had an adverse effect on economic management and outcomes. But countries have responded differently to external shocks. Some have adjusted sharply and resumed growth, while others have launched into a long downward spiral of declining incomes and policy disarray. What made the difference? Indicators of social tensions—such as income inequality and weaker and less democratic institutions—are associated with deteriorating policies and lower economic resilience in the face of a volatile external environment (Rodrik 1998b). Domestic factors may therefore be more important than external destiny.

Aid dependence. There has been a long debate on whether aid has been beneficial or detrimental to growth and development—and on how much its effects come by causing changes in policies or through other channels such as appreciating exchange rates, discouraging the development of exports, and sustaining inefficient patterns of investment, as in Tanzanian manufacturing (box 1.2). Recent research suggests that, historically, there appears to have been no significant net effect of aid flows on policies and that aid has fostered growth—but only in good policy environments (Dollar and Burnside 1997).

Economic management. Postcolonial African governments developed economic controls—comprehensive in only a few cases but invariably involving extensive and arbitrary regulation and frequently the prohibition of trade (Collier and Gunning 1999; see also World Bank 1989, 1994). Interventions were domestically as well as externally focused; some countries even banned interdistrict trade in food. Since the political base of governments was urban, agriculture was heavily taxed, and

Box 1.2 Industrial Productivity in Tanzania

AT INDEPENDENCE, MORE THAN 80 PERCENT OF THE manufactured goods consumed in Tanzania were imported, and manufacturing accounted for only 4 percent of GDP. A succession of government plans placed heavy emphasis on import-substituting industrial investments for basic consumer goods, construction, and related capital goods. Between 1965 and 1980 real investment in manufacturing grew by more than 21 percent a year, and in 1986–90 investment rose to the remarkable level of more than 100 percent of manufacturing value added. Despite this massive expansion, output per worker fell as production rose slowly and capacity use collapsed.

What constrained capacity use? By far the most important factor seems to have been a critical shortage of imported inputs and spare parts following the balance of payments crises after 1974. What sustained heavy capital investments and capital goods imports in the face of severe capacity underuse? One important factor was a substantial inflow of foreign assistance tied to the capital content of projects. Tanzania's industrial drive failed because investments could not generate enough manufactured exports to fund continuing imports of the materials needed to sustain production. Foreign aid sustained this neglect of export emphasis.

Source: Ndulu 1986; Devarajan, Easterly, and Pack 1999.

highly centralized public administrations paid little attention to rural services. At the same time, trade and exchange rate policies encouraged firms to produce under noncompetitive conditions for small, captured, domestic markets, undermining the basis for industrial growth. Unstable, capital-hostile environments contributed to massive capital flight (see table 1.3).

Public employment was emphasized over service delivery. The economic decline after 1973 may have increased pressure to expand employment, which was reconciled with limited revenues by lowering wages, compressing pay at upper levels, and leaving little space for operations, maintenance, and nonwage spending. Civil service became the arena for ethnic groups to contest for resources, often with the costs of poor service and endemic corruption. Poor service raised costs to firms—weak telecommunications, for example, was estimated to lower African growth by up to 1 percentage point (Easterly and Levine 1997). Poor service also handicapped households through inefficient spending on education, health, and infrastructure. Simple quantitative data cannot easily capture many of these and other domestic policies. But growth studies and case studies show that they hurt Africa's economic performance in the second half of the 20th century.

How important were trade policies? On a range of indicators, Africa imposed higher trade barriers and sustained more severely overvalued exchange rates than did other regions. These policies discouraged exports and may have been more damaging because of the small size of Africa's economies. But there is some controversy over the specific impact of trade restrictions relative to that of a policy environment that hurts efficiency, productivity, and investment. Supporting this view—that trade restrictions should be seen as part of a range of broader and more comprehensive policies and institutions that affect performance (Rodrik 1999)—is the fact that Africa's exports have changed little relative to GDP (see figure 1.2). They have moved together, influenced by common external factors and domestic policies. Trade reforms alone will not offer a simple fix, though increasing and diversifying exports will be critical in reversing Africa's marginalization.

The bottom line. Africa's performance is influenced by its history and its geography. But sound policies and strong institutions can moderate exogenous factors, and Africa's economies will, like others, respond to better economic policies. Studies suggest some of the focal points for ensuring that Africa embarks on a long-term process of rising incomes and falling poverty.

The first area is governance and leadership. Adopting sound, growth-oriented policies on a sustained basis will be all the more essential as further globalization brings risks of external shocks and instability. Successful countries must approach globalization armed with a "business plan" that includes developing indigenous institutions for mediating conflict without undermining economic stability and deterring investment and entrepreneurship, as well as improving public regulation and service delivery. Effective policies for Africa must therefore be win-win policies: to both strengthen the economy and to contribute to the formation of effective states (chapter 2).

A second important area is investment in people. Some of the most important "exogenous" variables in growth studies, including poor health and adverse demographics, are partly the outcome of ineffective policies and long economic decline. With its population growing rapidly relative to natural resources, Africa must reverse the marginalization of many of its people—notably its women—and strengthen their capabilities and capacity. Africa loses twice as much labor through illness as any other region. This disparity will only increase as HIV/AIDS incapacitates 2–4 percent of the active labor force and depletes skills (chapters 3 and 4).

A third area involves the high costs and risks of the business environment, which owe much to government policies since independence. Efficient

Sound policies and strong institutions can moderate exogenous factors

investment in infrastructure—physical, financial, and information—is essential if Africa is to overcome geographic isolation, and this requires the formation of public-private partnerships (chapter 5). Moreover, policies for productive sectors, particularly agriculture and industry, need to encourage investment, employment, and export diversification (chapters 6 and 7).

Finally, especially given Africa's high aid dependence and the important influence of donors, aid needs to be reassessed to ensure that it contributes to these objectives (chapter 8).

Where Is Africa Now? Reforms and Their Legacy

Most African countries have embarked on reform programs intended to regain macroeconomic balance, improve resource allocation, and restore growth

MOST AFRICAN COUNTRIES HAVE EMBARKED ON REFORM PROgrams intended to regain macroeconomic balance, improve resource allocation, and restore growth. These substantial reforms contributed to the resurgence of growth in the second half of the 1990s. Nevertheless, Africa has emerged from the reforms with a difficult legacy. And at current and projected growth rates of 4–5 percent, the performance of Africa's poor countries still falls short of the levels needed to reduce poverty and offset decades of stagnation.

Progress with Reform

Reforms in Africa have been substantial in three important areas: macroeconomic balances, market forces, and private initiative.

Macroeconomic balances. Many countries have made major gains in macroeconomic stabilization, particularly since 1994. Consider the 31 poor, aid-dependent countries covered by the Special Program of Assistance for Africa (SPA).[1] Their fiscal deficits dropped to 5.3 percent of GDP in 1997–98 and averaged only 2.5 percent of GDP net of grant financing (figure 1.5). And most financed part of this residual deficit through concessional credits, making budgets more sustainable than otherwise.

Macroeconomic balances are still fragile, however. Although inflation is now less than 10 percent in most African countries, deficit estimates do not fully reflect quasi-fiscal losses and contingent liabilities, such as guarantees to state enterprises. Some governments still run sub-

Figure 1.5 Fiscal Deficits in Special Program of Assistance Countries, 1984–98

Percentage of GDP

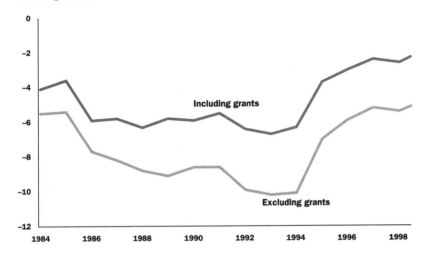

Many countries have moved toward sustainable macroeconomic balances

Source: World Bank data.

stantial arrears to suppliers. In addition to large external debt obligations, countries such as Ghana, Kenya, Malawi, Tanzania, and Zimbabwe face high domestic debt burdens, in some cases because domestic financial markets were liberalized before fiscal deficits were brought under control. Nevertheless, many countries have moved toward sustainable macroeconomic balances, assuming that concessional financing continues at recent levels.

Fiscal improvements have not been stress-free. Public capital spending, heavily supported by donors, has remained roughly constant as a share of GDP. But since 1993 tax revenues have increased relative to GDP while current spending has fallen. Many countries have taken steps to broaden their tax bases, creating autonomous revenue authorities, curbing arbitrary exemptions, and implementing value added taxes. But the combination of weak tax administration and rising tax effort on a narrow tax base has sometimes hit business profitability and reinvestment (Reinikka and Svensson 1998). Relative to other regions, statutory tax rates in Africa are quite high (table 1.5), and tax administration is sometimes seen as predatory by the small number of formal sector firms that contribute most direct taxes. High statutory taxes encourage informal activity and employment.

Table 1.5 Public Finance, External Support, Economic Management, Political Participation, and Risk Ranking Indicators by Region

Indicator	Africa excluding South Africa	Africa	South Asia	East Asia	Latin America
Public finance					
Government revenue/GDP, 1997	21	25	22	—	26
Government spending/ GDP, 1997	25	30	28	15	31
Highest marginal tax rate, 1998 (median, percent)					
Individual	35	35	35	37	30
Corporate	35	35	38	30	30
External support					
Debt stock per capita (dollars), 1997	338	358	120	373	1,426
Foreign direct investment per capita (dollars), 1970	1.49	1.49	0.10	0.24	3.86
Foreign direct investment per capita (dollars), 1997	4.61	7.13	3.40	35.71	120.09
Aid per capita (dollars), 1997	—	26	3	4	13
Economic management and political participation					
Country Policy and Institutional Assessment (CPIA) rating (scale of 1 to 6), 1998[a]	3.0	3.0	3.6	3.2	3.7
Top third	3.8	3.8	3.9	3.9	4.3
Middle third	3.2	3.2	3.7	3.1	3.9
Bottom third	2.2	2.2	3.1	2.8	3.1
GNP per capita (dollars, at market exchange rates), 1997 (CPIA countries)	315	511	384	1,244	3,957
Top third	344	866	616	1,324	5,134
Middle third	387	387	377	884	4,024
Bottom third	249	249	435	520	1,976
PPP GNP per capita, 1997 (CPIA countries)	1,045	1,466	1,587	3,507	6,775
Top third	1,081	2,198	3,261	3,650	8,623
Middle third	1,245	1,245	1,611	2,871	6,546
Bottom third	900	900	1,418	1,320	5,103
Political rights and civil liberties (scale of 1 to 7)					
1990/91	2.6	2.6	3.2	4.0	6.4
1998/99	3.5	3.6	3.5	4.4	5.4
Corruption perceptions index (scale of 1 to 10)	—	3.6	2.8	3.3	3.4
Euromoney *risk ranking* (average rank among 116 countries)					
September 1992	70	68	34	35	49
March 1999	83	81	49	40	41

Note: PPP stands for purchasing power parity.

a. The top third of countries under CPIA ratings for 1998 were Botswana, Cape Verde, Côte d'Ivoire, Eritrea, Ethiopia, Ghana, Lesotho, Malawi, Mauritania, Mauritius, Namibia, Senegal, South Africa, Tanzania, Uganda, and Zambia. The middle third were Benin, Burkina Faso, Cameroon, Chad, Gabon, The Gambia, Guinea, Guinea-Bissau, Kenya, Mali, Mozambique, Niger, Rwanda, Swaziland, Togo, and Zimbabwe. The bottom third were Angola, Burundi, Central African Republic, Comoros, Democratic Republic of Congo, Republic of Congo, Djibouti, Equatorial Guinea, Liberia, Madagascar, Nigeria, São Tomé and Principe, Seychelles, Sierra Leone, Somalia, and Sudan.

Source: World Bank data; Freedom House 1991, 1999; Transparency International 1998; *Euromoney.*

On the spending side, many countries suffer chronic shortages of current funding, especially for operations, maintenance, and nonwage inputs. There are also large deviations between planned and actual spending, partly due to the need for cash-based expenditure management to achieve aggregate fiscal targets. Tight fiscal restraints—including on public sector salaries—and the proliferation of donor-driven initiatives have created perverse financial incentives for public sector employees. These problems have probably worsened due to the intensity of aggregate fiscal pressure. And they need to be addressed in the next stage of reform, especially in countries that have most consolidated their macroeconomic balances.

Market forces. A second area of reform has been the opening of Africa to market forces. Most prices have been decontrolled and marketing boards eliminated—except in a few countries for such key exports as cotton and cocoa. Current account convertibility has been achieved and, except in a few countries, black market premiums average only 4 percent. Trade taxes have been rationalized from high and arbitrary levels. Average rates of 30–40 percent of the mid-1990s have given way, in many countries (including those in the West African Economic Union), to trade-weighted average tariffs of 15 percent or less. Trade-weighted tariffs are now below 10 percent in more open countries such as Uganda and Zambia. Arbitrary exemptions, though still numerous, have also been rationalized.

Much of Africa has been opened to market forces

This opening to market forces continues in West Africa through the movement to a common external tariff with a maximum rate of 20 percent—and in East and Southern Africa through country-by-country reforms supported by several regional associations. Trade policies are still more restrictive than in the world's more open developing countries, and many countries still confer substantial protection on domestic industry. But much of the gap in the early 1990s has been closed.

Private initiative. A third change in Africa's economic landscape has been wider space for private initiative. Thriving business networks have arisen in West, East, and Southern Africa, and in politically and economically stable countries private investment has increased by almost 3 percent of GDP in recent years. In a 1997 survey of 22 African countries, fewer businessmen saw the state as an opponent than had in 1987 (Weder, Brunetti, and Kisunko 1998). Foreign direct investment also rose in the second half of the 1990s—to about one-sixth the average level per capita for all developing countries. But it was still concentrated in a few countries, especially those with mineral resources. The number of funds seeking investments in Africa has grown from almost none to about 30. So, Africa is becoming a viable business address.

In many African countries privatization has accelerated and become more widely accepted. With more than 3,000 transactions totaling $6.5 billion, privatization has entered a new phase, one marked by private participation in providing infrastructure services (box 1.3). Private operators have substantial involvement in telephone systems in 18 countries and in water distribution in 23 countries. Railways and ports have been concessioned to private operators. Even when the lead investor is foreign (as is usually the case for the largest transactions), privatization is opening the door to domestic businesses, including as suppliers and distributors, and to better services.

Privatization is opening the door to domestic businesses and to better services

Regulations have not always advanced with privatization to ensure adequate competition, however, and most countries still need to expand the pool of investors. In some countries case-by-case privatizations have offered new owners exclusive rights to provide services to small national markets, whereas a subregional approach would have enabled more competitive service provision. Better regulations and more transparent privatization will need to remain a focus in many countries.

Box 1.3 Privatization in Côte d'Ivoire

OVER THE PAST EIGHT YEARS CÔTE D'IVOIRE'S AMBItious privatization program has wholly or partly privatized more than 60 firms—and yielded more than $450 million in return. The program gained momentum after the 1994 devaluation, which restored the profitability of a number of agribusiness companies. It has been successful in attracting investors: in the past four years $1.4 billion were invested in agribusiness and more than $1 billion in infrastructure. The private sector is now involved in almost all infrastructure sectors. A recent study, conducted using the same methods as in other regions, concluded that the program has been a success: employment in privatized firms has grown by 4 percent a year (it had been falling before), labor productivity has risen, and so has government's corporate tax yield.

Despite this track record, a number of questions remain. Côte d'Ivoire has not yet succeeded in attracting a diverse group of private investors. Doing so would increase competition. The country also needs to nurture a solid base of small and medium-size enterprises. Regulations need to be rationalized to clarify the roles of technical ministries and regulatory bodies, including the Competition Commission. And despite the increasing participation of private firms in infrastructure, the public sector still bears a significant part of market risks. Most contracts—power, water, railways—are of the *affermage* (lease contract) type, with investment still the responsibility of the state. Further transfers of risk to private operators will require policies that emphasize transparency and the building of confidence.

Figure 1.6 Growth in Output, Investment, and Exports in Africa, 1981–98

Percent

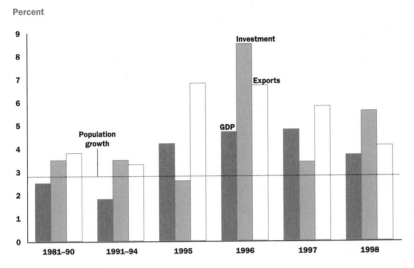

Source: World Bank data.

By all indicators, Africa's performance improved in the second half of the 1990s

Recovery—and Other Legacies

No single measure captures the rhythm of Africa's economies. Aggregate output is dominated by South Africa, a country facing unique economic and political challenges. Population-weighted growth rates or median country performance offer broader-based measures. But all indicators show that performance improved in the second half of the 1990s (figure 1.6). In the typical country annual output growth rose to about 4.3 percent in 1994–98. Agriculture also performed well, growing 3.7 percent a year in the median country, well above previous levels. In 1995–97 exports also grew rapidly. While this period was one of exceptional growth in world trade, especially in demand for key African products, it also saw a reversal of falling trade shares—suggesting that African exports were becoming more competitive (Yeats 1999). Although estimates of poverty headcounts are available for only a few countries over time, they show that rising aggregate consumption usually results in substantial declines in the percentage of the absolute poor (chapter 3).

This improving picture came under stress in 1998 in a way that underscores Africa's vulnerability to external shocks and internal conflicts. Except for South Africa (where growth fell sharply), African countries were less integrated with world capital markets than most other regions and less exposed to the direct effects of the East Asian crisis. Still, many

Macroeconomic and structural reforms in Africa have been highly controversial

countries suffered sharp declines in commodity prices. Oil exporters felt a massive terms of trade loss, but until late 1999 many oil importers were cushioned from the immediate effects of their slumping export prices by lower costs of oil imports (box 1.4). Even so, they faced intensified competition in depressed primary export markets. Another factor was the intensification of conflict in Central Africa, in parts of West Africa, and in the Horn of Africa with the resumption of war between Ethiopia and Eritrea. While many countries continued to grow strongly in 1998, the region's population-weighted growth slumped, leaving little growth space to cut poverty. Growth appears to have picked up in 1999 and 2000, though not to the peak levels of 1996, and sharp increases in fuel prices shifted terms of trade losses back to oil-importing countries.

Reform and recovery. Macroeconomic and structural reforms in Africa have been highly controversial.[2] Some studies using information through the mid-1990s failed to find a link between reform and performance. Perhaps this is not surprising. It is not easy to disentangle the relative contributions of external developments, domestic economic policies, and deeper institutional factors over the long run, because they work together. Nor is evaluation easy in the medium run, because of lagged effects and

---

Box 1.4 The East Asian Crisis and Africa

THE SWING IN THE CURRENT ACCOUNTS OF EAST ASIAN countries in 1998 sent a massive deflationary shock through the global economy—equal to 3 percent of world GDP. But except for South Africa, which suffered from a speculative currency attack, Africa was less exposed to international capital movements than many other developing regions. The main transmission effects from the Asian crisis were through a halving of growth in world trade and 20–40 percent declines in terms of trade for primary products.

The net effects were felt sharply by African oil exporters, which suffered a terms of trade loss of 7 percent of GDP. While other countries also suffered losses (particularly those exporting metals and tobacco), until late 1999 most were shielded from the immediate effects of export price declines by sharp cuts in their oil import bills. The net effect of the crisis—coupled

with increased conflict, adverse weather in East Africa, and political uncertainty in Nigeria—pulled growth down in Africa, especially in larger countries.

The longer-run impact of the crisis will be felt more widely. Second rounds of commodity price declines are hitting some producing countries severely. Oil prices doubled, benefiting producers but hurting importing countries. World trade growth may be slower than anticipated, and competition will come from other regions where exchange rates have depreciated sharply. For example, processed fish from Thailand has made severe inroads on Senegal's exports. Investors may also show less interest in projects to extract and process raw materials. Thus all the more pressing is the need to boost Africa's international competitiveness.

Source: World Bank 1998b.

because structural and institutional measures are difficult to quantify. Many African countries have moved in and out of compliance with macro-economic and structural reform programs, so formally being on a program has meant little for the policies actually pursued over longer periods. And short-term reforms have failed to address some difficult underlying institutional problems—and in some cases may have worsened them.

Despite all this, and recognizing the difficulty of specifying a clear counterfactual, some recent studies indicate that adherence to sound policies pays off in the medium run. But good economic management must be sustained for some time to have a substantial effect. An independent assessment of the Special Program of Assistance (SPA) cited eight African countries as being generally "on track" in 1992–96.[3] This group did better in 1992–97, both relative to its previous record and relative to a comparator group of SPA countries: GDP per capita grew 1.1 percent in the on-track group but fell 0.5 percent in the others. Export growth, import growth, investment rates, and government spending were also higher for the on-track group. The combination of sustained reforms and financial assistance was associated with better performance, at least at the aggregate level. The on-track group also performed better on intermediate social indicators, though it still fell well short of what was required to achieve poverty reduction goals.

Another way to assess the impact of economic management on performance is to group countries by broader indicators of macroeconomic, structural, and social policies and economic institutions. One such measure is the Country Policy and Institutional Assessment (CPIA), carried out each year by the World Bank for all borrowing countries and used—along with population and income—to allocate International Development Association resources among recipient countries. Macroeconomic sustainability has a 25 percent weight in the CPIA, and structural and financial sector policies and legal institutions about 30 percent. The remainder is based on financial and budget management, social policies, safety nets, and environmental policies (IDA 1998). Worldwide, few if any countries appear able to make progress toward a middle-income level without also achieving a high CPIA rating.

CPIA ratings for the late 1990s suggest that an upper tier of African countries has a good basis for further development. But a lower tier, including many very poor countries, is in danger of slipping ever further behind. Africa has many well-managed economies, especially in macro-economic terms (see table 1.5). The top third of its countries are not rated

Good economic management must be sustained for some time but then has a substantial effect

Figure 1.7 Africa's Annual Growth, Investment, Exports, and Deficits by Country Group, 1995–98

Percent

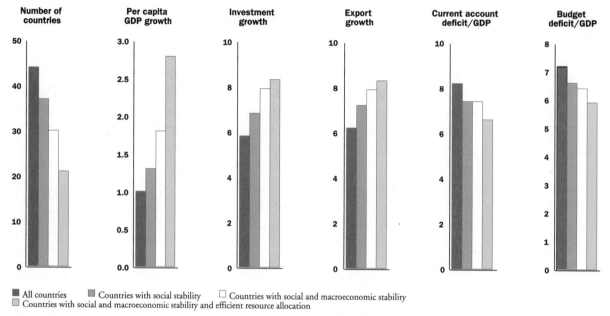

■ All countries   ■ Countries with social stability   □ Countries with social and macroeconomic stability
□ Countries with social and macroeconomic stability and efficient resource allocation

Source: World Bank data.

much differently from their counterparts in other regions. And while this tier includes some of Africa's richer countries, it also includes many poor ones. But the lowest tier of Africa's countries is both poorer and rated far lower than their counterparts elsewhere.

Countries are also distinguished by whether they have preserved a peaceful base for development. As discussed further below, for many countries avoidance of conflict has been critical in the ability to sustain development. Figure 1.7 shows how growth, investment, exports, and current account and budget deficits have differed across countries according to whether they have been at peace and, if so, whether their economic management has been deemed effective. Both peace and good economic management have been important for Africa's recovery, with better-managed countries seeing higher growth per capita and investment and export growth of more than 8 percent. There have also been signs of export diversification (chapter 7) and, in some countries, such as Uganda, of a reversal in capital flight. A number of countries have also advanced in international risk ratings, although few (with the notable exception of South Africa) are at the level required to attract appreciable private capital.

Other legacies of the crisis decades. Thus reforms have been instrumental in Africa's recovery and have laid the basis for deeper changes. But the focus on macroeconomic management over an extended period has also left deeper and difficult legacies for African countries: "hysteresis effects," which are not quickly reversed.

Perhaps unavoidably, economic management focused on short-term concerns. Thus reforms—for example, of the civil service—have restored macroeconomic balance rather than increased effectiveness. Many countries have seen improvements in capacity within central banks and ministries of finance. But with weaknesses in governance and severe erosion of pay, especially at higher levels, the adjustment decades also saw a substantial deterioration in the quality of public institutions, a demoralization of public servants, and a decline in the effectiveness of service delivery in many countries. Together with falling incomes, these effects—which cannot be speedily reversed—translated into falling social indicators and capabilities in many countries, and to losses of human capital, especially (though not exclusively) in the public service.

Cash management limits to control aggregate spending and continued macroeconomic instability increase the difficulty of assuring a predictable flow of resources to agreed programs. The divergence between budgeted and actual spending is often gaping, with at least a 30 percent deviation in one of every five African countries for national budgets, and in half of African countries for sector and program budgets (Kostopoulos 1999). This discrepancy has undermined the accountability of sector ministries for agreed outcomes—and left programs poorly performing and subject to the diversion of funds.

As external funding became more critical, African governments increasingly turned to external advisers, often those connected with the provision of funding. Conditionality became ever more intrusive, and the shaping of reforms was seen to lie mainly outside the region. This further weakened internal capacity for economic management and reduced African governments' sense of ownership and accountability for economic outcomes. Reforms were not "marketed" or explained to the population. Arrangements between governments and donors often weakened the role of representative institutions, particularly parliaments, with essential legislative and budgetary functions. The effect was lower credibility for both the reforms and the programs that tried to enforce them. Foreign assistance, largely shaped by the strategic considerations of the Cold War, was not allocated in a par-

The long period of macroeconomic adjustment also left some difficult legacies

37

ticularly discriminating way between better-managed and worse-managed countries. This too did little to encourage credible reforms.

The long crisis also lowered expectations of Africa and within Africa. In the 1960s governments actively strove for accelerated development. By the mid-1990s simply restoring growth to allow rising per capita income was seen as an achievement for many countries.

The end of the 20th century, however, marked the emergence of a fragile consensus between Africa and its donors, at least on broad principles. There was far greater understanding within Africa of the need for a stable macroeconomy, for working markets, for private initiative, and for the need to increase global competitiveness. Donors had accepted the limits of narrow approaches. Market-driven development could not succeed without strong social and institutional infrastructure—including a strong and capable state—and without active measures to alleviate severe poverty and raise the capacity of the population. Africans and their development partners had also begun to ask how to deliver assistance in ways that strengthen the accountability of governments to their people in Africa's emerging but aid-dependent democracies.

The end of the 20th century marked the emergence of a fragile consensus between Africa and its donors

Toward An Agenda for the Future

> It is not sufficient for African governments merely to consolidate the progress made in their adjustment programs. They need to go beyond the issues of public finance, monetary policy, prices, and markets to address fundamental questions relating to human capacities, institutions, governance, the environment, population growth and distribution, and technology.
>
> ——World Bank 1989

WHAT, THEN, IS NEEDED FOR ACCELERATED PROGRESS? WITH so many challenges—and so many interactions among them—it is hard for governments and donors to set priorities. How can African countries develop comprehensive development plans or "business plans" that will help guide them through the increasingly competitive and fast-moving 21st century, but that are sufficiently prioritized to guide implementation?

Circles of Causation

One approach is to focus on blocks of issues with strong cumulative interactions—circles of cumulative causation, which can be virtuous or vicious (figure 1.8). Success in one element of a circle will ease improvement in others, but it is difficult to envision Africa claiming the 21st century unless there is progress in all the circles. The unfinished agenda can be framed in four such circles: improving governance and preventing conflict, investing in people, increasing competitiveness and diversifying economies, and reducing aid dependence and strengthening partnerships.

Circle 1: Improving governance and resolving conflict. Governance, conflict, and poverty intertwine on several levels in Africa. At one end of the spectrum, the countries that made the greatest gains in political rights and

Figure 1.8 Africa's Circles of Cumulative Causation

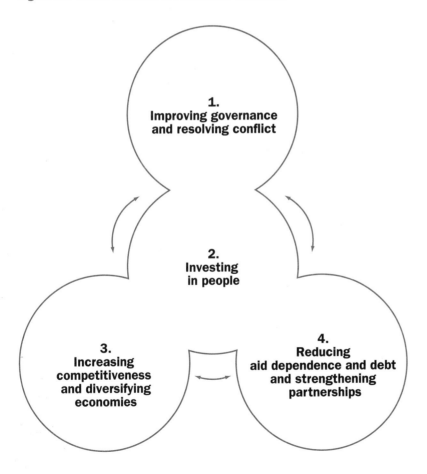

Figure 1.9 Political Rights, Civil Liberties, and Economic Management in Africa by Country Group, 1990–99

With highly diverse, multiethnic states, African countries will need to search for inclusive constitutional models and institutions

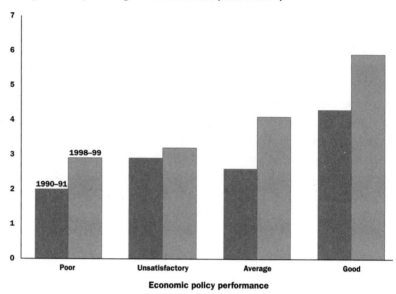

Average score for political rights and civil liberties (scale of 1 to 7)

1990–91

1998–99

Poor   Unsatisfactory   Average   Good

Economic policy performance

Source: Freedom House 1991, 1999.

civil liberties in the 1990s are also those with better economic management and performance (figure 1.9). This does not prove that political liberalization caused better economic management. But the relationship suggests that stronger and more accountable economic management has been associated with more participatory political systems and governments less accountable solely to narrow interest groups. Conversely, increased accountability and decentralized service delivery that comes closer to the people can strengthen political participation, contribute to a stronger state, and raise efficiency.

At the other end of the spectrum, about one African in five lives in a country formally at war or severely disrupted by conflict that, on average, lowers growth by at least 2 percentage points for every year that it persists. The direct annual costs of conflict in Central Africa and West Africa have been estimated at $1 billion and $800 million, and this does not include the costs associated with refugees and displaced persons—another $500 million in Central Africa alone. Indirect costs, including for neighbors not involved directly, are incalculable. Economic management has been far less effective in conflict-ridden countries, which make up most of the lower third in the CPIA ratings. A growing body of evidence shows that poverty, lack of employment, and low education levels are important determinants of conflict—more so, perhaps, than ethnic diversity.

Economic development is vital for political stability. But with highly diverse, multiethnic states, African countries will need to search for inclusive constitutional models and institutions that build consensus, facilitate the participation of diverse groups, entrench good governance, and lay a stable basis for development. These are themes taken up again in chapter 2.

Circle 2: Investing in people. Even with hidden growth reserves such as reversing capital flight (Collier and Gunning 1998) and reallocating aid flows to better-managed countries (Collier and Dollar 1999), Africa's savings are too low to sustain growth in income and consumption at rates needed to rapidly reduce poverty. In addition, Africa's productive base is rapidly shifting from natural resources toward people. The second circle of causation facing African countries is the strong interrelationship between investing in people, accelerating the demographic transition, and promoting savings and growth.

Savings respond to higher and growing incomes, as well as to falling dependency ratios. Elbadawi and Mwega (forthcoming) suggest that a drop in Africa's dependency ratio to levels prevailing in East Asia could increase private savings by 9 percent of GDP. Demographic trends, in turn, respond to higher incomes and to better health and social services—including female education and contraceptives, demand for which is substantial in many African countries. Kenya shows that the demographic transition can be speeded by effective public policy even without rapid economic growth. Raising the efficiency of delivery mechanisms to invest in people—especially women and poor rural residents—is thus a key entry point into any poverty-reducing growth strategy, from a demographic perspective as well as for savings and productivity.

All this is threatened by a new factor, however. Although the full impact of the HIV/AIDS epidemic is not yet apparent, it promises to impart a massive shock to this interrelated system. Countries will experience a reverse demographic transition as life expectancy falls by up to 20 years. Population growth will be lower, but the number of children orphaned by AIDS will explode. Age-based dependency ratios will rise despite a decline in fertility, because AIDS mainly affects young adults in their productive years. With 2–4 percent of the potential workforce

Confronting AIDS is essential if African countries are to prevent a long-term downward spiral

41

incapacitated at any point in time, actual dependency rates will increase even further.

AIDS depletes scarce human capital. Firms, farms, and households are already seeing the impact in lower output, much higher health and funeral costs, increased family insecurity with the loss of breadwinners, and increased training needs to replace lost skills across a wide range of professions. AIDS will also further reduce the incentive to save, given the increased risk of mortality. And it will deplete public and private resources: caring for one AIDS patient costs as much as educating 10 primary school children (World Bank 1997). Confronting AIDS and reversing rising transmission rates are essential if African countries are to prevent this second development circle from turning into a long-term downward spiral. Political commitment to address this problem is urgently needed. These themes are taken up in chapters 3 and 4.

Circle 3: Increasing competitiveness and diversifying economies. With their close links to other sectors and importance for employment and exports, raising the productivity of agriculture and protecting the natural resource base are essential for Africa's structural transformation (chapter 6). Eighty percent of Africa's poor live in rural areas, but forested area per capita will halve in less than 20 years. And productivity in agriculture is rising only slowly.

Africa is also urbanizing rapidly. At 4.9 percent, urban population growth is the highest in the world. Rural-urban migration reflects many factors, including the lack of access to essential services in rural areas, low productivity and incomes in agriculture, and, in some countries, conflict and insecurity. On current trends, Africa's urban population will exceed the rural in the first quarter of the 21st century. By 2025 the urban population will be three times larger than today. But Africa's urbanization is unique—accelerating without rising incomes and without the usual structural transformation that accompanies development, including in agriculture.

Urban agglomeration can have advantages. It is easier to deliver services to denser populations, and urban concentrations offer possibilities for building new industrial and service sectors that are impossible for sparsely populated rural economies. But Africa's urban economies have not been sufficiently dynamic to diversify and create rapid employment growth. Real wages are down in most countries, and formal employment has been falling or stagnant, with informal activities taking up the slack. Open unemployment, which averages about 20 percent in a sample of

Africa's economies have not been sufficiently dynamic to diversify and create rapid employment growth

African countries, is becoming an urgent economic and political problem. Unemployment rates are higher among the young and the better educated. And recent studies suggest that spells of unemployment are getting longer (Agenor 1998; Dabalen 1999). Cuts in public employment contribute to this dismal picture in a few cases, but the real culprit is the wider failure of private employment to expand.

Why have Africa's economies failed to diversify and create jobs in response to macroeconomic reforms? Labor costs and flexibility are a key issue in South Africa. But business surveys and comparisons with other regions suggest that the problem lies elsewhere in most other countries—in poor infrastructure services, including for the information economy (chapter 5), and in other factors and policies that cause high costs and risks for investors (chapter 7).

The sharp decline in aid since the mid-1990s is cause for concern

The third development circle therefore involves the interaction of population growth, urbanization, and economic diversification. The political economy of this circle is important. Without productive urban centers, tensions will rise as cities fail to generate resources for their infrastructure needs and employment for growing populations. These trends will further undermine political and economic stability and degrade the business environment.

Export diversification is essential to avoid these outcomes (chapter 7). Without exports, including of agroindustrial products, producers will be confined to tiny home markets and have fewer avenues to import global knowledge. No strong exporter lobby will arise to press for competitive service standards, including those needed to facilitate trade, whether in agroindustrial products, tourism, or manufacturing. Some African governments still need to forge a trusting and supportive relationship with their business communities, stressing entry and competition while phasing out informal, personalized links between government and business. Understanding why Africa's economies have been slow to diversify and to grow strong productive sectors (including agriculture) is essential to understanding the challenge of the 21st century.

Circle 4: Reducing aid dependence and strengthening partnerships. Africa is in the midst of an intense debate on aid dependence—on the size and allocation of assistance, on delivery mechanisms (including debt relief), and on the relationship between donors and recipients. There is wide agreement that past aid programs have been disappointing, but also recognition that the objective of much of the Cold War aid flow was strategic and political rather than developmental.

Aid is a two-edged sword for Africa. On the one hand, foreign savings are essential to permit both higher investment for growth and higher consumption to reduce poverty. Even under favorable conditions for private inflows and Asian levels of investment efficiency, the typical African country faces a resource gap of more than 12 percent of GDP relative to the investment needs of a growth rate likely to achieve the poverty reduction goal for 2015. Continued assistance is therefore essential, and the sharp decline in aid since the mid-1990s is cause for concern.

On the other hand, while high aid dependence and debt service are not the direct cause of weak capacity and accountability, they can make these problems worse and prolong them, especially when the institutional and capacity base is already weakened. With few exceptions, African countries face severe constraints on capacity and skills. Although weak education systems are a serious concern, capacity constraints are not simply a matter of low supply. The region has been losing more than 23,000 professionals a year, partly replaced by some 100,000 foreign advisers funded by technical assistance at an annual cost of $4 billion. The factors underlying Africa's massive brain drain are not just economic. They also reflect security concerns and, in some countries, violent political upheavals. But economic factors have been important too. Since the mid-1970s capacity has been weakened in many countries by the politicization of service under autocratic governments, severe wage compression, and inadequate working conditions. Only in the 1990s have reforms begun to redress pay and working conditions in the public sector, and only in a few countries.

Political participation has increased, but Africa's civil society and representative institutions are far from economically empowered A survey of government audit institutions in 22 countries showed that few satisfied criteria for professionalism, standards, staffing, independence, timely reporting, and quality of follow-up. Only five produced timely reports, and in only two cases were these publicized to encourage scrutiny of public spending by civil society. Few African parliaments have access to the information and technical support they need to monitor the use of public funds.

Limited resources and ineffective delivery—and in some cases, administrative barriers to cost-effective procurement—create massive inefficiencies in translating inputs into outcomes. It has been estimated that Africa receives benefits worth only $12 for every $100 spent on medicines (chapter 4) and that, in parts of West Africa, achieving one 6-year primary school graduate can require the equivalent of 21 student-years,

Limited resources and ineffective delivery create massive inefficiencies in translating inputs into outcomes

given high dropout and repetition rates. Cross-country relationships between inputs and outcomes are therefore weak.

How does this relate to aid? Net transfers (which take into account debt service paid on public and publicly guaranteed debt) may have compensated for terms of trade losses (see table 1.4), but most of this assistance has not supplemented normal flows of private income and public revenue. Commitments under SPA programs, which are largely untied and represent the closest equivalent to budget support, represent about one-quarter of net disbursements and in total are less than the debt service payments made by recipient countries.

There is still a long way to go in improving aid effectiveness

The rest of the aid flow sustains a parallel, multidonor, multiproject economy, obscure to host governments and where donors are sometimes reluctant to share information. This parallel economy fragments public programs in key sectors—for example, donors are estimated to fund 40 percent of health spending in a typical African country (World Bank 1999b)—and makes integrated budget management impossible. Because donors prefer to fund capital spending on physical projects, aid also distorts recurrent and capital spending in favor of the latter. Recipient governments become cash poor and project rich, a trend exacerbated in the phase of fiscal stabilization with the tightness of current spending limits.

Recipient governments also cannot compete with better-paying project implementation units that draw the best-trained staff out of public service. Moreover, negotiating aid programs and debt relief with multiple donors absorbs valuable time of key officials in aid-dependent countries. Informal surveys suggest that these officials may spend half their time on donor-related activities rather than on internal administration.

Particularly in countries that have only recently moved toward participatory political systems, aid dependence can make governments less accountable to their civil societies. Donor flows are equivalent to half or more of fiscal revenues in many countries—and finance a major part of social and infrastructure spending. Donors are concerned about the financial integrity of their projects, so governments have to account for aid resources using a variety of donor-specific procedures. But at the same time, governments face less pressure to be accountable to their societies.

Institutions, accountability, capacity, and aid dependence thus constitute a fourth development circle. The weaker are the institutional capacity and accountability at the core of government, the stronger is the incentive for donors to rely on their own institutional controls, further undermining government accountability and weakening capacity. Resolving this dilemma will require a fundamental rethinking of the relationships among Africa's civil society, governments, and donors. Major changes are under way, notably the World Bank's Comprehensive Development Framework and the initiation of country-led poverty reduction support programs (chapter 8). But there is still a long way to go in improving aid effectiveness—and in formulating a realistic long-run exit strategy from aid.

A Window of Opportunity

Africa faces daunting challenges. But the start of the new century offers a unique window to address them.

■ *Political opening.* The sharp rise in political participation opens the way for greater public accountability and pressure from civil society for better management of public resources. Today's African leaders are more focused on proper economic management than many of their predecessors, and they have the maturity to address weaknesses of previous policies. These are crucial developments, because the fate of Africa in the new century will be determined not by outsiders, but by Africans.

■ *End of the Cold War.* After World War II, Africa became a strategic and ideological battleground where external powers sought reliable allies rather than effective development partners. The end of the Cold War signaled a reduction in external support for peacekeeping and in aid flows due to waning geopolitical competition. But it also opened a window for donors and recipients to attend to development effectiveness.

■ *Globalization and new technology.* Globalization and new technology offer great opportunities for Africa. World markets are far more open now than ever before. Trade will probably continue to grow faster than world GDP. And the pool of capital seeking diversified international investments is growing rapidly, partly because of the demographic transition in industrial countries. Advances in the information economy offer huge gains to Africa, historically a sparse region with a population largely excluded from information.

But these trends also pose risks. Technological change will continue to put long-run pressure on primary commodity prices. Countries that can-

Globalization and new technology offer great opportunities for Africa

not take advantage of trade and investment opportunities face further marginalization and a longer technological lag. As falling protection in major markets reduces the value of special concessions to poor countries, policies will need to emphasize competitiveness and productivity rather than (or in addition to) preferential trading arrangements.

Will Africa be able to take advantage of the window? Will Africa's development partners be able to support the needed trends? The first set of priorities emerging from these cumulative circles—the interaction of governance, conflict, and poverty—is perhaps the most difficult to address from the perspective of economics alone, but it is also the most fundamental. For countries able to maintain peace and security, entry points into the three other circles must be found. Investment in people is essential for the second circle—involving investment, growth, the demographic transition, and HIV/AIDS. The ingredients of effective programs are known; they can now be priced and budgeted. Addressing the structural and institutional issues in the third and fourth circles will also be fundamental for sustaining the transition from adjustment to growth, social development, and poverty alleviation. This will require more than simply "staying the course" and deepening current reforms in macroeconomic and structural areas, even though they are far from complete.

Notes

1. The Special Program of Assistance was created in 1987 to mobilize concessional, quick-disbursing assistance for poor, debt-distressed African countries with adjustment programs led by the International Monetary Fund and International Development Association. For more details, see OED (1998b).

2. IMF (1997) provides a detailed assessment of performance under Enhanced Structural Adjustment Facility programs; Guillamont and others (1999) find that consistent management contributes to good performance. IMF (1998) provides an external evaluation of the Enhanced Structural Adjustment Facility. For a critical view of adjustment programs, see Mkandawire and Soludo (1999).

3. The eight countries judged to be on track were Benin, Burkina Faso, Ghana, Malawi, Mali, Mozambique, Uganda, and Zambia, although Ghana and Zambia had lapses of discipline (see OED 1998b, p. 98).

CHAPTER 2

Improving Governance, Managing Conflict, and Rebuilding States

Rapid changes in Africa's political landscape have created opportunities for development and growth

Poverty brings about instability and insecurity, which breed underdevelopment. The reverse is also true. Democracy must deliver on the bread and butter issues, otherwise the Continent could slide back into situations where the politics of poverty gives rise to the poverty of politics.

—Dr. Salim Ahmed Salim, Secretary-General, Organization of African Unity, 24 October 1999

GOVERNANCE, CONFLICT MANAGEMENT, AND STATE reconstruction are interrelated issues. Governance is the institutional capability of public organizations to provide the public and other goods demanded by a country's citizens or their representatives in an effective, transparent, impartial, and accountable manner, subject to resource constraints. Conflict management refers to a society's capacity to mediate the conflicting—though not necessarily violent—interests of different social groups through political processes. State reconstruction combines national and supranational competencies for resolving violent conflicts, sustaining peace, and undertaking economic and political postconflict reconstruction. In the past decade this nexus of governance, conflict management, and state building has moved from relative obscurity to being a central issue on Africa's development policy agenda. Why?

The first impulse has come from within Africa, where the political landscape has been changing rapidly. After years of authoritarian regimes and political and economic decline, there has been resurgent popular demand for multiparty elections and accountability in public resource management. Since the early 1990s, 42 of 48 Sub-Saharan states have held multiparty presidential or parliamentary elections. Though these elections have not always been completely fair, they have often generated high voter turnout—sometimes more than 80 percent. This trend has been bolstered by the end of the Cold War, which has made donors less inclined to favor trusted allies over competent development partners (chapter 1). New aid relations emphasize ownership, accountability to domestic stakeholders, and good governance (chapter 8). Moreover, a number of African countries are ready to undertake "second generation" reforms, which require building social consensus and bargaining among social groups.

Globalization also explains the increased importance of these issues. Like other countries, African states face growing pressures both to decentralize and to adapt to emerging global governance structures and standards. These extend beyond trade to encompass many areas once considered within the purview of national policy. Globalization also brings risks of increased economic instability, which can lead to social conflicts. All these factors have increased the importance of sound governance and institutions for mediating conflicts and promoting social cooperation.

This chapter analyzes Africa's postindependence performance in governance and conflict management and highlights opportunities for resolving conflicts, building peace, promoting social cooperation, and improving governance in the 21st century. A first theme of the chapter is that it is wrong to think that Africa's ethnic diversity dooms it to endemic civil conflicts. Poverty, underdevelopment, unemployment, and political exclusion are the root causes lurking behind social fractionalization. But socially fractionalized societies—like most in Africa—require careful management. Thus African countries need to seek inclusive, participatory, and democratic polities compatible with their ethnic diversity. Under the right conditions diversity can promote, rather than impede, social cooperation and stable growth. Active and collaborative involvement by regional institutions and international donors is also critical for resolving conflicts and building peace in Africa.

A second theme involves options for improving institutions for national economic management. Africa has seen many such initiatives as part of reform programs, but success has been limited. One reason for past failures is that externally inspired technocratic measures to streamline and strengthen the bureaucracy have not been matched by complementary action by incumbent states, or by measures to generate demand

African countries need to seek inclusive, participatory, and democratic polities compatible with their ethnic diversity

for good governance by local constituencies. This too is changing. A new breed of African reformers now places far more emphasis on transparency and on measures to empower the users of public services, in part through decentralization. Such measures have significance beyond their immediate impact, helping over time to develop the civic organizations and the capacity needed to sustain a robust democratic system.

Together these two themes point to the following implication: political and economic governance are inseparable, and together they underpin sustainable development. Especially with the spread of modern communications, a corrupt, ineffective state is unlikely to meet the popular and economic demands of the 21st century. As East Asia's experience suggests, states that successfully manage and develop their economies are likely to strengthen their legitimacy. Indeed, African countries with well-managed economies saw an increase in stability, political rights, and civil liberties in the 1990s. Conversely, states in conflict perform poorly on political criteria and have weaker economic policies and institutions (chapter 1).

Political and economic governance are inseparable—and together they underpin sustainable development

Characteristics of a Well-Functioning State

WELL-FUNCTIONING STATES SHARE CERTAIN CHARACTERISTICS. Not all of these are necessarily preconditions for development—many countries, including many industrial ones, fall short on a number of relevant attributes. Nor is there a single model toward which all African countries should aspire. Successful options include "consensual democracy" in Japan, unitary liberal democracy in parts of Europe, and federalist democracies and confederacies in other regions. All of these approaches preserve political competition through popular participation in regular elections, but they differ in many ways.

Yet while the diversity among successful democracies suggests a variety of functional institutional arrangements, effective public institutions generally have some common fundamental characteristics. The first is the capacity to maintain nationwide peace, law, and order, without which other government functions are compromised or impossible. Second, states must secure individual liberty and equality before the law, a process still working itself out in the West and elsewhere. This has been a major institutional inadequacy in many African states. Secure property rights and transparent adjudication of disputes arising thereof are critical in shaping investment decisions. Third, the state needs workable checks and balances on the arbitrary exercise of power. Public decisionmaking must be transparent and predictable. Oversight mechanisms should guard against arbitrariness and ensure accountability in the use of public resources, but need not eliminate the flexibility and delegation needed to respond quickly to changing circumstances.

Once this institutional infrastructure is in place, the public sector has an important role in financing and providing key social, infrastructure, and dispute resolution services. Effective states raise revenue and supply these services in ways that contribute to development. Where corruption is detected, legal and administrative sanctions are implemented, regardless of the social and political status of perpetrators. A free press and public watchdog organizations guard against abuse of power and reinforce checks and balances and effective service delivery. The political process is broadly viewed as legitimate and provides an anchor of predictability for private investment and economic development more broadly. Besides enhancing individual liberties, a participatory civil society, free speech, and an independent press are indispensable for promoting productive and healthy investment.

It would be naïve to expect these characteristics to be adopted automatically as the political platform of any country's leadership. Governments the world over are susceptible to factional contests for political power, motivated by incentives other than those that encourage good governance. But without political stability and checks and balances on power, public responsibility for key services and social legitimacy for government are in jeopardy and economic development may not be achieved. Without these foundations of good political and economic governance, Africa's development will be sluggish—or stalled.

Without the foundations of good political and economic governance, Africa's development will be sluggish—or stalled

African Governance since Independence

PERCEPTIONS OF AFRICAN GOVERNANCE HAVE BEEN BEDEVILED BY A tendency toward sweeping generalization—an unwillingness to acknowledge not just failures but also mixed outcomes and some successes. Any review of Africa's governance track record since independence thus confronts the challenge of both describing general patterns and highlighting variations across countries.

A complex patchwork of old and new state institutions produced a varied but generally disappointing record in national governance

By definition, colonial rule tended to be unaccountable to Africans and overly reliant on the military to suppress dissent. Its departure was rapid and unanticipated by both colonizer and colonized. Part of the early caution about the departure of colonialists was perhaps a response to the recognition that local skills were inadequate and the institutional foundations of incoming African governments were poor. For example, when Congo gained independence in 1960, it had just 16 postsecondary school graduates—for a population of 13 million.

The constitutional innovations introduced at independence partly sought to promote long-repressed local values. But these were unavoidably blended with the formal structures of national governance introduced by European colonialism. With notable exceptions like Kenya and Zimbabwe, British colonialism bequeathed to its former dependencies the legacy of "indirect rule," which provided considerable autonomy to "traditional" rulers—whether these were genuinely traditional or not—against the backdrop of English common law.

In contrast, former French colonies inherited a metropolitan-centered system of direct rule extending to the remotest rural cantons, circles, and communes. Belgian administration in Burundi, Congo, and Rwanda was comprehensive and highly autocratic. Until its cataclysmic end in 1974, Portuguese colonialism in countries like Angola, Guinea-Bissau, and Mozambique abjured local participation in governance, much less indigenous representation. This complex patchwork of old and new state institutions produced a varied but generally disappointing record in national governance. But there were exceptions—like Botswana, Côte d'Ivoire (until the 1980s), Kenya, and Mauritius—where public institutional capability was considerable. Overall, the political transition between the 1960s and the early 1990s can be divided into three phases:

- *Guarded experimentation—1960s to early 1970s.* Former British colonies inherited variants of the Westminster system, with competitive parties, independent judiciaries, and cabinet governments based on a merit-recruited, politically neutral civil service. Former French-ruled states got a powerful presidential system wielding strong executive authority. Under this system the comparatively weak office of the prime minister headed the public service and was answerable to a chamber of deputies elected on a run-off constituency-majority system. But confronted by the divisive, ethnic-driven politics of redistribution in the 1960s, innovations were made to introduce all-purpose nation-building ideologies. Single parties emerged encompassing dissidents and competitors, sometimes using patronage to consolidate power—and not always peacefully. Thus conceived, national unity was expected to facilitate faster, friction-free growth.

Though many presume that economic and institutional decline set in almost immediately after independence, that was not the case. With limited aid, African economies grew by more than 5 percent a year between 1965 and 1973. Primary school enrollments rose sharply, and new universities, infrastructure, and public service training programs were developed. At the same time, driven by the development orthodoxy of the day, the supposed scarcity of indigenous entrepreneurs, and the fear of commercially dominant expatriate minorities, many countries laid the foundations for increased state control and centralization of resource allocation in a broad range of economic activities.

With limited aid, African economies grew by more than 5 percent a year between 1965 and 1973

- *Military rule, dictatorships, and economic regress—mid-1970s to 1990s.* After military takeovers in the early 1960s in Congo-Brazzaville, Dahomey (Benin), and Togo, the first gush of military coups in 1965–66 in Burundi, Central African Republic, Congo-Kinshasa, Ghana, Nigeria, and Upper Volta (Burkina Faso) opened the way to autocratic military rule. External involvement played a major role in such cases. Many proved disastrous from an economic and institution-building point of view, as evidenced by Ethiopia (1974–91), Ghana (1966–69 and 1972–83), Mali (1968–91), Nigeria (1983–98), Somalia (1969–91), Uganda (1971–79), and Zaire (1965–97). By 1990 half of Africa's states had military or quasi-military governments. In parallel with authoritarian military governments came a trend toward single-party rule under autocratic civilian leaders, largely pursuing interventionist economic policies, in some cases under the banners of socialism or Marxism. Especially when combined with external shocks, the resulting economic decline and politicization of the bureaucracy eroded much of what remained of institutional governance capacity and undermined many of the accomplishments of the 1960s.

- *Political and economic liberalization—late 1980s and 1990s.* Recurrent balance of payments crises and economic regress, together with pressure from donors, led a number of African governments to adopt structural adjustment policies in the 1980s, opening up markets, encouraging deregulation and private initiative, and reducing state economic intervention. The popular processes that led to the collapse of Benin's military government in 1989, the fall of the Berlin Wall in late 1989, and the release of Nelson Mandela from prison in early 1990 increased demands for constitutional reform. Under popular pressure, some francophone states (Benin, Congo-Brazzaville, Mali) held national conferences that replaced authoritarian constitutions with French-style democratic ones. Especially after 1989, popular discontent with military or autocratic regimes found vent in mass demonstrations in favor of individual freedoms and multiparty government. Most remaining African governments conceded the principle of democracy in the first half of the 1990s. By 1999 nearly all countries had held multiparty elections with varying degrees of credibility.

A few African states have built effective national governance institutions on the foundations of genuinely competitive democracy and the rule of law...

Variations across Countries

A closer look at the experiences of individual countries also points to much greater diversity than is commonly imagined.

Capable and effective governance. A few states, like Botswana and Mauritius, have demonstrated a capacity to build effective national governance institutions on the foundations of genuinely competitive democracy and the rule of law. Although Botswana's dominant party (Botswana Democratic Party) has been in office since independence in 1966, it has provided wide freedom to opposition parties and maintained the rule of law. Mauritius—with its medley of ethnic and religious groups, including Hindus, Muslims, Creoles, Africans, and Europeans—has defied the view that ethnolinguistic diversity undermines economic growth. This has been achieved through regular multiparty elections where competition cuts across the ethnic divide and—significantly—by a delicate balance of ethnic representation at the top levels of government. South Africa's transition since 1994 also points in this direction. The linchpin of the 1994 transition was an ethnically inclusive government of national unity underpinned by the visionary leadership of Mandela.

Violent conflict and state disintegration. At the other end of the spectrum are states where governance has disintegrated into protracted civil wars and lawlessness. These states include Angola (since 1975), Burundi (since 1993), Democratic Republic of Congo (since 1997), Guinea-Bissau (1997–99), Liberia (1989–97), Sierra Leone (1992–99), Somalia (since 1991), and Sudan (since 1983). In addition, large slices of states bordering these countries have suffered the spillover effects of conflict.

The vulnerability of these countries to conflict mirrors a global pattern. Since 1980 more than half of all low-income countries have been involved in conflict, including 15 of the world's 20 poorest countries. Africa is no exception. In 1999 one African in five lived in countries severely disrupted by wars or civil conflicts, and 90 percent of the casualties were civilians. There were more than 3 million refugees and 16 million internally displaced persons. And an estimated 20 million landmines had been laid in Africa, including 9 million in Angola alone.

...but many have been caught in a low-level equilibrium of poor institutional capability and ineffective economic transformation

State crisis and institutional decay. About two-thirds of African states have neither enjoyed the opportunities created by development success nor endured the violent risks inherent in the opposite extreme. By the 1990s many of these countries were caught in a low-level equilibrium of poor institutional capability and ineffective economic transformation. Some had initially showed high promise. Kenya, for example, was an African "miracle" in the 1960s and early 1970s, growing by 7.9 percent a year between 1965 and 1973. Internal security, working infrastructure, and capable public institutions staffed by competent Kenyans underpinned that performance. But since the mid-1980s the country has been a victim of corruption and institutional decay. Since 1989 it has seen rising internal violence, economic mismanagement, and declining external aid. Other countries struggling to escape a low-level equilibrium trap include some with enormous economic potential and large populations, including Cameroon, Nigeria, and Tanzania.

What Accounts for the Evolving Patterns of Governance?

Broadly speaking, there are two types of explanations for Africa's governance patterns. The first focuses on conditions inherited at independence—political and economic—along with structural factors that reflect Africa's development experience. The second focuses more on successive generations of leaders and the political and economic policies they have pursued. Rather than arbitrate between these competing views, the discussion here highlights the relevance and the implications of each.

The administrative heritage of colonialism. Although colonial rule generally provided poor preparation for African self-rule, some countries emerged from it better prepared than others. This is evident in the cross-country differences in investment by colonial powers in the skills needed to govern an independent state—good leadership, administration and management of public resources, understanding of the formulation and application of laws.

There is no difference in performance between multiethnic and homogeneous states that sustain democratic institutions

In this regard the British dependencies in West Africa—Ghana, Nigeria, Sierra Leone, arguably The Gambia—had a head start. Indirect rule and the absence of European settlers in West Africa facilitated a greater presence of trained Africans in the governments of these states at independence relative to British colonies in East Africa, Zambia, and Zimbabwe. So did the output of Gordon Memorial College in Sudan. In contrast, the first institution of higher learning in East Africa—Makerere College in Uganda—opened its doors only in 1930. Segregated public service systems in most of East and Southern Africa did not permit much African participation in government—as elected representatives or civil servants—until well into the 1950s, on the eve of independence.

French-governed territories were also not as well prepared for self-rule as was anglophone West Africa. French colonial policy advocated assimilation into an empirewide public service and recruitment into one imperial French army. Only a few Africans studied at French universities and served in the French public service, many of them in what is now Benin. Similarly, education opportunities for Africans at top French schools—like Ecole Normale William Ponty in Dakar, Senegal—were limited. Only in the 1950s were university-level institutions opened in Dakar and Tananarive (Madagascar) to serve French colonies.

Under the French Union (1946–60) a few Africans were elected to the French legislature and served as government ministers, but the system called for African acquiescence. Its limits are best demonstrated by the precipitous departure of French colonial officers after the Guinean vote for independence in 1958—leaving Guinea without effective administration almost overnight. Education opportunities for Africans in Belgian, Portuguese, and Italian colonies were even more sparse. The impacts of these colonial inequalities have long persisted.

Ethnic diversity. African states are exceptionally diverse in ethnic and linguistic terms. Some have argued that such diversity damages or destroys national consensus on infrastructure, macroeconomic reform, and the allocation of public goods. But while ethnic conflict is a major factor in African politics, recent research suggests that its impact on economic performance is mediated by a country's institutional structure. There is no difference in performance between multiethnic and homogeneous states that sustain democratic institutions (Collier 1998). Without such institutions, however, multiethnic states grow far more slowly. This finding is consonant with the argument that faction-ridden societies are best administered by a decentralized democracy.[1]

Tanzania illustrates the potential for ethnic harmony in a racially diverse setting. With an estimated 120 ethnic groups, it has avoided all ethnic conflict or political appeal to linguistic units. National unity cuts across ethnic boundaries, leading to a widespread rejection of tribalism. This outcome can be attributed to former President Julius Nyerere's integrative political efforts and his government's promotion of Swahili as a common language.

Political leadership. How much has Africa's governance been shaped by the quality of its leaders? And might good leadership, where it exists, shape the political institutions of the 21st century? Some imaginative governments have turned supposed liabilities (ethnic and linguistic diversity in Tanzania, for instance) into a nation-building asset. In contrast, some states with religious, ethnic, and linguistic homogeneity (like Somalia) have slid into political disaster. Leadership is important, and many studies of African leadership since independence distinguish four types (box 2.1). But in few cases have African leaders been successful in promoting sustained development in their countries.

Civil war lowers per capita GDP by 2.2 percentage points a year

Civil Conflict

ABOUT ONE-FIFTH OF AFRICANS LIVE IN COUNTRIES SEVERELY DISrupted by conflict. Excluding independence wars, nearly 20 African countries have experienced at least one period of civil strife since 1960. This unfortunate legacy has huge direct costs (box 2. 2) and incalculable indirect costs, including the destruction of physical infrastructure, loss of institutional capacity and social capital, and flight of financial and human capital. Civil war lowers per capita GDP by 2.2 percentage points a year. Moreover, dynamic sectors that use or supply capital and transact intensively—manufacturing, construction, transport, distribution, finance—suffer disproportionate losses (Collier, Hoeffler, and Pattillo 1999). Civil wars also leave a social and political legacy that can affect development for decades.

Conflict has reinforced perceptions of Africa as a doomed continent with inescapable ethnic cleavages and tribalism. But recent analysis of the determinants of civil wars in Africa and other regions points to deep political and economic development failures as the root causes. In diverse societies where intergroup interactions have been uncooperative, the

Box 2.1 Four Types of African Leadership

■ *Successful and conservative leaders.* Recognizing the complex mix of peoples and cultures arbitrarily enclosed within colonial boundaries, these leaders introduced ethnically inclusive policies and informal power-sharing arrangements. They also pursued growth-oriented economic policies and increased human resource investments. Botswana's founding president, Sir Seretse Khama, provides a leading example—one that has been maintained by his successors—as does Felix Houphouet-Boigny in Côte d'Ivoire between 1960 and the mid-1980s. Under Jomo Kenyatta, Kenya enjoyed stability and high economic growth rates, though complaints about ethnic inequalities emerged toward the end of his rule.

■ *Radical and ideological leaders.* Motivated primarily by African (or Marxist) socialism, these leaders sought an economic and social transformation of their societies through state intervention and the leadership of a mass-based one-party state. In some cases (Kwame Nkrumah in Ghana, Julius Nyerere in Tanzania) there was success in molding national consciousness. Elsewhere the policy proved socially divisive. Economically, state intervention yielded disappointing results. When combined with war in states such as Guinea-Bissau and Mozambique, the result was economic regress.

■ *Predatory leaders.* Instead of focusing on efficient national resource management and growth-enhancing policies, predatory leaders did the opposite. National and state offices were treated as personal money-making positions. The archetypal case of Zaire under Mobutu Sese Seko has been duplicated to a lesser degree in a number of other states. Conditions in Nigeria under Sani Abacha (1993–98) also fit that mode.

■ *Tyrants.* Because of the eccentricity that often marks tyrants, and the shocking human rights abuses that they perpetrate, this form of leadership has received more international attention than the rest. Besides the cost in lives, its economic legacy is the most catastrophic. Uganda under Idi Amin (1971–79) and Equatorial Guinea under Macias Nguema (1968–79) are the worst examples. The Rwandan regime that organized the 1994 genocide represents tyranny at its most extreme, costing more than 500,000 lives and cutting GDP by two-thirds in a matter of months.

Source: Chege 1999.

fundamental problem has been a failure to develop political institutions able to accommodate such diversity. The highly centralized governance systems in most African countries have failed to take into account sociopolitical differences. This becomes explosive when mass poverty enters the picture. And once started, civil wars retard economic and social development and aggravate poverty—completing the vicious circle of conflict, poverty, and exclusionary politics.

Causes of Conflict

The high incidence of civil wars in Africa is commonly attributed to ethnic diversity. This inference might seem self-evident, given that rebel movements almost always have ethnic identities. But more systematic analysis suggests that Africa's civil wars conform to a global pattern explained by political and economic factors as well as by ethnic, cultural, and religious diversity (Collier and Hoeffler 1998, 1999; Collier, Hoeffler, and Soderbom 1999; Collier, Elbadawi, and Sambanis 2000a, b). Civil wars are less likely when the young men who otherwise provide ready recruits to rebel causes have earning power in productive activities (as proxied by indicators of economic development, such as per capita GDP or education attainment). To a certain degree, extensive natural resources—including diamonds and other minerals—are associated with a higher risk of war. Resources provide a convenient way to sustain "justice-seeking" rebel movements and are easily lootable assets that can encourage "loot-seeking" rebellion. They can also help governments fund armies or buy popular support. The risk of civil wars has also been associated with political repression and the absence of political rights.

This literature also suggests that the influence of social diversity on civil wars is more complex than a casual reading would suggest. Ethnic, reli-

Africa's civil wars conform to a global pattern explained by political and economic factors

---

Box 2.2 Costs of Conflict in Africa

CONFLICT IMPOSES HEAVY SOCIAL AND ECONOMIC COSTS in the countries where it occurs. It also imposes costs on neighboring countries by generating refugee flows, increasing military spending, impeding key communication routes, and reducing trade and investment (domestic and foreign). The resources diverted from development uses by conflict—over and above any additional assistance provided by the international community—are estimated at $1 billion a year in Central Africa and more than $800 million in West Africa. To this must be added the costs of refugee assistance, estimated at more than $500 million for Central Africa alone.

These estimates do not include the costs of environmental degradation occasioned by the disruptive movements of large numbers of people. With an estimated 400,000 refugees, Guinea has suffered severe deforestation. Sudan's high military spending—more than three times the African average—may have caused investment to fall by 16 percentage points of GDP. Its civil war may have reduced growth by up to 8 percentage points.

Less dramatic but also significant in many countries has been an increase in violence and crime. One survey of South Africa put the cost of crime and violence at about 6 percent of GDP; this is not out of line with estimates for a number of countries in Latin America. In addition to its direct economic and human costs, violence inhibits development in many ways. Farmers in predominantly agrarian economies cannot cultivate and harvest in bandit-infested regions. Vendors cannot operate beyond limited hours because of the security risk. Factories cannot operate more than one shift because employees cannot commute safely to work. High and in some cases growing criminal violence has many causes, including unemployment, high inequality, and the limited legitimacy and responsiveness of police forces and public security structures.

Source: World Bank; *Sunday Times,* 14 February 1999.

gious, or cultural diversity becomes problematic when it approaches polarization between two dominant groups. In such polarized societies it is easier to start and to sustain a rebellion. But further diversity can actually reduce, rather than increase, the risk of civil war, because maintaining the unity of a rebel movement composed of diverse groups tends to become harder over time.

What, then, accounts for Africa's high risk of civil wars?

Better political rights, higher living standards, and more diversified economies are key in reducing the risk of civil war

- *The median African country faces a high risk of civil war*—though not higher than countries in some other regions.
- *Four factors drive Africa's propensity for violent conflict.* First, many countries are dependent on natural resources. Second, income in Africa is low—the fact that young men are very poor and often have little education has increased the risk of civil conflict. Third, a lack of democratic rights has also increased the risk of violence. Until the 1990s the only prospect for power transfer in many countries was through violence. Fourth, African countries tend to be small. Even though countries with smaller populations have a lower risk of war, Africa as a region has a higher risk because the risk does not increase proportionately with population size.[2]
- *Allowing for other factors, Africa's ethnic diversity is a deterrent rather than a cause of civil war.* Globally, countries with homogeneous or highly diverse societies are significantly less prone to violent conflicts than are polarized countries.

How effective are political reforms and economic development in reducing the risk of civil war? Better political rights, higher living standards, and more diversified economies are key—achievements in any of these areas are associated with a lower risk of conflict. And while the most effective strategy is to make progress on all fronts, better political rights appear to be most important in reducing the risks, both directly and because they are associated with stable economic growth (chapter 1).

Conflict Resolution, Peacebuilding, and State Reconstruction

The previous section discussed a broad framework for preventing civil wars. Ideally the same framework should provide guidance for resolving conflict and building peace after a war. But once a civil war starts, it takes on a life of its own. Especially during protracted conflicts, mistrust among warring factions increases, destruction of economic and social capital is substantial, and opportunistic behavior dominates, including by groups who benefit from continuation of the war. Hence resolving conflict and building peace are much more complex than preventing war. This constitutes one of the main challenges facing African countries.

Unless a government is committed to political reforms, it is in its best interests to renege on peace agreements once rebels lay down their arms. This credibility problem suggests the important role that an external agency (such as a supranational regional body) can play in conflict resolution. Conflict resolution and peacebuilding efforts in Mozambique offer important lessons. A commitment to peace by the key protagonists was essential. But without active regional and international assistance it would have been difficult to rebuild public confidence, establish government legitimacy, and persuade interest groups to support peace (box 2.3).

An end to violence does not ensure sustainable peace. Once hostilities have ceased, peacebuilding and postconflict reconstruction must begin—otherwise violence can easily recur. Peacebuilding is multidimensional, involving activities ranging from demobilization and reintegration of former combatants and resettlement of refugees to demining, emergency

Resolving conflict and building peace are much more complex than preventing war

---

Box 2.3 Reversing a Spiral of Decline in Mozambique

MOZAMBIQUE OFFERS A STRIKING AND UNLIKELY EXAMple of the reconstruction of national governance institutions after a brutal civil war. Colonized by Portugal in the 16th century, it served primarily as a colony of last resort for that country's poor. Political discontent with Portuguese rule produced a guerrilla war and victory in 1974, led by the current ruling party FRELIMO. But before long FRELIMO's failing Marxist program was sabotaged by RENAMO, a guerilla force supported by Rhodesia and South Africa. The indiscriminate destruction of infrastructure and killing of civilians by RENAMO and by FRELIMO counteroffensives left most of rural Mozambique a vast killing field.

Discussions between the two sides began in 1989, leading to full-fledged negotiations in 1992. Unlike talks elsewhere in Africa, neither FRELIMO nor RENAMO

sought a zero-sum solution. Negotiations produced a new democratic constitution, multiparty elections in 1994, full demobilization of both armies, and the building of a new party-neutral army. Though not part of government, RENAMO enjoys a share of state resources and local support in its central Mozambique bailiwick. A second round of elections was held in late 1999.

Peace and economic liberalization have changed Mozambique beyond recognition. Though still very poor, it was one of the fastest-growing economies in Africa in the 1990s. Strong macroeconomic management has attracted considerable external aid and higher private investment than many of its wealthier neighbors. Much remains to be done, however, especially in the countryside—and especially with the massive destruction wrought by recent floods.

relief, food aid, and economic rehabilitation, including infrastructure repair. The move from war to peace is a long-term process of political, economic, and social transformation. A core element is the development of institutions, such as fair courts and inclusive electoral processes, that facilitate negotiation and nonviolent resolution of disputes.

Different wars pose different challenges for peacebuilding. Long wars and ethnic and religious conflicts are more difficult to end through peace settlements. On the other hand, war weariness can reinforce the desire to maintain peace. How and when third-party intervention is used, and the nature of the intervention, affect its chances of success. Early intervention can prevent hostility from rising over time, but in cases of extreme hostility not even a peace treaty and a multilateral peace operation can assure peace.

What are the policy implications of these findings? A number of general lessons emerge, although the circumstances and nature of the conflict will determine the required approach. A peace treaty is an important first step, because such treaties are highly correlated with peacebuilding success. But efforts must also be made to address the sociopolitical problems that caused the war and to develop institutions that encourage economic growth, equitable distribution of resources, and political inclusion.

Regional organizations can make a major contribution. In most conflicts international intervention is needed to end hostilities. The United Nations is the primary institution for peacekeeping and peacebuilding, and in some cases a multinational operation under the United Nations is essential. But attention is increasingly being given to regional approaches, and the Organization of African Unity and subregional organizations have taken on conflict management responsibilities. The establishment within the Organization of African Unity of a conflict management mechanism has increased its capacity to initiate and manage diplomatic interventions and conflict mediation efforts. Subregional organizations such as the Economic Community of West African States and the Southern African Development Community have added security cooperation to their mandates and engage in joint military training and peacekeeping exercises. The ability of subregional organizations to mount peacekeeping operations has evolved considerably as experience has been gained and capacity built.

Because effective collective security arrangements depend on the national security forces that comprise them, attention must be given to creating coherent and efficient national security structures. At the same time, regional security protocols can promote security reform at the

International and regional intervention can underpin the credibility of measures to end hostilities

national level. For example, there is considerable scope for greater regional cooperation to curb cross-border trade in small arms—as has happened in West Africa.

The international development community also has a role. The emphasis on African solutions to African problems should not, however, be seen as an excuse for disengagement by the international community. Even when African institutions mount operations, they need considerable financial and logistical assistance. Recent peacebuilding operations also suggest that security initiatives must be supplemented by efforts to help war-affected regions develop economically. Multilateral and bilateral development institutions have to actively cooperate with other regional and international organizations to ensure coordination and implementation of initiatives. They also need to find different approaches to address the problems of postconflict countries. Postconflict reconstruction necessitates a comprehensive approach; it is long and costly, requiring both considerable resources in the early stages of recovery and commitment over the long term.

Countries coming out of conflict usually face difficult choices and adverse initial conditions. They are faced with the immediate need to provide security, both to protect against violence and to prevent a recurrence of hostilities. But conflict usually undermines individual security and weakens state and civil society institutions that could provide law and order and engender trust. Rebuilding such institutions takes time and resources, but the need to restore fiscal discipline, usually with few options to raise revenue, leaves little room for major new spending.

Other factors also reduce the scope for redeploying budget resources. Civil wars normally fail to produce decisive peace, and the creation of a smaller unified national army does not necessarily save money, particularly in the short term. Countries in or emerging from protracted conflict often face unsustainable debt and arrears to international creditors—debt that stalls the involvement of multilateral institutions in their reconstruction programs.

The policies adopted by governments and their development partners can help build and sustain peace. These include measures for:

- Resolving institutional breakdown, through the creation of a fully accountable, transparent, and participatory system of government that protects the rights of ethnic, religious, and cultural minorities.
- Reducing individual insecurity and consolidating the broader political process—for example, shifting financial and human resources to

Security initiatives must be supplemented by efforts to help war-affected regions develop economically

63

strengthen institutions of law and order, coupled with demobilization and the creation of a professional, capable, and unified military.

- Improving laws and incentives. Efforts should be made early on to create the legal and incentive environment required to restore professional ethos and ensure the effectiveness and vitality of formal and informal institutions of civil society.
- Undertaking economic reforms and restoring growth and development. Certain policies could be particularly helpful for repatriating flight capital and recovering assets and investments. As Uganda suggests, debt relief in support of a sound postconflict reconstruction program can be one such instrument (box 2.4).

Better governance should aim at the 3 E's: Empower citizens Enable governments Enforce law

Restructuring and Reforming Africa's Institutions of Governance

BETTER GOVERNANCE IS A DEVELOPMENT IMPERATIVE FOR MOST African countries. Most stories of African governance in recent decades are stories of shortcomings. Good governance should aim to achieve the "three E's":

- *Empower* citizens to hold governments accountable through participation and decentralization.
- *Enable* governments to respond to new demands by building capacity.
- *Enforce* compliance with the rule of law and greater transparency.

Box 2.4 The Contribution of Debt Relief in Uganda's Repatriation of Flight Capital

TO SUPPORT UGANDA'S REMARKABLE ECONOMIC reforms after 1992, international financial institutions made it the first country to qualify for debt relief under the Heavily Indebted Poor Countries initiative. This move had dramatic effects on confidence. Institutional investor risk ratings jumped from 5.2 to 20.3, overtaking countries such as Côte d'Ivoire.

In 1992, $15 million in flight capital left Uganda. By 1997 the government had turned the tide: $311 million—17 percent of private wealth—was repatriated. Still, there was enormous potential for continued repatriation. Were all flight capital to return, the stock of private capital could be doubled.

Source: Collier 1999; Collier, Hoeffler, and Pattillo 1999.

These objectives are not simply current fashions. Comparative studies point to the importance of creating durable and inclusive systems of political representation, especially in ethnically diverse societies. Improving the capacity of the state is also key, not only for economic management but also for strengthening and legitimizing the state (box 2.5). To achieve these goals, Africa needs institutional reform tailored to each country's social, political, and economic priorities.

Building on recent gains in political participation, most countries need to develop systems and structures that facilitate political pluralism, tolerance, and inclusion; to institutionalize constitutional government, the

---

Box 2.5 Can Stable Development States Emerge in Ethnically Diverse Africa?

AT THE DAWN OF AFRICAN INDEPENDENCE, W. ARTHUR Lewis (1965) recognized that cultural diversity called for consensus-based, decentralized, and inclusive governance rather than centralized one-party authoritarianism. Lewis's insight has been corroborated by recent studies stressing the importance for development of political arrangements able to foster compromise and resolve conflicting claims. A functioning democracy offsets the adverse effects on growth of high ethnic diversity, whereas political rights have little effect on growth in ethnically homogeneous societies.

In a study of Europe, Tilly (1993) finds that representative institutions and successful states emerged out of intergroup bargaining where the state gradually assumed functions—including the provision of security—previously provided through ethnic groups. Under the right conditions this can lead to a development-oriented state, which ensures that economic growth is equitably distributed to reduce economic disparities (Collier and Binswanger 1999). For such coalition politics, a polarized society divided into just two contesting ethnic groups will find a development-oriented bargaining equilibrium more fragile than one with many groups, provided political arrangements enable these groups to represent their interests.

In Africa these principles imply, first, the need for open information on policies and budgets. A trans-parent budget process enables repeated and stable bargaining that leads to an outcome owned by all parties. There is also a need for reliable information and contract enforcement for the business community, to level the playing field between individuals and groups—say, in access to credit. A third point concerns the role of governments in ethnically diverse societies. Public sectors in such countries are faced with continuous pressures to dispense patronage along ethnic lines. Active measures are needed to contain this, such as competitive examinations for entry, tighter definitions of job functions, and performance-based assessments. In addition, the boundary between public and private service provision might be shifted toward the latter.

All these observations point in a similar direction. Acquiring capacity—to provide information, manage resources transparently, and provide services effectively to businesses and households—will be essential to the consolidation of stable, representative systems of government in Africa. The use of ethnic identification to meet needs and perform functions will be replaced by other means, facilitated by the state. Governance reforms that increase such state capabilities are win-win—contributing both to the quality of economic management and to the consolidation of durable political systems.

rule of law, and respect for human rights; and to promote accountability and transparency in democratic institutions. Measures to bring service delivery closer to the people can provide a useful entry point in creating constituencies for broader public sector reform. At the same time, regional initiatives can improve enforcement of legality and the rule of law—and hence better governance—within countries.

Political Dimensions of Governance

Proactive measures are needed to build political accountability and power sharing, starting with the public service

The sociopolitical environment in most African countries is in flux. Countries are trying to break away from patterns of authoritarianism, but most have not yet fully instituted participatory systems of governance. Multiparty electoral systems can be put in place relatively quickly, but developing accountable, credible, and durable democratic institutions is a longer process. The role of political leaders in this process cannot be overemphasized: proactive measures are needed to build political accountability and power sharing, starting with the public service. Political leaders can lead by example and instill the principles of democracy in society. Over time nondemocratic practices will weaken and democratic progress will take hold, helping to create national unity.

Individual African countries have to determine the political structures that suit them best. Democracy can have many faces, but some general principles must be shared by all: constitutional government, respect for human rights, adherence to the rule of law, and freedom of expression and association. Reforming countries are struggling to institutionalize these principles. To succeed, reforms will need to strengthen the capacity of citizens to engage in collective action and hold governments accountable, while increasing government capacity to be responsive.

Given the increased availability of small arms, the question of providing security for the state and its people is at the center of the debate on political reform in Africa. Better governance should promote the democratic oversight of security forces and protect people against violence and crime. There are positive examples of security reform in Africa—including South Africa's open discussions on defense policy since the end of apartheid, as well as its integration of disparate forces into a national army, Mali's public debate on military restructuring and promotion of a moratorium on small arms, and Zimbabwe's police reforms, which focus on accountability and responsiveness to community needs.

Elections and Electoral Systems

Elections alone do not create functioning democracies, and many African states that have moved to free elections need to fortify basic democratic tenets. Several factors stand in the way, including the incongruence between Western electoral systems and Africa's ethnic politics. African countries must develop democratic systems that facilitate political inclusion and representative parliaments, able to respond to the needs of a citizenry that defines itself largely in terms of ethnic kinship.

African countries must develop inclusive representation—but have many options for doing so

Most countries have adopted electoral systems from established Western democracies, making little attempt to adapt them to local realities or needs. In many countries elections have been conducted on a winner-takes-all basis, excluding some groups from political power. There is a high development price to be paid for this, as the most economically successful and best-educated minorities have sometimes been among those excluded.

Ways must be found to make electoral systems more inclusive, through diverse arrangements at the national and local levels. These might include proportional representation or hybrid systems. Even when people vote in ethnic or religious blocs, electoral systems can promote factional representation and stability. What is required is more consensus-based, decentralized, federalist-oriented, inclusive forms of governance.

Although a strong state is needed and economic policy considerations should inform proposals for political reform, there are a number of options for broader and more inclusive representation in Africa:

- Informal power sharing among elites.
- Proportional representation that protects minorities.
- Bicameral legislatures in which one (upper) chamber represents diverse regional or ethnic groups, giving them equal power regardless of their numerical or economic strength.
- Regional autonomy, with compensation mechanisms for less advantaged regions.
- Federalism with national-level guarantees of individual rights so that discrimination against minorities in specific states can be assuaged by higher intervention.
- Confederacy, providing constituent groups with wide powers short of national defense and foreign policy.

Innovative structures that facilitate broader participation and representative governance can more readily be put in place at the local than at the national level

All these national governance concepts provide more space for autonomous local initiatives than the political systems currently in place in most African countries. Though most attention has been given to presidential and national elections, devolution of political power can promote good governance. Locally elected officials are more easily held accountable and have greater incentives to respond to community demands for better services. Population groups that may not be well represented at the national level can still assume responsibility for managing their affairs at provincial levels. In many cases innovative structures that facilitate broader participation and representative governance can more readily be put in place at the local than at the national level. Traditional and formal governance structures can also be more easily blended and power-sharing arrangements worked out at subnational levels.

Although electoral systems can facilitate political inclusion and representation, effective political parties are also needed. Throughout Africa, greater political freedom has increased the number of political parties. But these parties often lack a broad constituency or distinctive platforms. New parties also need to develop organizational skills and access financial resources. Further, political parties must ensure that women have opportunities to participate in the political process, both as candidates and as informed members of the electorate. Local and provincial politics can provide a useful training ground for participation in national politics.

The high cost of elections and political campaigns must be contained if elections are to be sustained without substantial external support. In many African countries the costs of campaigning are very high relative to income levels—in Uganda, for example, campaign costs for parliamentary candidates were as high as $60,000 in 1998. This is partly because of widely dispersed rural populations, poor and costly transportation and communications, and limited media coverage. But in some cases campaign costs are driven up by traditions and expectations of political patronage. The high cost of campaigning undermines political competition by excluding those who lack sufficient resources.

The appropriateness of state funding for political parties and campaigns is widely debated. A legislated limit on campaign spending could help control the cost of campaigns and broaden the pool of candidates. Appropriate and frequent access to media channels by all parties—as well as more press freedom—would guarantee public exposure at a fixed cost, even where the government media dominates. Finally, to preserve public confidence in the political process, elections must be transparent. Independent electoral institutions can help ensure this, as in Ghana (box 2.6).

A further challenge for many African countries is achieving peaceful political succession. For this, a sound institutional base and commitment to democratic principles are required. The rule of law and due process should apply to political leaders, who must be held accountable for their actions while in office. Violations of human rights cannot be tolerated. At the same time, political leaders need to be assured that they will be financially and physically secure upon retirement. In countries undergoing political transition it may be necessary to consider special arrangements, such as amnesty, to ensure a peaceful political change. A number of African countries have already adopted constitutional mechanisms, such as presidential term limits, to facilitate orderly political succession. Leaders who have served with integrity and diligence and who are accorded adequate provisions, both financially and in terms of function, can continue to play an active role in the development of their countries and their continent.

Peaceful political succession requires a sound institutional base and commitment to democratic principles

Institutional Development and Better Governance

In a democratic, participatory political system, all three branches of government—executive, legislative, and judicial—have important roles

---

Box 2.6 The Electoral Commission of Ghana

AS AN INDEPENDENT INSTITUTION CHARGED WITH REGistering voters and candidates, organizing polling, counting votes, and announcing results, the Electoral Commission of Ghana has earned a reputation for professionalism and integrity since the multiparty elections of 1992. It operates at arm's length from the ruling party and is widely seen as impartial—which is why Ghana's opposition party accepted defeat gracefully in the 1996 elections.

In preparing for the 1996 elections, the electoral commission undertook reforms that contributed to fair elections and general acceptance of the results. It responded to concerns about the electoral system and created a transparent election process that helped resolve electoral conflict. The innovative Inter Party

Advisory Committee brought together representatives of political parties and the election authority, providing a forum for constant dialogue. Soliciting the active involvement of and collaborating closely with domestic poll-watching groups also enhanced transparency and greatly boosted public confidence in the outcomes of the elections.

In preparation for the December 2000 elections, the electoral commission has helped draft a bill that seeks to address some of the remaining concerns of political parties. It has also convened meetings of the Inter Party Advisory Committee to discuss outstanding issues and problems in the electoral process. The commission is making a marked contribution to strengthening Ghana's nascent democracy.

to play. Each branch must function effectively, and a balance of power must be established among them. Few African countries have reached this point. The nature and type of government, and its responsiveness to public demands, will be determined by the ability of the executive to provide leadership while respecting the independence and institutional integrity of the legislature and the judiciary. In turn, the legislature and the judiciary are the primary vehicles for upholding constitutional provisions, promoting the rule of law, and protecting citizens' rights.

Political reform has led to a renewed emphasis on constitutionalism. But constitutions can only provide for predictable and stable governance and protect human rights if they are recognized as the ultimate source of authority. To the extent that constitutions are repressive, they will not institutionalize democracy. Further, political leaders must adhere to constitutional principles, and the military and the judiciary must uphold them—processes that can be promoted by popular awareness of constitutionally defined rights and duties.

State institutions. Institutional development cannot be limited to building technical capacity—institutional accountability is also critical. Public involvement is essential for reforms to be sustained, and institutional development needs to be embedded in broader political and governance reforms. Good governance requires a competent executive that respects the constitution and the rule of law and that exercises sound leadership. It also requires institutions that counterbalance executive power and hold the executive accountable.

Parliament is especially important, particularly in performing legislative duties such as scrutinizing budgets. To enhance parliamentary performance, most new African democracies need better information, equipment, technical resources, and professional staff. Efforts to build parliamentary expertise, especially of key committees, would also facilitate legislative oversight. Some of Africa's development partners are helping to make parliaments more effective by providing equipment and training. They could also help by reviewing their procedures and ensuring that development assistance agreements, which fund a large part of public spending in many countries, are subject to legislative review (chapter 8).

In many countries political liberalization has led to the creation of independent agencies that report to parliaments, including ombudsmen, human rights and legal commissions, auditors-general, and anticorruption agencies. But these bodies often lack the autonomy and resources needed to carry out their tasks. Few auditors-general, for exam-

> *Public involvement is essential for reforms to be sustained, and institutional development must be embedded in broader political and governance reforms*

ple, have the resources and support needed to provide timely, high-quality reports (chapter 1). Strengthening such agencies would increase parliamentary effectiveness. While this is primarily a domestic responsibility, development partners can also help—at relatively little cost. Kenya's Office of Controller and Auditor-General offers a good, and perhaps unexpected, example of how this complementarity can work, though the dividend from its findings has been limited by the weak follow-up to its recommendations (box 2.7).

The rule of law is essential for a predictable, stable environment in which conformity to formal rules—rather than reliance on patronage and connections—prevails. It is as necessary for facilitating investment and business transactions as it is for protecting political rights and freedoms. But upholding the rule of law also requires an independent, professional, and competent judiciary. Access to justice is still denied many Africans, particularly in rural areas, because of weaknesses in the legal system. In some cases private sector development is constrained by limited legal expertise in areas such as financial and contract law. In others corruption and delays in the administration of justice have undermined public confidence in the judicial system. For all these reasons, legal reform has become a priority in many countries, and one that Africa's development partners are beginning to assist.

A comprehensive legal sector review can help countries prioritize reforms. A well-functioning and credible legal system requires a merit-

The rule of law is essential for a predictable, stable environment in which conformity to formal rules prevails

---

Box 2.7 Kenya's Office of Controller and Auditor-General

THE KENYAN OFFICE OF CONTROLLER AND AUDITOR-General is an independent body established to audit all government accounts and to report annually to parliament. It has fulfilled its obligations without fear or favor since Kenya's independence in 1963. Despite constant intimidation and attempts to whittle down its authority, the office has consistently provided full accounts of the abuse of public funds at all levels of government. Although the state has never been quick to prosecute the culprits, the office's reports provide a forum for parliamentary debates in which cabinet ministers are held accountable for gross malfeasance in their ministries.

Parliament's public accounts committee has the power to summon civil servants to explain abuses of public funds based on the office's reports—and it does so. The press uses the reports to embarrass offenders. The reports are useful in assembling Kenya's fiscal statistics and in keeping donors informed of trends in public spending. In a country facing entrenched corruption in the public service, the Office of Controller and Auditor-General is an island of institutional integrity whose output could support future reforms.

Source: Chege 1999.

based career structure, adequate compensation, and mechanisms to ensure accountability. Specific training is often needed to meet new demands on the legal system. Streamlining legal procedures and increasing the transparency of legal decisions can help contain corruption. In addition, a stronger legal infrastructure and the use of computer technology can expedite legal decisions, reduce opportunities for corruption, and increase transparency by helping to disseminate a public record of court proceedings at low cost. Alternative dispute mechanisms and provision of legal aid improve access to justice.

A vibrant and diverse civil society is needed to hold governments accountable

Civil society. Good governance is not the sole responsibility of governments. A vibrant and diverse civil society is also needed to hold governments accountable. The freedoms of association, information, and assembly resulting from political transition have expanded civic activism throughout Africa. Civil society organizations have an important role to play in articulating popular interests, monitoring government performance, and facilitating participation in governance.

But this role has to be earned. Not all nongovernmental organizations are genuinely representative or democratic. Some are formed around prominent individuals; others serve narrow interest groups. In some cases groups that helped bring about political transition find it hard to adapt to new circumstances. Nonetheless, vibrant interaction between civic groups—whether traditional councils of elders, ethnic mediators, or contemporary religious and secular organizations—has been indispensable in resolving conflict in African societies. Civil society organizations have also been at the forefront of efforts to combat corruption.

Public education and dissemination of information are among the most significant functions of civil society organizations. The media have an important role to play in this regard, and new technologies have radically improved public access to information. Although political liberalization has usually increased press freedom, private print and electronic media are often still subject to censorship and restrictions, information that should be in the public domain remains difficult to access, and journalistic harassment continues in some countries. Continued state domination of the media also reduces the possibility of objective, nonpartisan reporting during elections.

In most cases private media are underfunded and poorly equipped, and training is needed to enhance skills and professionalism. Better coverage of economic and security issues would increase public awareness of policies in these areas. Expansion of independent radio and television would also increase public access to information. Although newspapers and magazines have become an important source of information in cities, the difficulties and expense of distribution—coupled with low literacy—mean that radio is still the primary means of reaching mass audiences.

Although the private sector is relatively weak in most African countries, political and economic reforms are creating a more enabling environment for private activity. A growing private sector and the resulting increase in economic and employment opportunities outside government contribute to economic growth and better governance. A diverse and capable private sector can also provide and attract the investment that helps open up the economy and society and create options for people to act on their own initiative. In addition, private actors can function as countervailing forces to executive power. Business associations, such as those developing in West, East, and Southern Africa, also provide a way to articulate business interests in the provision of public services (chapter 7).

A growing private sector contributes to economic growth and better governance

Creating Demand for Good Governance

Accountability and transparency are at the heart of efforts to improve governance in Africa. Corruption often flourishes where institutions are weak, where the rule of law and formal rules are not rigorously observed, where political patronage is rife, where the independence and professionalism of the public sector have been eroded, and where civil society lacks the means to generate public pressure. Once entrenched, corruption hinders economic performance, increases the cost of public investment, lowers the quality of public infrastructure, decreases government revenue, and makes it burdensome and costly for citizens—particularly the poor—to access public services. Corruption also undermines the legitimacy of governments and erodes the fabric of society.

Combating corruption is not straightforward or easy. But it is not impossible, especially with increased public awareness of the problem. Indeed, as the costs and consequences of corruption have become more publicly known, efforts to fight it have intensified throughout Africa. Although results take time, civil society organizations and the press have made corruption a public issue and challenged governments to address it. For example, business associations in West Africa are documenting the incidence of unofficial transport levies that are often twice as high as formal levies. Broad coalitions of civil society, the private sector, and governments are required to combat corruption, underpinned by reforms that increase accountability and transparency and enhance public participation in decisionmaking.

Anticorruption strategies must be realistic, achievable, and consistently implemented. They also have to be country specific, because what works in one country may not work in another. Some countries have made a lot of progress by reforming tax laws and investment codes, eliminating price controls, reducing permits and licenses, and revising public procurement procedures. Constitutional and legal requirements for assets disclosure by political leaders and senior officials can also make a difference.

By contrast, stop-start efforts, a piecemeal approach, overemphasis on legal measures, and sporadic anticorruption campaigns are unlikely to yield lasting results. Specialized agencies and anticorruption bodies can only be effective if they have sufficient independence, authority, and resources. Ineffective bodies that lack real power can undermine rather than enhance public accountability.

Public sector management. A professional, meritocratic, and qualified public service is essential to ensure effective and efficient delivery of public services and to combat bureaucratic corruption. For too many Africans, public agencies—their most direct point of contact with government—are synonymous with poor service, corruption, and inefficiency. Popular dissatisfaction undermines confidence in public institutions, undermining government legitimacy. Just as other state institutions need to adapt to changing circumstances and be made more efficient, cost-effective, and accountable, so does the public service. In most countries this will require a fundamental change in orientation. Instead of exercising control, agencies have to move toward facilitation and public service delivery.

Efforts at civil service reform have mostly been in the context of adjustment programs negotiated with the World Bank and International Monetary Fund, and have focused on reducing the wage bill rather than on improving quality. While capacity has increased in some areas (central banks, ministries of finance), there has been little progress in developing the capacity of employees more broadly or in reversing the decline in public service institutions. Revitalizing public service agencies will require transparent, merit-based recruitment procedures, promotion based on performance, sound management, in-service training and career development, and interlocking checks and balances to counter corruption. Internal rules that deal with professional ethics have to be

Anticorruption strategies must be realistic, achievable, and consistently implemented

consistently and impartially applied. Piecemeal reforms are unlikely to be more than a short-term palliative—what is needed is an overarching strategy for sequencing changes. Political commitment at the highest level is also needed if reforms are to be successfully and consistently implemented.

Pay policy in the public sector is especially challenging. Since the early 1970s most public sectors in Africa have been subjected to severe wage compression, as tight as a factor of two to one in Tanzania. Salaries of public employees at the low end of the pay scale are often commensurate with or higher than in the private marketplace. But at the high-skill end, even after a recent trend toward widening differentials as part of reform programs, earnings are often far below market levels. Trained in accordance with European qualifications and fluent in the main international languages, African professionals are highly mobile. As a result many African governments cannot, for example, retain qualified auditors and accountants.

Unless a way can be found to improve pay at the higher levels, it will be impossible to attract, retain, and assure the integrity of highly skilled public officials. The problem is often not one of total resources, as the number of senior officials is quite small, but of willingness to accept significant differentials in pay between top administrative officials and lower-level employees in an integrated civil service. Countries could consider introducing a senior civil service for highly qualified civil servants. Entry to such a cadre would be competitive and meritocratic, and would be rewarded by higher salaries and better professional opportunities.

Political liberalization has generated a number of examples of participatory public sector initiatives. User surveys and other quantitative scorecards of public services are increasingly used in African countries, and the results are increasingly publicly available. User participation in service delivery and oversight is rising, empowering parents to participate in the governance of schools, allowing user groups to manage irrigation systems, involving community groups in the delivery of urban water and waste systems, and so on. Social funds have supported efforts by communities and nongovernmental organizations to invest in and deliver services to the poor in some countries. Increased transparency and participatory service delivery can be mutually reinforcing, as illustrated by Uganda's education reforms (box 2.8; chapter 4).

Decentralization. Decentralization is increasingly seen as a way to improve service delivery and increase popular participation in gover-

Without higher pay, it will be impossible to attract, retain, and assure the integrity of highly skilled public officials

---

Box 2.8 Toward Transparent Funding: Uganda's Education Reforms

IN UGANDA A 1996 BUDGET TRACKING SURVEY HIGH-lighted a stark gap between intent and reality: less than 30 percent of the resources targeted by the Ministry of Finance for nonwage education spending actually found their way to schools. Uganda is committed to universal primary education, to devolving responsibility for delivering services to local authorities, and to involving citizens directly, including through active parent-teacher associations. To eliminate the diversion of funds for overhead and other purposes by government bureaucracies, reforms included the writing of checks directly to individual schools. The amounts of these checks were posted publicly in each locality—empowering parent-teacher associations and others to monitor how the resources were used. In addition, random audits were initiated to follow up.

---

nance. Decentralizing responsibility for the delivery of front-line services—or, more broadly, for decisions on the allocation of scarce public resources—from central to local governments can bring government closer to the people. But decentralization is no panacea. Nor should it be used as an excuse for central governments to reduce their responsibilities to regions. Decentralization has to be part of a national policy to create more responsive and equitable governance, and has to be managed carefully. Effective communication between local and central governments needs to be maintained, and measures of accountability implemented to counter corruption. Equitable allocation of central resources is also needed, as is the ability of decentralized authorities to generate and allocate their own resources.

Decentralizing government may also require additional resources, at least in the short term, unless local government structures already function effectively. In most cases local institutions are weak and need to be strengthened before taking on additional responsibilities. Providing infrastructure, equipment, and training can be costly, and government employees accustomed to working in central offices are often unwilling to relocate to provinces and districts. Decentralization can facilitate innovation and experimentation, but local structures need to deliver results if they are to improve governance. There is no guarantee that decentralized authorities will be more responsive than central government agencies to the needs of women and other marginalized groups. South Africa's approach to decentralization offers some suggestions on overcoming these constraints (box 2.9).

Setting a course of action. Given the range of issues to be addressed with limited resources, all countries have to decide which actions to prioritize. This involves more than just copying what has worked elsewhere—close attention to the minimum package of required governance measures and to the country's initial conditions are essential.

In countries where governance is reasonably strong and where macroeconomic reform and state restructuring are well advanced, public management reforms can move to the forefront of the governance agenda. But such reforms pose a formidable challenge, because the seemingly disparate elements of a high-performing public sector are in fact closely interdependent. Priority social needs can only be met if the budget system enables politicians to choose among competing initiatives and, once they have made these choices, to resist pressures to reverse their commitments. Even with sufficient resources, public agencies are likely to deliver results only if they have strong incentives to perform—that is, if they are in some way held accountable.

Public agencies are likely to deliver results only if they have strong incentives to perform

Box 2.9 Decentralization in South Africa

FEW COUNTRIES HAVE TAKEN SUCH A FUNDAMENTAL approach to reforming their intergovernmental systems as South Africa, which has embarked on an ambitious program of political, fiscal, and financial decentralization. At the political level, racial jurisdictions were eliminated with the end of apartheid. New elections were held for all tiers of government, including several new provinces. A new constitution was introduced to define and protect the powers and responsibilities of each tier.

Fiscal reform sought to improve the distribution of income by reassigning expenditures (education and health are centrally funded provincial responsibilities), providing central funding for redistributive subsidies, and developing stable and predictable intergovernmental grants. The amount of redistribution to a local jurisdiction is based on the average income per capita of households residing there, as well as the share of rural inhabitants for provinces. Local authorities can set user charges, property taxes, and certain business taxes, but provinces are under the strict oversight of central authorities.

On the financial side, a program has been created to transfer capital grants from the center to local levels, and a regulatory framework is being established to enable local governments to access capital markets directly, while ensuring clear rules on disclosure and public sector bankruptcy. In addition, governments are allowed to form partnerships with the private sector, including nongovernmental organizations, for service delivery.

As in other countries, many local governments lack capacity for effective management. So, South Africa has introduced an innovative demand-driven approach to capacity building. A fund has been created to help municipalities hire experts and strengthen their ability to work with private agents.

Though South Africa's decentralization is far from complete, several lessons are apparent. First, decentralization can be compatible with macroeconomic stability and pro-poor distribution policies. Second, a comprehensive approach is required in which institutional and fiscal restructuring precedes financial decentralization. Third, the overall approach need not be completely uniform—as between major urban concentrations and other local jurisdictions—and some aspects may require tight central oversight. Finally, a demand-driven capacity-building mechanism can greatly assist the process, especially for new or poor provinces or local authorities.

Technocratic or top-down public management reforms require the most robust governance foundation if they are to succeed. This is because they focus on the core operation of the bureaucracy rather than on the provision of specific goods and services. Thus they are less easily subjected to civic scrutiny and monitoring. These reforms are more likely to succeed in countries where sustained civic engagement, functioning oversight institutions, accountability to the legislature, and progressive and competent political leadership have already created a culture of commitment to development performance throughout the bureaucracy.

Where institutions are weaker, public management reforms need to proceed in tandem with measures that raise awareness—such as an anticorruption initiative that draws civic attention to how politicians and bureaucrats use and abuse public resources. This approach should be handled with care, however. If governance institutions are too weak, reforms may be implemented inadequately—with the net result not of better governance and reduced corruption, but of heightened civic frustration and disillusion. At the limit, public institutions might prove too brittle to absorb the heightened conflict, raising the risk of precipitating a debilitating downward spiral.

For many African countries the most manageable public governance reforms, at least in the initial stages, will focus on increased transparency and greater participation in service delivery. Both reforms aim to empower citizens and their government counterparts to engage more directly with one another and to build demand for results-based good governance. Progress—or lack of it—is also easy to monitor. Once a firm basis has been built, more complex governance reforms can be undertaken. Ongoing efforts in Ghana and Guinea show how different countries are striking the balance between technocratic and participatory reform (box 2.10). While the outcomes of these efforts will only be seen in the longer term, they represent attempts to devise workable institutional reforms and improve government.

Regional and Global Dimensions

Just as regional economic cooperation and integration can help African countries economically, regional initiatives and institutions can strengthen governance in individual countries. Evolving geopolitics may create opportunities to strengthen international monitoring and enforcement even in countries where judicial independence is lacking. Regional cooperation to combat corruption could also support the anticorruption efforts of individual countries.

Regional institutions. Regional and subregional organizations can put pressure on member governments to conform to norms of good governance and democratic behavior. In recent years the Organization of African Unity has emerged as a strong advocate of democracy throughout the continent, and election observation is now one of its functions. At its Algiers Summit in 1999 it passed a resolution to exclude governments that come to power through extraconstitutional means. Though commendable and bound to send a strong signal to potential coup-makers, this resolution does not address those who retain power by refusing to submit to elections or by rejecting the free and fair results of the ballot box.

Box 2.10 Different Routes to Better Government in Ghana and Guinea

GHANA AND GUINEA ILLUSTRATE ALTERNATIVE EMphases in reforms—technocratic and participatory—that aim to make government more effective and responsive. Building on previous reform, the reform launched by Ghana in 1997 aimed to reinvent and modernize the core public sector. Its agenda included:

- Reforming subvented agencies that employ more than 400,000 of the country's 600,000 public employees, providing them with a coherent mandate and sufficient resources, defining their relations with line ministries, and strengthening their planning and monitoring.
- Strengthening regulation within the public sector, improving incentives and human resource management.
- Realigning line ministries to adapt to decentralization and to enhance public-private partnerships, and introducing targets for service improvements, such as reducing the average time for delivery of services from one month to a week or less.

Departing from its long tradition as a top-down, centralized bureaucracy, Guinea's reform program seeks to bring government closer to the people. Initiated in mid-1996, its agenda includes:

- Enhancing the responsiveness of the 33 urban and 303 rural communes by broadening their membership to include a wide range of social, cultural, ethnic, and economic groups, and by making regional administration increasingly accountable to these communes.
- Creating a demand-driven local investment fund to support communal social and infrastructure projects with matching grants, as well as introducing revenue-sharing mechanisms and other systems of matching finance.
- Realigning subnational administration to reflect the shift in accountability to local communities. This includes revising the administrative frameworks that define roles and responsibilities of different levels of government, improving participatory mechanisms (such as parent-teacher associations, health center management committees, and farmer groups), building capacity at local levels, and introducing an incentive system to reward well-working communes.

Today almost three-quarters of budgeted funds are spent on administrative functions upstream, but Guinea hopes that within 10–15 years at least 70 percent of operating funds will reach the service delivery level. It also hopes for an 80 percent increase in the quality of and access to services for the rural population.

Harmonization of rules and procedures within subregional groups can help institutionalize the rule of law within individual countries. Subregional conventions can help strengthen country-level property rights, financial regulation, and contract enforcement. Similarly, agreements to exchange information and collaborate on investigations can counter crime and corruption within subregions and individual countries. There is considerable scope for involving regional nongovernmental organizations to monitor compliance and develop expertise. OHADA provides an example of such an initiative (box 2.11).

Other regional mechanisms could encourage observance of human rights, democratic principles, and governance practices by African countries by providing opportunities to exchange experiences and monitoring progress. Regional initiatives to engage former political leaders in advocacy for issues such as HIV/AIDS or regional integration could also be considered. There is also scope for building capacity within parliaments and independent agencies by sharing information on a regional basis.

Subregional conventions can help strengthen country-level property rights, financial regulation, and contract enforcement

---

Box 2.11 The Organization pour l'Harmonisation en Afrique du Droit des Affaires

IN THE EARLY 1990S SOME FRANCOPHONE AFRICAN countries realized that a lack of confidence among private investors was hurting their efforts to promote the private sector. Problems included obsolete legislation dating from the colonial period; difficulties in enforcing contracts, particularly in the banking sector; and unpredictable court judgments. To address these issues, 15 countries signed a treaty establishing the Organization pour l'Harmonisation en Afrique du Droit des Affaires (OHADA) in 1993.

The treaty aims to facilitate regional economic integration and international trade by providing unified, modern business legislation for member states, strengthening legal and judicial security for enterprises, promoting arbitration to settle contractual disputes, and providing continuing education to magistrates and judicial personnel. To date, uniform laws have been enacted for general commercial law, corporations and economic interest groups, secured transactions, bankruptcy proceedings and discharge of liabilities, debt collection proceedings, and arbitration.

OHADA's institutions comprise a council of ministers of finance and justice with a secretariat in Yaounde (Cameroon), a common court of justice in Abidjan (Côte d'Ivoire) with final jurisdiction over business transactions in member countries, and a regional school of magistrates in Porto Novo (Benin) to provide continuing education.

OHADA has increased confidence among the business community, and several contracts have been signed under its provisions. But it still faces a number of challenges. There is insufficient dissemination and knowledge of OHADA laws. There have been substantial delays in setting up a court registry. There is insufficient financing for OHADA institutions. And there is a need to monitor implementation, build OHADA jurisprudence, identify additional legal areas requiring harmonization, and assess best means to establish links with anglophone countries.

Global institutions. Globalization increasingly demands adherence to international standards. Faced with a variety of choices, serious long-term investors are unlikely to be attracted to countries with rampant corruption and weak contract enforcement and property rights. International agreements will increasingly complement regional and subregional arrangements to promote good governance. African membership in rules-based organizations such as the World Trade Organization will support compliance with international norms in certain areas. The development of international legal institutions and criminal tribunals means that countries are subject to much greater scrutiny of internal affairs than before. Recourse against abuse of human rights is increasingly found in the international arena.

Throughout the world, the impulse is toward integration and cooperation through the creation of trading blocs as well as political and security arrangements. New technologies have permitted the free movement of information and ideas. Ease of travel and communications has strengthened cross-border connections between countries. This process is under way in Africa in both formal and less formal ways. Although Africa has long had regional integration groupings, they and their individual member countries need to come to terms with the governance implications of these potentially far-reaching changes.

Much more can be done internationally to promote good governance in Africa, focusing on actions in industrial countries. Some steps, such as the OECD convention against bribery, are being implemented. Tighter regulations on money laundering and international crime will also help African countries by, among other things, countering capital flight. Increased attention is also being paid to weapon flows, including through binding international codes of conduct for arms exports. Concern about conflict in Africa and how it is funded has raised the question of whether tighter international controls on the export of natural commodities—such as diamonds—can reduce the resources available for financing wars without harming legitimate exporters. Formulating a broader regional approach toward conflict management and economic progress will be a priority for Africa and its development partners in the new century.

Development partners. Development agencies have both a special responsibility and an unusual opportunity to support efforts to make Africa's governments more transparent and accountable to their people. The responsibility arises from their obligation to ensure that aid is used for its intended purposes. More fundamentally, it arises from the need to direct

Countries are subject to much greater scrutiny of internal affairs than before

Donors have a special responsibility and an unusual opportunity to support efforts to make Africa's governments more transparent and accountable

assistance to countries willing to make effective use of all resources, not just those of the agency.

The opportunity arises from donors' access to the full range of stakeholders in recipient countries—not just government officials but also the media and opposition groups. Donors are only beginning to take advantage of this opportunity. The African Development Bank has recently taken steps to promote good governance by including governance criteria in its lending decisions. This is in line with the trends in bilateral assistance agencies and international financial institutions. Governance has also been a criterion in allocations of funds from the World Bank's International Development Association (IDA), and the weight of performance in IDA allocations has been increasing.

Africa's development partners can also promote better governance by providing assistance to strengthen institutions such as the judiciary and the legislature, or to support a fledging independent press. Many are already doing so, and hopefully will continue over the long term, recognizing that democratic institutions and behavior cannot be created overnight. Donors can also ensure that their practices conform to standards of good governance and that they support openness and accountability not just to their own polities but also to Africans and their representative institutions (chapter 8). Just as private corporations are increasingly adopting codes of conduct to promote good corporate governance, so too Africa's development partners should consider adopting codes of conduct that cover their own practices and the ultimate use of funds. The Cold War promoted a culture among African countries and their development partners of nontransparent management of aid resources. But these expectations are changing rapidly—a process that it is in the interests of Africa's people to move even faster.

Notes

1. This argument goes back as far as James Madison's Federalist Paper 10. Granting political factions—be they ethnic, geographic, racial, or religious—political space for self-expression increases confidence in the larger unit as long as the factions operate within the law and the constitution. This perspective is contrary to the centralizing tendencies that African leaders adopted after 1960.

2. If a hypothetical nation of 100 million people is divided into 10 nations of 10 million people, then the risk of civil war occurring somewhere among the 100 million people triples. There is also a much higher risk of international war simply because there are many more nations.

CHAPTER 3

Addressing Poverty and Inequality

SOME 300 MILLION AFRICANS—ALMOST HALF THE POPULA-tion—live on barely $0.65 a day (in purchasing power par-ity terms), and this number is growing relentlessly. Moreover, a severe lack of capabilities—education, health, nutrition—among Africa's poor threatens to make poverty "dynastic," with the descendants of the poor also remain-ing poor. The rural poor account for 80 percent of African poverty, but urban poverty is substantial and appears to be growing.

Africa is not only poor, it also suffers from vast inequality in incomes, in assets (including education and health status), in control over public resources, and in access to essential services, as well as per-vasive insecurity. These dimensions of poverty and deprivation are worsening in many parts of the region. Primary school enrollment rates, after increasing sharply until the 1980s, show signs of decreas-ing. In some areas there are indications of a deterioration in the gen-eral health of the population, particularly among the poor and children.

Not surprisingly, the elimination of deep poverty has emerged as the overriding objective of development in Africa. Growth is essential to reduce the number of poor people, and will do so if sustained at high rates. But growth is less effective in the face of massive inequality. Given the depth of deprivation in Africa, growth will not be enough without attention to easing inequality and to eliminating the barriers that con-strain poor people's ability to benefit from a growing economy and to contribute to that growth.

Indeed, although African economies respond to better economic policies, a major acceleration of growth is unlikely without a dramatic improvement in human capital, particularly public health (chapter 1).

Growth is essential to reduce the number of poor people—but attention must also be paid to inequality

Vigorous action against HIV/AIDS is an essential component of that agenda. Similarly, a higher savings rate is unlikely without an accelerated demographic transition. This requires lower child mortality and higher female education. So, reducing poverty and improving social conditions are not simply consequences of development—they are essential components of any viable development strategy.

For these reasons Africa's development strategies cannot be focused solely on growth. They will need to take into account likely distributional implications and be grounded in a solid understanding of who the poor are and why so many have such trouble escaping from poverty. Development strategies will also need to be adequately financed; people cannot increase consumption while sharply raising investment to support growth.

Poverty on the African scale is more than an individual phenomenon. It is also a social and political one, entering into the workings of economies and societies in a multitude of ways that differentiate the initial conditions of poor countries from rich ones. The poor are not simply the rich with less money. They often live in different areas, frequently in the most degraded environments. Poverty also makes it harder to avoid further environmental degradation. At the margin of existence, concern for security can inhibit the adoption of new, potentially advantageous cropping patterns or technology, reducing growth potential. Failing to address growing poverty in Africa risks rising violence and crime and imperils the peaceful development of viable states (chapter 2). Thus measures to reduce poverty are not a luxury; they are essential for the peaceful development of Africa and for other regions.

Measures to reduce poverty are not a luxury—they are essential for peaceful development

Dimensions of Poverty

PARTICIPATORY ASSESSMENTS AND SURVEYS HAVE INCREASED understanding of African poverty in recent years, both as seen by the poor and in terms of statistical coverage. Poverty has many facets. In addition to low incomes and assets, participatory assessments draw attention to exclusion and isolation, as well as lack of trust in public agencies. Almost everywhere, poor people say that new ways have to be found that allow them to participate in development programs and ensure that such programs reach their intended beneficiaries (box

3.1). With new technology, rapid assessments such as the Core Welfare Indicator Questionnaire are enabling speedy assessment of other factors that affect the capabilities of the poor, including access to essential public services. Almost all countries now have at least one household survey, and these are being made available on CD-ROM to enable wider analysis. These surveys typically allow an assessment of income or consumption poverty, which reflects the economic opportunities available to the poor.

Box 3.1 Voices of Africa's Poor

"Poverty is like heat: you cannot see it, you can only feel it; so to know poverty, you have to go through it."
—A man from Adaboya, Ghana

"Women are beaten at the house for any reason...They may also be beaten if the husband comes home drunk or if he simply feels like it."
—A researcher from Ethiopia

A RECENT SURVEY, VOICES OF THE POOR, BROUGHT together the voices of 60,000 poor women and men from around the world. The study used participatory research to explore poverty realities, experiences, and priorities. While poverty is often specific to certain groups and locations, some broad patterns cut across groups. Most of those surveyed believed that things had gotten a lot worse for the poor and that traditional systems of social support had eroded—leaving poor households in deeper poverty and greater vulnerability. Africa was the only region where food insecurity was the most common descriptor of poverty: many poor people were preoccupied with where their next meal would come from. Poor people also spoke extensively about the importance of assets for getting loans and making it through rough periods; they rarely spoke about income. Entrepreneurship and multiple sources of income contributed to the movement out of poverty.

Poor people also spoke extensively about the social and psychological dimensions of poverty. They craved a sense of belonging, a future for their children, safety and security for their families. Being poor means being excluded—being treated "like dogs" by service providers and traders, unable to negotiate fair prices for crops or make one's voice heard at community meetings. The most important trigger for downward mobility was illness and injury—everywhere, illness was dreaded.

Gender relations are often traumatic. As poor men lose their jobs and women are forced to earn cash incomes, gender relations based on men as breadwinners and women as homekeepers are being challenged. While in many places poor women are taking a stand and becoming involved in household resource decisions, violence against women remains widespread. Since all poverty interventions affect gender relations in households, gender discussions must include both men and women.

Finally, there is a fundamental distrust of state institutions. Almost universally, poor communities expressed more trust in church organizations and indigenous or local institutions. There was less confidence in nongovernmental organizations, though more than in government institutions. Government services rarely work, and even when they do, government servants are corrupt, rude, and exclusive. Poor people encountered corruption on a daily basis. The "us versus them" attitude toward the state is a serious problem that will take time to fix. It takes just days to destroy trust, but decades to rebuild it.

Source: World Bank 1999b.

Better health, nutrition, and education are likely to have major effects on labor productivity and income growth

But much more needs to be done in monitoring poverty, including obtaining a better understanding of its dynamics—how poverty evolves for individuals and groups and how it is influenced by changes in economic policies. It is also important to strengthen capacity in Africa to analyze survey data. A number of initiatives, including by the African Economic Research Consortium, are making a contribution in this area. A final critical dimension of poverty is insecurity; the poor face continued risks of further impoverishment, while the near-poor face threats of falling into poverty traps.

Capabilities and the Poor

Capabilities such as good health, nutrition, and education are important in their own right. Poor health, malnutrition, illiteracy, powerlessness, and social or physical isolation measure directly the low levels of well-being in most of Africa. But these capabilities can also be considered human capital, which has enormous potential to raise incomes and living standards. Much literature emphasizes education as the key to higher incomes, both for individuals and countries. But especially in an agriculture-based region, better health and nutrition are also likely to have major effects on labor productivity and income growth (chapters 1, 4). Two of these dimensions—mortality and education status—show Africa far behind the rest of the world (see table 1.3).

Mortality. Child mortality is particularly sensitive to the well-being of the population. In Africa infant mortality is close to 10 percent, and on average 157 of every 1,000 children die before the age of 5. But in many countries the mortality rate exceeds 200 per 1,000. This compares with 53 in East Asia and 9 in high-income countries.

Even taking into account its low income levels, Africa's under-5 mortality rates are exceptionally high (figure 3.1). The region has had the smallest improvement in under-5 mortality since 1970, and some countries—including Kenya and Zimbabwe—saw mortality increase in the 1990s. AIDS is also wreaking havoc on Africa's people: life expectancy has declined in almost one-third of its countries, in Botswana by almost 10 years (chapter 4).

Nutrition. Anthropometric indicators of weight, height, and age provide further evidence of deterioration in the health of Africans. Children with low weight for their height are considered to be wasting; this indicates low recent nutrition levels. Children with low height for their age are considered stunted, a condition resulting from longer-term malnutrition. The overall picture is mixed (table 3.1). In some countries there have been improvements in urban populations but deterioration in rural ones. In other countries, notably Mali and Senegal, nutrition levels appear to have deteriorated overall.

The poorest 20 percent of the population has been the most affected by this deterioration. Among the eight countries in table 3.1, stunting has worsened among the poorest in four (Ghana, Mali, Senegal, Tanzania). But wasting has worsened among the poorest in six (Ghana, Madagascar, Mali, Senegal, Uganda, Zimbabwe).

Education. Outside Africa, most of the developing world has achieved almost universal primary enrollments, though with significant dropout rates. But in Africa primary enrollments dropped between 1980 and 1993, from 80 to 72 percent. Moreover, less than a quarter of secondary school-age children were enrolled in secondary school. And many adults have little or no education. This is important because in Africa

Mortality in Africa is high, even considering its low income

Figure 3.1 Under-5 Mortality by GNP Per Capita and Region, 1995

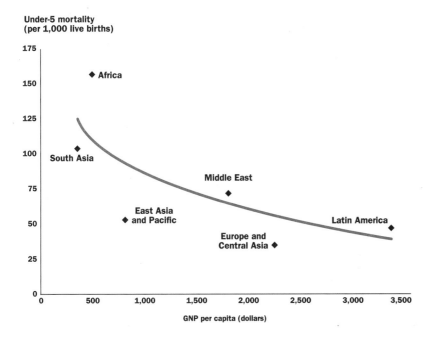

Source: Demery and Walton 1998.

Table 3.1 Nutrition Measures for Children in Eight African Countries (percent)

Region/country (years)	First year		Second year		Change (percentage points)	
	Low weight for height	Low height for age	Low weight for height	Low height for age	Low weight for height	Low height for age
Urban						
Ghana (1988 and 1993)	7.3	24.6	9.1	17.0	1.8	−7.6
Madagascar (1992 and 1997)	3.8	40.5	5.3	44.8	1.5	4.3
Mali (1987 and 1995)	9.9	19.6	24.9	23.9	15.0	4.3
Senegal (1986 and 1992)	3.5	17.5	8.8	15.2	5.3	−2.3
Tanzania (1991 and 1996)	5.1	38.0	8.1	32.6	3.0	−5.5
Uganda (1988 and 1995)	0.6	24.8	1.4	22.7	0.7	−2.1
Zambia (1992 and 1996)	5.4	32.8	3.3	32.9	−2.1	0.1
Zimbabwe (1988 and 1994)	1.4	16.0	6.5	19.0	5.0	3.0
Rural						
Ghana (1988 and 1993)	8.5	31.4	13.1	32.3	4.6	0.9
Madagascar (1992 and 1997)	6.0	50.6	8.3	49.5	2.3	−1.1
Mali (1987 and 1995)	12.3	26.2	24.4	36.2	12.2	10.0
Senegal (1986 and 1992)	7.1	26.5	13.4	32.7	6.3	6.3
Tanzania (1991 and 1996)	6.4	45.0	7.3	46.1	0.9	1.2
Uganda (1988 and 1995)	2.0	45.2	3.2	40.7	1.3	−4.5
Zambia (1992 and 1996)	5.0	46.5	4.9	48.9	−0.1	2.4
Zimbabwe (1988 and 1994)	1.1	34.3	5.6	25.0	4.5	−9.3

Source: Sahn, Dorosh, and Younger 1999.

parents' education is an important determinant of whether their children attend school.

Income, region, and gender also help determine whether children are enrolled. Primary enrollments are low overall, but particularly among poor rural females—in the 1990s only 24 percent of this group was enrolled among 16 countries surveyed (table 3.2). In Ethiopia, The Gambia, Guinea, Mali, and Niger enrollments were less than 10 percent; only in Ghana, Kenya, and Zambia were more than 50 percent of primary school-age children enrolled.

Secondary enrollments were almost uniformly low. On average only 7 percent of the poorest rural group (male and female combined) was enrolled, and in 13 of the 16 countries enrollment was negligible for this group (3 percent or less). This compared with an average secondary enrollment of 44 percent among the urban upper-income quintile.

Judged by these measures, the capabilities of African populations have shown little improvement in recent years—and in some cases have deteri-

Table 3.2 Net Enrollments in 16 African Countries by Region, Consumption Quintile, and Gender, 1990s (percent)

| | Rural areas | | | | | Urban areas | | | | | |
| | Poorest quintile | | Richest quintile | | | Poorest quintile | | Richest quintile | | | |
Level	Male	Female	Male	Female	All	Male	Female	Male	Female	All	All
Primary	32	24	50	42	36	53	48	75	70	63	40

| | Rural areas | | | Urban areas | | | |
	Poorest quintile	Richest quintile	All	Poorest quintile	Richest quintile	All	All
Secondary	7	15	11	21	44	33	19

Source: Demery 1999.

orated considerably. Poorer parts of the population are largely excluded from acquiring the capabilities they need to partake in and contribute to the growth of a modern economy. Low female enrollment is also slowing the demographic transition, reducing the prospect that African countries will move toward a virtuous circle of growth, demographic transition, and savings (chapter 1).

Measures of Poverty

There is no single measure of poverty, and all choices have their advantages and weaknesses. For welfare levels, consumption is the preferred criterion. But many surveys—especially those outside Africa—measure income.

Poverty lines. The choice of a poverty line is always arbitrary. Two options are available. One is to set an absolute standard common across all countries, such as $1 a day per person adjusted for purchasing power parity (PPP). This approach facilitates cross-country comparisons of poverty, although the conversion from national currencies into PPP dollars is subject to error. A second option is to define the poor as those falling below the poverty lines of their countries. This relative approach allows for differences in poverty lines depending on a country's level of development. But it also makes it harder to compare countries.

A choice must also be made on how to show the prevalence and depth of poverty. The headcount ratio, or percentage of the population falling below the poverty line, is a widely used measure of the prevalence of poverty. The poverty gap takes into account the extent to which the consumption of the poor falls below the poverty line. It is a measure of the depth of poverty, as well as its prevalence. The squared poverty gap weights more heavily the poverty of the poorest parts of the population and so emphasizes extreme deprivation.

Analysis using an absolute poverty line of $1 a day shows that almost half of Africans live below this level and that the number of poor has been steadily increasing. The vast majority of Africans consume less than $2 a day. This is a reflection of the desperately poor conditions prevailing in the continent and indicates how vulnerable entire societies are to falling into poverty, with large tracts of the population just a little over the $1 a day poverty line. Dealing with poverty in the region must involve expanding the income opportunities of whole groups.

Dealing with poverty in the region must involve expanding the income opportunities of whole groups

The second approach, using relative poverty lines, yields a similar picture. In 21 countries surveyed in the 1990s, more then half of the rural populations lived below the national poverty lines (table 3.3). Rural poverty is both deep and severe. The average income of the rural poor is just $163 a year, barely half the average regional poverty line for rural areas. Ghana recorded the lowest rural poverty, with a headcount ratio of 29 percent. But nine countries had rural headcounts above 60 percent.

Urban poverty is also high, as judged by national poverty lines, and is moderately deep. More than 40 percent of the urban population is poor according to national criteria, and the average income of this group is only $352 a year. More than half of the urban population is poor in Ethiopia, Guinea-Bissau, Tanzania, Swaziland, and Zambia. With the rapid growth of Africa's urban populations, high urban poverty threatens political and economic stability.

Trends in poverty and growth. For some countries it is possible to trace recent trends in consumption poverty based on household data. These reveal a mixed pattern (table 3.4). Some countries, notably Nigeria and Zimbabwe, have experienced significant increases in poverty. Ethiopia,

Table 3.3 Poverty in 21 African Countries Using National Poverty Lines, 1990s

Indicator	Rural	Urban	Overall
Headcount ratio (percent)	56	43	52
Poverty gap (percent)	23	16	22
Squared poverty gap (percent)	13	8	12
Mean expenditure (dollars a person per year)	409	959	551
Mean poverty line (dollars a person per year)	325	558	

Source: Ali 1999.

Mauritania, and Uganda have experienced widespread improvements in economic well-being that have filtered down to the poor. Ghana shows a mixed picture for 1987–96. Poverty rose in urban areas (especially Accra) but fell in rural areas, apparently reflecting distributional shifts due to reform programs. More recent trends appear to have changed this pattern, causing urban poverty to decline.

How do these poverty trends relate to overall growth? On average, a 1 percent increase in consumption is associated with almost a 1 percent drop in the poverty headcount ratio (figure 3.2). Growth that translates into rising consumption is thus essential for poverty reduction. But growth is not sufficient, given Africa's low incomes and high inequality and exclusion, which result in the world's largest poverty gaps.

Africa has perhaps the world's highest income inequality...

Table 3.4 Consumption Poverty in Various African Countries

Country, years	Headcount ratio		Squared poverty gap		Change in per capita consumption (percent)
	First year	Second year	First year	Second year	
Ethiopia					
Rural, 1989 and 1995	61.3	45.9	17.4	9.9	8.2
Urban, 1994 and 1997	40.9	38.7	8.3	7.8	5.1
Ghana, 1987 and 1996	31.9	27.4			2.5
Rural	37.5	30.2			
Urban	19.0	20.6			
Mauritania, 1992 and 1996	59.5	41.3	17.5	7.5	11.5
Rural	72.1	58.9	27.4	11.9	
Urban	43.5	19.0	9.7	2.1	
Nigeria, 1992 and 1996	42.8	65.6	14.2	25.1	−16.3
Rural	45.1	67.8	15.9	25.6	
Urban	29.6	57.5	12.4	24.9	
Uganda, 1992 and 1997	55.6	44.0	9.9	5.9	22.4
Rural	59.4	48.2	10.9	6.56	
Urban	29.4	16.3	3.5	1.65	
Zambia, 1991 and 1996	57.0	60.0	25.5	16.6	−1.4
Rural	79.6	74.9	39.1	23.2	
Urban	31.0	34.0	9.7	5.4	
Zimbabwe, 1991 and 1996	37.5	47.2	7.2	9.3	−1.8
Rural	51.5	62.8	10.2	13.0	
Urban	6.2	14.9	0.5	1.4	

Note: Headcount ratio and squared poverty gap are based on national (nutritionally based) poverty lines. Comparisons between countries are not valid. Ethiopia data are based on small samples. Nigeria data are provisional.
Source: World Bank data.

Figure 3.2 Changes in Headcount Ratios and Per Capita Consumption in Selected Countries and Periods

...but growth is still essential for poverty reduction

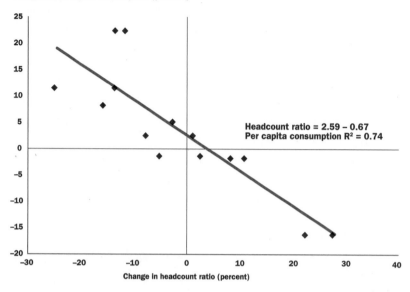

Change in per capita consumption (percent)

Headcount ratio = 2.59 − 0.67
Per capita consumption R² = 0.74

Change in headcount ratio (percent)

Source: Table 3.4.

Inequality and Its Implications

AFRICA HAS PERHAPS THE WORLD'S HIGHEST INCOME INEQUALity. Both rural and urban incomes are unequally distributed. There is also considerable inequity in the distribution of social spending, with more going to higher-income groups than to the poor. To be effective in fighting the depth of African poverty, development strategies have to address inequality and exclusion. With current fiscal policies and service delivery systems, inequalities in capabilities will not soon be alleviated.

A Profile of Income Inequality

As conventionally measured, Africa has the world's second highest inequality after Latin America (table 3.5). But most of Africa's household surveys measure inequality using consumption, whereas most other surveys use income. Adjusting for this difference, Africa's inequality is as high as or higher than that in any other region. The poorest 20 percent of Africans account for just 5.2 percent of total household consumption, or about 4 percent of GDP. This is equivalent to less than half the foreign aid to a typical poor African country in the 1990s. At 58 percent, South Africa boasts the region's highest Gini coefficient (box 3.2).

Africa's inequality has two distinctive features. First, rural inequality is almost as high as urban inequality, with the poorest 20 percent of the population accounting for less than 6 percent of consumption in both cases (Ali 1999). Because most land is held communally in Africa, in most cases rural inequality does not stem from severe inequality in landholdings. Rather, it reflects geographic differences in the quality of land, in climatic conditions, and in access to markets and to remittances from urban areas. (The exception is Southern Africa, where in addition to the above factors, inequality in land holdings is a major determinant of rural inequality.) Africa's poor, sparse economies are not well integrated, and communities far from roads are typically far poorer than others. Spatial factors, including those relating to inadequate rural capital and infrastructure, therefore need to be taken into account in designing antipoverty policies (chapters 5, 6). In urban areas job creation and economic diversification are crucial challenges (chapter 7).

Rural inequality is almost as high as urban inequality

A second feature of African inequality is its high level despite low average income. A stylized (though debated) feature of development is the Kuznets hypothesis—that income distribution tends to become more unequal as countries develop, before tending to equalize again at relatively high income levels. Ali and Elbadawi (1999) suggest that the income at which African income inequality will naturally start to

Table 3.5 Income Inequality by Region (percent)

Region	Gini coefficient	Share of top 20 percent	Share of middle	Share of bottom 20 percent
Africa	45.0	50.6	34.4	5.2
East Asia and Pacific	38.1	44.3	37.5	6.8
South Asia	31.9	39.9	38.4	8.8
Latin America	49.3	52.9	33.8	4.5
Industrial countries	33.8	39.8	41.8	6.3

Note: Data for Africa are calculated on a consumption basis. Adjustment to an income basis (as is common in other regions) involves raising the Gini coefficient by 6 percentage points, making Africa's Gini 51 percent.
Source: Deininger and Squire 1996.

Box 3.2 Inequality in South Africa

ALONG WITH BRAZIL, SOUTH AFRICA IS PERHAPS THE world's most unequal economy. The poorest 20 percent of the population disposes of just 3 percent of income, while the richest 20 percent disposes of 42 percent. What underlies this high inequality?

Inequality within racial groups accounts for about 60 percent of overall inequality, but inequalities between racial groups account for 40 percent—a great deal relative to other countries. (In Malaysia, for example, inequalities between racial groups account for just 13 percent of overall inequality.) The share of income held by white households fell from 72 percent in 1960 to 60 percent in 1991, but some of the decline was due to slower population growth among whites. The average per capita income of Africans, 9.1 percent of that of whites in 1917, had risen to just 13.5 percent in 1995. For any poverty line, the fraction of African workers below it is far greater than the fraction of white workers. For example, if the line is set equal to monthly adult equivalent poverty income, 4 percent of the white labor force is poor—but more than half of the African workforce is.

But other factors are important as well. The unemployed, household domestic workers, and farm workers are the poorest and most vulnerable groups. The poor, especially the poorest, are disproportionately found in rural areas. Labor market factors are also central. Many Africans are unemployed, so many households do not have access to wage income. Age and education are also factors. New entrants to the labor market have trouble finding jobs, while lower education means far lower probability of finding work and almost no chance of finding well-paid work.

How can this situation be remedied? Policies should follow two broad strategies. The first is to narrow the mismatch between the supply of unskilled labor and the demand for skilled labor. This involves changes in both labor market policy and education: younger cohorts need to have better access to secondary education and higher-quality education, with a focus on technical and vocational training. The second strategy is to strengthen safety nets and poverty alleviation efforts for people—especially in poor rural areas—with few prospects for long-term sustainable employment. Both planks will require robust growth to create new jobs and fund the social safety net.

Source: African Economic Research Consortium, comparative research project on poverty and inequality in Africa.

decline is $1,566 (in 1985 PPP dollars)—several times average income today. This implies that pronounced inequality is likely to be a feature of African economies for a long time, and reinforces the importance of including distributional elements in development programs.

The Distributional Impact of Reform

Income distribution reflects deep structural features of an economy and so usually does not change much over time. Yet some African countries have experienced substantial changes—whether toward or away from equality—over short periods. Some of these changes may reflect changes in macroeconomic policy, which has considerable potential to shift incomes between social and economic groups.

Until recently little evidence was available of the impact on income distribution of policy reform, but that is beginning to change. Many poor groups—those linked to markets and public services—have benefited from the reforms and economic recovery of the 1990s (box 3.3). But other poor households, notably those in remote locations and relying on subsistence crops, as well as those without work, have fared badly. Reforms can lift many out of poverty. But there is a danger that many of the very poor will be left behind.

Box 3.3 Winners and Losers from Reform and Recovery in Ghana and Uganda

MANY AFRICAN COUNTRIES EXPERIENCED ECONOMIC recovery in the 1990s, partly because of major economic reforms. How these reforms affect poverty and inequality is of massive significance for the long-run sustainability of growth. In Ghana and Uganda reform and recovery led to surprisingly similar results for households and their living standards. In Uganda real GDP per capita grew by some 5 percent a year in 1992–97, and real private consumption per capita grew by just over 4 per cent a year. Real GDP and private consumption growth rates were also high in Ghana in 1992–98. Who were the main beneficiaries of this growth, and did the poor benefit?

In both countries GDP growth appears to have significantly lowered consumption poverty. Mean household consumption per adult equivalent in Uganda increased markedly in the 1990s, causing the poverty headcount ratio to fall from 56 percent in 1992 to 44 percent in 1997. In Ghana the headcount ratio dropped from 51 percent in 1991/92 to 43 percent in 1998/99. The declines in poverty in both countries are robust with respect to the choice of poverty line (and poverty index).

Income distribution also improved in both countries. In Uganda decreases in inequality explain 10 percent of the decline in the headcount index. (The remainder came from an increase in mean household consumption.) Similarly, in Ghana an improvement in income distribution explains just under a quarter of the decline in the headcount index for the country as a whole. Inequality did not fall in all parts of these countries, however—and in some areas it rose.

Trends in consumption and poverty were also not even across all groups and regions. Central Uganda gained the most, while the eastern region lagged behind. In Ghana the declines in poverty were concentrated in the west, Greater Accra, Volta, and Brong Ahafo, while the poorest ecological zones (the center, north, upper east) saw poverty increase. How households fared also depended on the main source of livelihood. In Uganda there were sharp falls in consumption poverty among households engaged in cash-crop production, noncrop agriculture, and manufacturing. The higher living standards of those growing cash crops accounted for more than half of the observed fall in poverty. But poverty among food-crop farmers (representing more than half of consumption poverty) declined only marginally. And poverty actually increased among those in miscellaneous services and those not working. A similar picture emerges for Ghana: economic well-being improved significantly for export farmers and those in formal and nonformal wage employment, but much less for nonexport (mainly food) farmers. And as in Uganda, poverty increased in Ghanaian households where the head was not working.

Thus in both countries many poor groups benefited from the reforms and economic recovery of the 1990s. But other poor households—notably those in remote locations, those relying mainly on subsistence food crop production, and those not working—fared badly.

Source: Appleton 1999; Ghana Statistical Service 1999.

Unequal Access: Public Spending and the Poor

Improving the human capital and capabilities of Africans, particularly the poor, is crucial to reduce poverty and to improve people's lives. Actions to develop human capital must be seen across a broad front. Reducing child mortality might require, in addition to higher incomes, increased food consumption, cleaner water, more female education, reduced disease-bearing vectors, better immunization programs and postnatal care, and more widespread basic clinical services. Not all of these objectives involve public services and public spending, but many do. Chapter 4 discusses the need for better delivery systems for public services and offers examples of effective interventions. The question here is the degree to which current budget allocations and fiscal policies are focused on benefiting the poor.

The evidence is not encouraging. Health spending, for example, is not well targeted to the poorest (table 3.6). In seven countries for which data are available, the poorest 20 percent of the population receives only 12 percent of the subsidy—compared with more than 30 percent for the richest 20 percent of the population. The only exception is South Africa, where the richest 20 percent of the population mainly uses private health care. The overall picture for education is similar to that for health. Africa's poor, particularly its women, have less access to fiscal resources directed toward enhancing their capabilities. This gender dimension to inequality hinders growth and contributes to poverty and inequality (chapter 1).

Table 3.6. Benefit Incidence of Public Health Spending in Various African Countries (percent)

Country, year	Primary facilities		Hospital outpatient		Hospital inpatient		All	
	Poorest quintile	Richest quintile	Poorest quintile	Richest quintile	Poorest quintile	Richest quintile	Poorest quintile	Richest quintile
Côte d'Ivoire, 1995	14	22	8[a]	39[a]			11	32
Ghana, 1992	10	31	13	35	11	32	12	33
Guinea, 1994	10	36	1[a]	55[a]			4	48
Kenya, 1992[b]	22	14	13[a]	26[a]			14	24
Madagascar, 1993	10	29	14[a]	30[a]			12	30
Tanzania, 1992/93	18	21	11	37	20	36	17	29
South Africa, 1994	18	10	15[a]	17[a]			16	17

a. Includes inpatient spending.
b. Rural only.
Source: Castro-Leal and others 1999.

Security

SECURITY IS IMMENSELY IMPORTANT TO MOST AFRICANS. FOR THEM, life involves hazards that threaten livelihoods and capabilities (such as health). A participatory poverty assessment in Ethiopia investigated this dimension of well-being among both urban and rural communities. One striking finding was the value Ethiopians place on peace and the freedom it brings as a source of well-being, quite apart from its effects on economic opportunities. This message must resonate across Africa, given the wars and rumors of wars that are rife in the region.

Security is a source of both well-being and economic opportunity

Ethiopian rural households were asked to identify events in the past 20 years that had caused great losses of income or wealth. Four broad events were associated with serious household losses: harvest failure, due mainly to drought; policy failure, highlighting the disastrous effect on rural areas of the Derg regime; labor problems, such as the death of a breadwinner; and livestock problems, especially with oxen (table 3.7). While respondents highlighted the 1984 drought as a catastrophic harvest shock, there is continuing concern about harvest failure. Erratic rainfall is a major preoccupation among the poor. Annual variations in the agricultural harvest are a source of great uncertainty and seriously undermine household well-being.

Surveys confirm these fluctuations in well-being. Just 31 percent of the rural population surveyed was poor in both 1989 and 1995 (table 3.8). But three-quarters of the population experienced poverty in one or more of the two years.

Table 3.7 Events Causing Hardship in Ethiopia, 1975–95 (percentage of respondents)

	Village location				
Event	*Tigray*	*Amhara*	*Oromiya*	*SEPA*	*All*
War	15	10	3	5	7
Harvest failure	96	86	66	74	78
Labor problems	50	29	34	54	40
Land problems	36	14	17	14	17
Oxen problems	73	47	25	33	39
Other livestock	69	36	30	30	35
Policy	40	44	35	50	42
Crime/banditry	5	2	1	4	3
Asset losses	13	18	15	15	16

Source: Dercon 1998.

Table 3.8 Movements In and Out of Poverty in Rural Ethiopia, 1989 and 1995 (percent)

Category	Poor in 1995	Nonpoor in 1995	All households
Poor in 1989	31.1	30.2	61.3
Nonpoor in 1989	14.8	23.9	38.7
All households	45.9	54.1	100.0

Source: Dercon 1998.

Assistance must be based on an understanding of the coping mechanisms employed by the poor, and their limitations in protecting welfare

Some of the variation in these data is due to rainfall—1989 was a bad year for the harvest, and 1995 was a relatively good year. But idiosyncratic shocks must also have been at work, dragging some households into poverty and helping other out of it. Similar results have been found for short panels in Côte d'Ivoire (Grootaert, Kanbur, and Oh 1997).

Year-to-year insecurity in livelihood is only part of the story for an agrarian economy like Ethiopia. The participatory assessment found that most communities were also preoccupied with variations in consumption (especially food consumption) within the year. Seasonal fluctuations in food availability and prices are second only to drought as perceived causes of insecurity in rural communities. Seasonality was even cited by urban respondents as a problem for most households, especially the poor. The survey also points to large within-year fluctuations in household consumption, with significant seasonal variations in poverty.

Households are also concerned about the effects of a death of a working adult. High burial costs and income losses represent a major catastrophe for a household. AIDS has obvious and massive implications for household welfare in communities that have little cushion above bare survival.

How can policies help households cope with these unforgiving uncertainties? Assistance must be based above all on an understanding of the coping mechanisms employed by the poor, and their limitations in protecting welfare. Participatory assessments have found that rural communities reduce consumption during shocks or during lean seasons, or cope by borrowing cash or by generating other income through migrant work or petty trade.

There are two broad kinds of policies to deal with risk and uncertainty. First, governments can help reduce the risks by providing better water storage and management and by assisting with crop research and diversification. Second, governments can provide a safety net that is triggered by a shock such as drought or harvest failure. The safety net can also be designed to smooth consumption within the year. Community-based public works programs can meet both these safety net objectives. To the extent that policies enable the rural sector to recapitalize itself (chapter 6), the poor will also have more assets to buffer uncertainties.

Strategies for Reducing Poverty in Africa

Macroeconomic and structural policies that encourage growth and employment are essential for any poverty reduction strategy

WHATEVER THE MEASURE—CONSUMPTION POVERTY, direct indicators of well-being—the situation in Africa is serious. Income poverty increased in the 1990s. Malnutrition (wasting) appears to have worsened. Some countries have experienced increased child mortality—and lower life expectancy, in part because of AIDS. School enrollments have backslid. Growth has not been high or sustained enough to offset the previous decline, and the population has limited capacity to take advantage of income opportunities. Given these challenges, what are the key ingredients of a poverty reduction strategy for Africa?

Growth and Jobs

Macroeconomic and structural policies that encourage growth and employment are essential for any poverty reduction strategy. Raising the growth rates of African economies would have two main benefits. It would enhance the consumption potential of the population, improving food consumption, raising nutrition levels, and reducing the number of poor people. It would also generate resources that could be used to increase spending on basic needs such as health and education—which, if well targeted to the poor, would enhance their ability to take advantage of better employment opportunities and contribute to growth. How much growth is required? More than 5 percent a year seems needed simply to prevent the number of poor from rising, whereas meeting the International Development Goals for 2015 will require growth of more than 7 percent a year (chapter 1).

Inclusive Policies

But growth is not enough. Africa's high inequality increases the importance of inclusive policies. High initial inequality implies higher growth requirements to achieve a given poverty target, and can adversely affect growth prospects (Alesina and Rodrik 1994; Deininger and Squire 1996). Changes in inequality could have a considerable impact on the number of Africa's poor. For example, a 10 percentage point rise or drop in the region's Gini coefficients could move 50 million people in or out of poverty. Such a variation is within the range of historical experience of countries over a 15-year period.

Attacking the depth and severity of poverty, as measured by the poverty gap and the squared poverty gap, requires attention to sources of persistent inequality. Different aspects of poverty respond differently to changes in income and inequality. Changes in the distribution of income—as measured by the Gini coefficient—are more powerful for attacking deep poverty, as shown by the response of the poverty gap and the squared poverty gap (figure 3.3). Geographic targeting of assistance, including for the construction of essential rural infrastructure, is key for reducing high rural inequality. And in Southern Africa and a few countries elsewhere in the region, land redistribution measures may be required as well. Addressing constraints to economic diversification, investments, and job creation will also have to be an essential feature of any development strategy (chapters 6, 7).

Better Capabilities

Improving human capital is crucial for Africa, both to reduce income poverty and to directly improve people's lives. Accelerating programs to fight HIV/AIDS is perhaps the most pressing priority for many countries. But efforts to boost human capital in the region must cover a broad front. As noted, efforts in one area—such as reducing child mortality or raising education levels—are often linked to other objectives for well-being. Not all involve public services and public spending, but many do.

Africa's fiscal policies have been ineffective in achieving these better outcomes. Major efforts are needed to ensure that poor and excluded groups receive a larger share of public spending for essential social services and infrastructure, so that better capabilities can help close the inequality gap.

Improving human capital is crucial for Africa, both to reduce income poverty and to directly improve people's lives

Figure 3.3 How African Poverty Responds to Changes in Income and Inequality

Elasticity of poverty measures

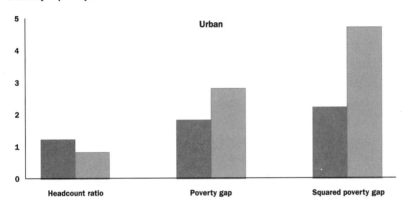

Government measures to help households cope with uncertainties must supplement the coping mechanisms used by the poor

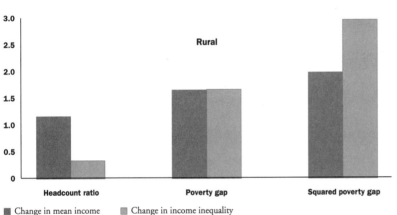

■ Change in mean income   ■ Change in income inequality

Source: Ali 1999.

Delivery Mechanisms and Accountability

Antipoverty programs will not succeed unless delivery systems are adjusted to deliver more public resources where the need is greatest, to increase transparency and accountability to beneficiaries, and to build the capacity of poor communities to help themselves. In highly centralized but poorly administered public bureaucracies, little public spending is likely to trickle down to the poor communities where it is most needed. Effective decentralization has both a governance component (chapter 2) and a service delivery component (chapter 4).

Stability and Security

Government measures to help households cope with uncertainties must supplement the coping mechanisms used by the poor. Participatory assessments are especially useful in improving understanding of these. Macroeconomic instability also hurts the poor disproportionately, because they have fewer mechanisms to cope with the consequences. Governments can help reduce risks by delivering better services (water storage and management, crop research and diversification) and by providing safety nets against shocks (drought, harvest failure). A safety net can also smooth consumption. Well-designed public works programs can meet both these safety net objectives.

CHAPTER 4

Investing in People

FRICA'S FUTURE LIES IN ITS PEOPLE. INDEED, AFRICA must solve its current human development crisis if it is to claim the 21st century. It can solve the crisis by replicating the decentralized service delivery mechanisms already in place in some African countries, by increasing international cooperation, by sustaining political commitment to the poor, and by using the extra financial resources that will come from the enhanced Heavily Indebted Poor Countries initiative (chapter 8). The crisis can be solved in one generation if countries focus on the basics: basic nutrition, education, health, and protection against increased vulnerability.

Investment in people is becoming more important for two reasons. First, Africa's future economic growth will depend less on its natural resources, which are being depleted and are subject to long-run price declines (chapter 1), and more on its labor skills and its ability to accelerate a demographic transition. Growth in today's information-based world economy depends on a flexible, educated, and healthy workforce to take advantage of economic openness. Accelerating the demographic transition to reduce population growth will require education, especially of women, and widely available contraceptive and reproductive health services.

Second, investing in people promotes their individual development and gives them the ability to escape poverty. This again requires education and health care as well as some measure of income security.

Africa's households and governments have invested heavily in human development since independence. By the 1980s this investment had started to pay off in much improved human development indicators. But in the last 10–15 years of the 20th century these indicators, still lagging

Africa must solve its human development crisis if it is to claim the 21st century

Figure 4.1 Fertility Rates by Region, 1960–2015

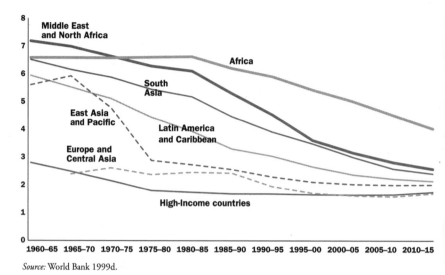

Africa's demographic transition remains slow— and well behind other poor areas of the world

Source: World Bank 1999d.

behind those of other regions, started to stagnate or even decline. Not only is Africa still well behind the rest of the world, there is also a major danger the gap will widen unless major changes are introduced.

This chapter makes no claim to be comprehensive. Instead it focuses on some critical factors that account for this slowdown in progress and on the major actions needed if progress is to be resumed and, indeed, accelerated so that Africa's people can claim the 21st century.

Africa's Human Development Crisis

I N ONLY A FEW AFRICAN COUNTRIES HAS FERTILITY STARTED TO decline, marking the last stage in the demographic transition, and they are the ones with higher per capita incomes and, especially, high health spending and fairly good access to contraception. Overall, however, Africa's demographic transition remains slow—and well behind other poor areas of the world, notably South Asia (figure 4.1). Africa's continued high fertility rates result not only in rapidly growing populations but also in populations with large portions of young people. The momentum generated by past population growth means that Africa, including both Sub-Saharan and North Africa, is now the only region

Figure 4.2 Gross Enrollment Rates by Education Level and Region, 1980 and 1995

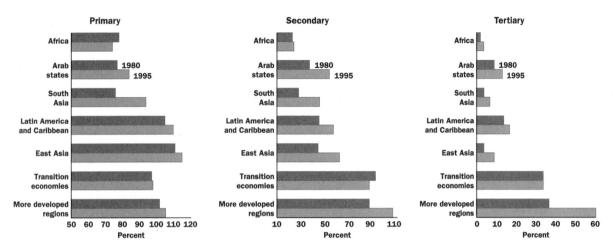

Source: UNESCO 1998.

where the absolute number of 6–11 year olds is growing (World Bank 1995). Coupled with the impact of HIV/AIDS on adult mortality, Africa's high fertility is resulting in 1.1 workers per dependent, compared with 1.4 in South Asia and 2.0 in East Asia (see table 1.1), with deleterious consequences for savings and investment.

So high has been the growth of the school-age population that African countries have had trouble keeping enrollment rates constant. Africa is the only region where primary enrollment rates were lower in 1995 than in 1980 (figure 4.2). Though there were improvements in the late 1990s, the primary enrollment rates of 1980 have not been reattained for boys or girls (table 4.1). Enrollment rates at all levels are far behind those in other regions (see figure 4.2).

Low primary enrollments seriously undermine economic growth and poverty reduction. Worldwide, no country has enjoyed sustained economic progress without literacy rates well over 50 percent. The consequences of low secondary and tertiary enrollments are harder to analyze but may be particularly critical in Africa. There is increasing evidence of positive backward links between secondary and higher education and other parts of the system, especially teacher education. Only in Africa, for example, does the correlation between female education and fertility reduction not kick in until the secondary level (UN 1987; Ainsworth 1996; NRC 1993). Tertiary education levels are so low that they limit the development of society's leaders. Moreover, universities have a potentially greater role to play in Africa than in many other regions—they are often the only national institutions with the skills, equipment, and mandate to generate new knowledge through research or to adapt global knowledge to help solve local problems.

Rapid enrollment growth in higher education, coupled with declining resources, has significantly lowered quality

The content and quality of African education are also in crisis. At the primary level the regular assessment of student achievement remains rare. The assessments that exist are not encouraging, however (figure 4.3). Poor quality not only produces poorly educated students, it also results in excessive repetition and low completion rates—at enormous cost. In 14 of 32 African countries for which data are available, more than one-third of school entrants do not complete the primary cycle. In 11 of 33 countries the input-output ratio is more than 1.5—that is, these countries use 50 percent or more resources than is necessary in an ideal system. At the university level religious studies and civil service needs have resulted in the development of the humanities and the social sciences and the neglect of natural sciences, applied technology, business-related skills, and research capabilities. Rapid enrollment growth in higher education, coupled with declining resources, has significantly lowered quality (World Bank 1999c).

Another major factor affecting school performance is the health and nutrition of students. Their health and nutrition also affect their future productivity in the workforce. Nutrition trends have yet to return to the levels of 1975 despite recent improvements in some countries. Population growth is causing a rapid increase in the

Table 4.1 Gross Enrollment Rates in Africa, 1960–97 (percent)

Level	1960	1970	1980	1990	1997
Primary total	43.2	52.5	79.5	74.8	76.8
Primary female	32.0	42.8	70.2	67.6	69.4
Primary male	54.4	62.3	88.7	81.9	84.1
Primary female as share of total	37	41	44	45	45
Secondary total	3.1	7.1	17.5	22.4	26.2
Secondary female	2.0	4.6	12.8	19.2	23.3
Secondary male	4.2	9.6	22.2	25.5	29.1
Secondary female as share of total	32	33	36	43	44
Tertiary total	0.2	0.8	1.7	3.0	3.9
Tertiary female	0.1	0.3	0.7	1.9	2.8
Tertiary male	0.4	1.3	2.7	4.1	5.1
Tertiary female as share of total	20	20	22	32	35

Source: UNESCO, *Statistical Yearbook,* 1978–79 and 1998.

Figure 4.3 Mean Scores of Primary Students on Three Dimensions of Reading Comprehension in Four African Countries, 1998

Percent correct

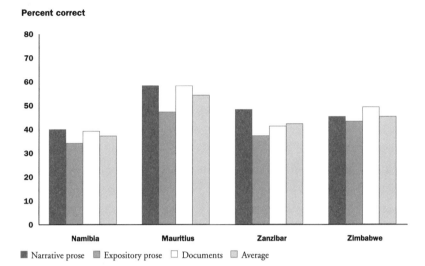

■ Narrative prose ■ Expository prose ☐ Documents ■ Average

Source: SACMEQ 1998.

Ill health in Africa results much more from infectious diseases and nutrition deficiencies than it does elsewhere

absolute number of underweight children, from 23 million in 1975 to 35 million in 1995.

Ill health in Africa results much more from infectious diseases and nutrition deficiencies than it does elsewhere (Feacham and Jamison 1991). This pattern affects Africans in their youth, when they may be too weak to attend school or to learn when they do attend, and remains with them as they grow up. The potential income loss from adult illness in Africa is about 6.5 percent, two to three times that in other regions, confirming cross-country evidence that poor health is associated with slow growth (chapter 1).[1]

Indeed, the burden of disease is dramatically higher in Africa than elsewhere (figure 4.4). And the disease pattern is different (figure 4.5). Malaria, onchocerciasis (river blindness), trypanosomiasis (sleeping sickness), and HIV/AIDS occur elsewhere in the world but are concentrated in Africa. Malaria, for which 80 percent of the world's cases occur in Africa, accounts for 11 percent of the disease burden in Africa and is estimated to cost many African countries more than 1 percent of their GDP (Leighton and Foster 1993; Gallup and Sachs 1998; Shepard and others 1991). (One estimate for Kenya puts it at 2–6 percent.). Onchocerciasis affects 18 million people, 99 percent of them in Africa. Trypanosomiasis

Figure 4.4 Variations in the Burden of Disease by Region, 1998

Disability-adjusted life-years lost (millions)

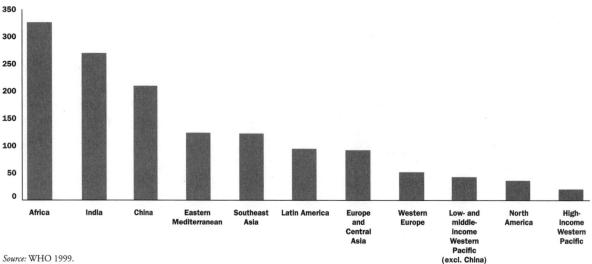

Source: WHO 1999.

Figure 4.5 Burden of Infectious Diseases in Africa, 1998

Disability-adjusted life-years lost (millions)

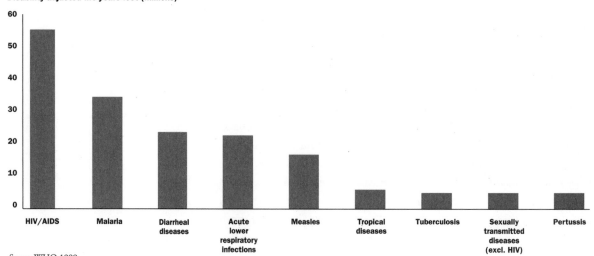

Source: WHO 1999.

108

occurs in 36 African countries and has recently surged. Two-thirds of the world's HIV/AIDS cases are in Africa.

Every three seconds an African child dies—in most cases from an infectious disease. In some countries one in five children die before their fifth birthday. Almost 90 percent of deaths from infectious disease are caused by a handful of diseases: acute respiratory infections, diarrheal diseases, HIV/AIDS, malaria, measles, tuberculosis, and sexually transmitted infections (see figure 4.5). These diseases account for half of all premature deaths, killing mostly children and young adults. Every day 3,000 people die from malaria—three out of four of them children. Every year 1.5 million people die from tuberculosis and another 8 million are newly infected. AIDS alone has orphaned more than 8 million children.

Life expectancy in Africa increased between 1950 and 1990, though at a lower rate than elsewhere. Since 1990, however, life expectancy has stagnated in the region, largely because of HIV/AIDS—and has dropped sharply in countries with a high adult prevalence of HIV/AIDS (figure 4.6). In 1982 only one African country, Uganda, had an adult HIV prevalence rate above 2 percent. Today there are 21 countries where more than 7 percent of adults live with HIV/AIDS. It is estimated that only 10 percent of the illness and death that HIV/AIDS will bring have been seen—despite more than 11 million deaths and 23 million cases

Since 1990 life expectancy has stagnated in the region— and has dropped sharply in countries with a high adult prevalence of HIV/AIDS

Figure 4.6 Estimated Life Expectancy at Birth in Selected African Countries, 1955–2000

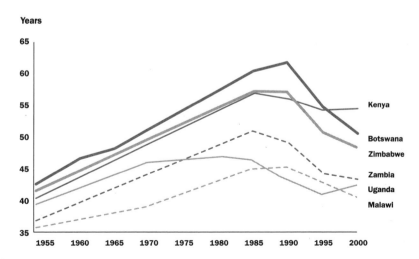

Source: UN 1999.

Family structures and income security are severely threatened by the increased vulnerability brought by HIV/AIDS, conflict, drought, and urbanization

among Africa's 600 million people. HIV is increasing child mortality (more than 1 million children are infected) and affects adolescents and women disproportionately, with half of new infections occurring among those 15–24 and six women infected for every five men in a number of the hardest-hit countries. HIV thus hits people in their prime productive years, profoundly disrupting the economic and social bases of families and dramatically reducing national income.

As noted, there are more than 8 million orphans in Africa as a result of HIV/AIDS, 1 million in Uganda alone. Dependency ratios are shooting up and economic insecurity is increasing. At the national and even the continental level, the illness and impending death of up to one in four adults in some countries will have an enormous impact on national productivity, earnings, and savings (World Bank 1999b). This impact will be strongest in Southern Africa, where HIV is most widespread and where much of Africa's GDP is located. The combination of HIV infection and malaria infection is especially insidious, weakening in a mutually destructive action the immune systems of both the pregnant mother and the fetus.

Though perhaps the most dramatic element undermining family structures and threatening income security, HIV/AIDS is not the only one. War and civil conflict became more common in the 1990s, and 28 percent of the world's 12 million refugees are now in Africa (UNHCR 1998). Increasing numbers of refugees and migrants, coupled with high urbanization, will exacerbate the spread of HIV/AIDS. As the new century opens, there is hope that the main recent conflicts are being resolved. But much peace is fragile, and the consequences for Africa's families are profound. Furthermore, many conflicts remain.

War and conflict come on top of other external shocks for many people, such as more than 30 years of drought in the Sahel. Indeed, 60 percent of Africa is vulnerable to drought, and 30 percent is extremely vulnerable. In addition, much of the poor's consumption is seasonal (chapter 3), and macroeconomic shocks have a greater impact on the poor than on others. Moreover, in Africa as elsewhere, urbanization, while generally promoting development through the concentration of populations, weakens traditional family structures. And in Africa particularly, employment growth appears to have stagnated along with economies more generally. Coupled with massive poverty, family structures and income security are severely threatened by the increased vulnerability brought by HIV/AIDS, conflict, drought, and urbanization (World Bank 1999a).

Why the Human Development Crisis?

I F AFRICA IS TO CLAIM THE 21ST CENTURY, IT MUST REVERSE THIS LATE 20th century pattern of rapid population growth, stagnating primary enrollments, declining health, poor nutrition, and growing income insecurity, all affecting children and women disproportionately as a result of poverty and deteriorating family structures. Reversing the pattern means understanding its causes. This section explores some possible explanations.

Households and communities are willing to invest in the future of their children

Do Africans Value Investments in Human Development?

It is sometimes suggested that African households do not invest in human development, especially education, because the private returns to that investment are not high enough to justify it. The evidence on private returns to education in Africa is mixed and somewhat dated. But it appears that market wage returns are usually high, as elsewhere in the world, especially for postprimary education.

There is considerable controversy about the absolute size of the returns to education in Africa. Psacharopoulos (1994), for instance, aggregates the private returns to primary education at 41 percent, to secondary education at 27 percent, and to higher education at 28 percent. Mingat and Suchaut (forthcoming) put them at 30, 21, and 28 percent. Others think that these estimates overestimate the returns to schooling. And indeed, issues of omitted variable bias and selection complicate the interpretation of wage-education gradients in Africa (as elsewhere).

Even studies that control for bias, however, find substantial private returns to education in Africa, on the order of an 8–10 percent increase in wages per year of schooling (van der Gaag and Vijverberg 1987). These data are largely static. Unresearched in modern Africa is the key question of whether returns to skills are rising because of increasing demand or declining because of increasing supply (Knight and Sabot 1990). Whatever the precise numbers, the private returns to schooling are significant in Africa—suggesting that households should want to invest.

This quantitative evidence is strongly supported by anecdotal evidence. In many countries the buildings erected through voluntary effort for primary and secondary education, for local training centers, and for health clinics attest to the willingness of households and communities to invest in the future of their children. Outlays on school fees, uni-

Extremely poor households have fewer mechanisms for coping with increased vulnerability

forms, and the like account for a substantial claim on households' cash income (Fine and others 1999). Given the poor and declining quality of education offered to many poor households, their continued willingness to forgo a considerable share of current consumption provides unambiguous evidence of a strong desire to invest in their children's future. In Mauritania and other countries, parents fund private tutoring (often by the same teachers) to supplement low-quality public schooling. Offered timely, comprehensible, and appropriate advice, African mothers will take appropriate measures to provide for their children's nutrition and development. Entire communities have often banded together to support a gifted child's secondary and university education.

Strauss (2000) has summarized the evidence on household and community factors affecting investment in human development in Africa. Household investment is largely determined by the education of the parents, by household income, and by income responses (at least for health care). There is almost no evidence on the response of households to school choice in Africa, but evidence from elsewhere indicates that there will likely be an income response. The implication of all this is that public, rather than private, health and education services are becoming more targeted at low-income populations.

At the community level there is considerable evidence that health and school facilities are more likely to be used when they are close to the community. The impact of distance on use seems to be greater than that of user fees, though there is not as much evidence on user fees in Africa (Strauss and Thomas 1988).

While households demand investments in education and health, and invest their own funds in these areas, a disturbing recent development is the inability of the poorest of the poor to cope with increased vulnerability. Traditionally, the poor have had diverse mechanisms for protecting themselves against vulnerability—joining labor-sharing clubs in Togo, taking children out of school to work in the household in Swaziland, selling cattle in Zimbabwe. But these traditional mechanisms have become less effective at managing household risks as the risks, and household vulnerability, have increased. In Burkina Faso, for example, cattle sales by households during the most extreme drought period finance only 20–30 percent of the village-level income shortfall.

In addition, Africa's traditional system of social protection—the extended family—is under extreme stress because of conflict, HIV/AIDS, drought, and migration, and can no longer provide the economic and social protection to households that it once did. This, in turn, is beginning to affect households' abilities to enroll their children in school, as in Côte d'Ivoire, Kenya, and Zambia. This increased vulnerability is not just a rural phenomenon: the primary enrollment rate in Nairobi (Kenya), for instance, has dropped to 61 percent from 103 percent in 1980. The increased attraction of education programs that include meals attests to this increased vulnerability.

Are Resources Used Efficiently?

Because of its young population, Africa's human development investment needs are great. Yet its resources are limited, even with external aid. Thus it might seem that Africa simply does not have enough resources to invest in its people.

But the reality is more complicated. In 1993 public investment in education averaged 3.8 percent of GDP in Africa compared with 2.7 percent in Asia and 2.8 percent in Latin America (table 4.2). In general, private spending adds another 50 percent to public spending. Health spending in Africa averages 5.6 percent of GDP, the same as the global average for low- and middle-income countries and significantly more than the 3.5–4.1 percent for Asia (table 4.3). Public spending accounts for about half of Africa's health spending.

Of course, these spending data refer to the continent as a whole. One of the most remarkable features of human development investments in Africa is their differentiation across countries. Public spending on education in francophone West African countries amounts to 5.5 percent of GDP; that in anglophone East African countries is 2.3 percent of GDP. Median per capita public spending on health is about $6 a year in

Relative to GDP, Africa spends as much—or more—on education and health as other regions

Table 4.2 Public Spending on Education in Africa, Asia, and Latin America, 1975 and 1993 (percentage of GDP)

Region	1975	1993
Africa	4.0	3.8
Asia	2.6	2.7
Latin America	2.9	2.8
Memorandum item		
All countries with GDP below $2,000	3.6	3.6

Source: Mingat and Suchaut forthcoming.

Table 4.3 Spending on Health in Africa, Asia, and Latin America and Caribbean, 1990s (percentage of GDP)

Region	Total spending	Public spending
Africa	5.6	2.8
East Asia and Pacific	3.5	1.5
South Asia	4.1	0.8
Latin America and Caribbean	7.2	3.0
All low- and middle-income countries	5.6	2.8

Source: World Bank 1997.

Investments in human development differ considerably across Africa

Africa—but averages $3 in the lowest-income countries and $72 in middle-income countries (Peters 1999).

The completely different patterns for education and health spending require caution in generalizing about human development. In education the main issue is the efficiency of resource use, as spending tends to account for a larger share of GDP in the poorest countries than in the richer ones. In health the issue is resource availability in the poorest countries and efficiency in all countries. In Burundi, for instance, annual public spending on health is only $1.5 per capita—a level that is simply insufficient for progress.

Moreover, especially in health, expressing available resources as shares of GDP obscures the need for significant spending in foreign exchange for drugs and other supplies. And, more generally, the youth of most African populations means that spending on education should probably account for a larger portion of GDP than in many higher-income countries. Yet African countries' high dependency ratios are just one reason it is hard to increase tax efforts.

There is enormous potential for more efficient human development spending in Africa:

■ *Internal efficiency.* Relative to GDP per capita, Africa's unit costs in education are twice as high at the primary level as in Asia and Latin America (table 4.4). This reflects not only high repetitions and dropouts but also high teacher salaries relative to GDP per capita, especially in the Sahel countries of West Africa (Mingat and Suchaut forthcoming). In health, patients at public health facilities may receive benefits worth just $12 for each $100 of public spending on drugs (box 4.1). The range of outcomes achieved with the same public spending (relative to GNP) is very wide for both health and education—higher spending is not necessarily reflected in better outcomes.

Table 4.4 Education Unit Costs in Africa, Asia, and Latin America, 1975–93 (percentage of GDP per capita)

	Primary			Secondary			Tertiary		
Region	1975	1985	1993	1975	1985	1993	1975	1985	1993
Africa	20	16	15	117	117	56	1,293	691	656
Asia	12	10	8	32	22	19	192	226	86
Latin America	8	8	7	12	12	11	149	82	66
All countries with GNP < $12,000	16	13	12	72	42	37	758	400	373

Source: Mingat and Suchaut forthcoming.

- *Allocative efficiency.* Despite low secondary and tertiary enrollment rates, education spending is biased toward these levels of education, which mainly benefit the better-off. The primary level offers higher returns, especially for the poor. Similarly, public health spending is not focused on the essential components of basic health care. Rather, it is significantly biased toward expensive secondary and tertiary care. The poorest 20 percent of the population receives only about 12 percent of public health subsidies (chapter 3). Combined with the inefficiency in the drug supply system, that means that this group may receive less than $2 in benefits for every $100 spent on drugs.

Are African Governments Committed to Human Development?

The persistence of such inefficiencies, coupled with the low volume and poor quality of many human development services, often leads to the charge that African governments are not committed to their people's development. This may be true in some cases, especially among countries in conflict. Generally, however, it is far off the mark. More than 40

Box 4.1 Waste in the Drug Supply System

AFRICA'S HEALTH DELIVERY SYSTEMS COULD BE MADE a lot more efficient through improved maintenance of equipment and facilities, better-informed investment in high-level training, and redeployment of redundant staff. Symptomatic of such inefficiencies is the waste in supplying drugs, a significant component of private and public health spending. Patients at public facilities may be receiving benefits worth only $12 for every $100 of tax revenue spent on drugs. The main sources of waste are noncompetitive procurement ($27), poor storage and management ($19), inappropriate prescriptions ($15), poor projections of requirements ($13), inadequate buying practices ($10), and incorrect use by patients ($3).

Source: World Bank 1994.

African countries have developed national "education for all" programs. And most have subscribed to the International Development Goals for 2015, which include targets for education and health along with those for poverty reduction, gender equality, and environmental sustainability (chapter 1; OECD 1996).

The problem is not necessarily a lack of political commitment but rather the wide range of actions needed and the intensely political nature of the reforms required to create effective service delivery systems. In recent years most governments have been preoccupied with improving macroeconomic policy (chapter 1). Political commitment is now needed not just to boosting human development in general but to improving nutrition, to implementing major health and education reforms, to confronting HIV/AIDS, to protecting the vulnerable, and so on. It is difficult for governments, however committed, to move simultaneously on many fronts, each of which is vastly more complicated than macroeconomic reform.

It is difficult—but not impossible—for governments to move forward on the many fronts needed to create effective service delivery systems

This difficulty is compounded by the political nature of the reforms. They involve overcoming massive vested interests, which requires steadfast political will and is not always feasible—especially given the new democratic climate and frequent elections in many countries and the political weakness of rural populations. Teachers tend to be heavily unionized, university students often represent a powerful political force though a tiny numerical minority, hospitals have more influence than clinics, and so on. Taken together, public education and health labor forces usually represent the bulk of the nonmilitary public service in African countries.

Despite these complex issues of political economy, many countries have made a major start. Burkina Faso, Guinea, and Senegal, for example, are making teacher salaries more flexible, partly by permitting the recruitment of community-based teachers who are off the civil service pay scales. More progress can be expected, linked to the growth of civil society throughout Africa and to the power of information. As Africans better understand what is at stake, they will increasingly demand better services through standard political channels and through civil society organizations.

At the same time, reform is always a lot easier when economies are growing and transition costs can be more easily absorbed through increased resources. Not only must vested interests be overcome, but human development programs must simultaneously focus on the needs of the poorest, through basic health and education, and on the need to build societies more generally, which involves an important role for other parts of the education system, including higher education. Balancing these priorities would not be easy even in the absence of problems of political economy.

In two areas, however, political commitment remains severely lacking: fighting HIV/AIDS and reducing fertility. Not all African leaders are convinced of the seriousness of the HIV/AIDS epidemic, nor do they realize the potential impact it will have on their countries. Because of this, not all have made HIV/AIDS a high priority. Strong political commitment to fighting AIDS is crucial to provide the resources, leadership, and enabling environment needed to control the epidemic's spread and care for the nation. Accurate and relevant data are a powerful tool for convincing leaders to increase their commitment to confronting HIV/AIDS (World Bank 1999b). Where there is political commitment, AIDS can be met head on—as in Uganda, where high infection rates have been brought down, and in Senegal (box 4.2).

Political commitment remains severely lacking in two areas: fighting HIV/AIDS and reducing fertility

Are Service Delivery Mechanisms Appropriate?

If Africa's households and communities want to invest in human development and if there is political will, why has the human development record been so poor in recent years? Mention has already been made of the difficulty of moving simultaneously on many fronts. But this is mainly true at the national rather than the local level. Africa's public institutions are relatively weak at the national level. Yet its communities, except in areas torn by war and conflict, are among the strongest in the world—especially in West Africa, as evidenced by their response to the availability of social funds and other community-based investment funds. Almost all human development programs, however, have been national

---

Box 4.2 Senegal Confronts AIDS

UNLIKE THOSE IN MANY AFRICAN COUNTRIES, Senegal's leaders chose not to deny the existence of the HIV/AIDS epidemic, but to face the challenge from the start. Enlisting all key actors as allies in a timely and aggressive prevention campaign has helped the country maintain one of the lowest HIV infection rates in Africa (1.8 percent). The small number of HIV positive individuals allows the government to consider using treatment schedules that otherwise would not have been affordable.

Source: World Bank 1999b.

programs, implemented by weak institutions and ignoring strong communities. External donors have exacerbated this pattern of excessively top-down delivery. A recent review of completed World Bank education projects in Africa, for instance, found that only 8 percent had resulted in institutional strengthening.

Centralized control often results in a focus on the wrong issues, on inputs rather than on results

Centralized control often results in a focus on the wrong issues, on inputs to programs rather than on results. Centralized recruitment and deployment of teachers, for example, leads ministries of education and health to focus on teacher and health worker interests and diverts them from education and health results in individual schools and clinics. It also diverts attention from delivering services to dealing with central public employees—who, as noted, tend to be predominantly education and health workers. It leads teachers to spend days away from their schools attempting to receive their pay, which is still rarely handled at the school level. Centralized procurement of drugs, contraceptives, and textbooks can lead to the all-too-common phenomenon of supplies stored in central warehouses long after clinics and schools needed them and to extensive inefficiency in the use of funds (see box 4.1). In social protection, centralized programs focus on coping with shocks, not mitigating or averting them.

Overly centralized management has resulted in human development programs that are perceived as distant by their beneficiaries, with low transparency and limited accountability (chapter 1). Around the world, there is a trend toward decentralized delivery of human development services, partly in response to the global growth of democracy and civil society. The jury is still out on whether decentralized programs are more effective and efficient in societies where institutions are relatively strong. But in Africa, where institutions tend to be weak, service delivery is superior when it is controlled by beneficiaries and implemented by them or by autonomous agencies (Frigenti, Hasth, and Haque 1998). This finding is increasingly confirmed by the World Bank's assessments of its projects: those based on community-driven delivery mechanisms have fewer problems than others.

Until recently autonomous local control of service delivery represented a political threat to central governments and elites in Africa. That is changing rapidly as civil society and democratic political institutions grow. Indeed, Africa is poised to adopt service delivery mechanisms more attuned to its political development, as has already happened in some countries (chapter 2).

Is There Enough International Cooperation?

International cooperation takes many forms. This section concentrates on partnerships among African countries and between them and their development partners. International cooperation is particularly important in human development—and above all in health, because disease knows no boundaries.

In education there is a vibrant partnership among African countries and external aid agencies through the Association for the Development of African Education. There are also other important forums, such as the United Nations Educational, Scientific, and Cultural Organization and the Organization of African Unity, in which African governments meet and share experiences. Yet something is lacking. Francophone education systems have been little influenced by anglophone ones, and vice versa. Similarly, in health there are various organizational forums, notably AFRO (the World Health Organization regional office for Africa) and the Organization of African Unity again. Particularly noteworthy has been the shared experience of implementing the Bamako Initiative, with its emphasis on community involvement in basic health delivery. But in health, as in education, something is lacking in the sharing of ideas and experience, probably because of the lack of forums for such exchanges to occur. Maternal mortality halved in three years in Inganga, Uganda, when traditional birth attendants were partnered with public health centers using modern communications. How can such innovations be replicated?

External partners can supply knowledge, finance, and research. Much aid to Africa is focused on human development. For example, the International Development Association, the World Bank's soft-loan window, targets 50 percent of its funding to Africa and 40 percent of that to the social sectors. Many bilateral donors have similar priorities. The multilateral Heavily Indebted Poor Countries initiative (chapter 8) will free resources for education and health programs in countries now saddled with high debt service obligations. External finance is available. Indeed, institutions such as the International Development Association have found it hard to use all their funding because of limited absorptive capacities resulting from weak institutions and inappropriate delivery mechanisms.

In knowledge and research, however, much remains to be done. The onus lies on African countries in terms of knowledge and on them and their OECD partners in terms of research. There is resistance in Africa, perhaps understandably derived from the struggle against colonialism, to

Africa is poised to adopt service delivery mechanisms more attuned to its political development

119

learning about human development from other parts of the world. Yet the experiences, especially of East Asia and Latin America, are profoundly important for Africa. More openness is needed to these experiences.

In research, Africa suffers from its uniqueness. Because the predominant diseases in Africa tend to be mainly African, there has been little international effort to develop appropriate vaccines and other medical interventions. But that is changing. Indeed, now that some of these diseases—like malaria and HIV—are spreading around the world, attention is finally focusing on them. Today there is a concerted international effort to develop vaccines against HIV, malaria, trypanosomiasis, and the like. Still, the African nature of these diseases has made it difficult to mobilize relative to, say, the successful global effort to eliminate smallpox 20 years ago.

Yet when international partnerships are mobilized against African diseases, the results can be tremendous and highly cost-effective. River blindness is on the retreat as a result of two successful programs: the Onchocerciasis Control Program in West Africa and the African Program for Onchocerciasis Control in East and Central Africa. Together these programs comprise the largest human disease control program in operation today, with 93 partners and an economic return on investment of 17–25 percent (box 4.3).

When international partnerships are mobilized against African diseases, the results can be tremendous and highly cost-effective

Tools for Investing in Africa's People

R EVERSING RECENT TRENDS AND INVESTING IN AFRICA'S PEOPLE SO that they can claim the 21st century will not be easy. The social development targets of the International Development Goals for 2015 offer a benchmark:

- Achieving universal primary education.
- Eliminating gender disparities in education (by 2005).
- Reducing infant and child mortality by two-thirds.
- Reducing maternal mortality by three-quarters.
- Achieving universal access to reproductive health services.[2]

These goals appear reasonable but are not going to be easy to reach. In some areas, such as primary education, it is only in the past few years that the declines of the 1980s and early 1990s have started to be reversed.

In others, such as child mortality, trends are worsening—largely because of HIV/AIDS. Achieving these goals will require resources, political commitment, appropriate service delivery, and increased international cooperation. Elements of all four are already partly in place throughout Africa, and they are yielding results. What is urgently needed now is to replicate them throughout the continent, adapting them to national and local circumstances.

Box 4.3 The Successful International Partnership against Onchocerciasis

ONCHOCERCIASIS IS A PARASITIC DISEASE, ENDEMIC IN West Africa, that causes debilitation, eye damage, and (eventually) "river blindness." The disease is caused by a parasitic worm and transmitted by the bite of the female blackfly, which breeds in rapidly flowing rivers. Two onchocerciasis programs are the essence of effective development partnerships: results-oriented, comprehensive, widely representative, international, instilling ownership, capitalizing on a diverse range of comparative advantages, and focusing on poverty reduction. These successful programs have seen nearly 100 partners come together with the sole purpose of providing a global public good: eliminating a disease that devastates the poorest in Africa.

The Onchocerciasis Control Program, begun in 1974, has halted transmission of the disease in 95 percent of the 11-country, 34-million-people program area by destroying the blackfly larvae in its river breeding sites using insecticides sprayed from the air. To complement vector control, the program also collaborated with a pharmaceutical company, Merck and Co., to develop a drug called ivermectin. Ivermectin has revolutionized the treatment and prevention of onchocerciasis by providing a safe and effective drug that, when dosed once a year, prevents the blinding and itching caused by the parasite. Merck announced in 1987 that it would donate as much ivermectin as needed for as long as necessary to eliminate onchocerciasis in Africa.

The Onchocerciasis Control Program has been sustained by a unique partnership involving 11 West African governments, sponsoring agencies (United Nations Development Programme, Food and Agriculture Organization, World Bank), bilateral donors, the private sector, and an international technical staff headed by the implementing agency, the World Health Organization. The parasite is dying out in the human population. People previously infected are recovering. More than 12 million children born in the program area since the program began are growing up without risk of contracting the disease. An estimated 25 million hectares of arable land have been freed from onchocerciasis and are being resettled. New villages are being established, and agricultural production is increasing. The cost: just $0.57 a person per year in 1987 constant dollars.

A second program, the African Program for Onchocerciasis Control, has extended the benefits of onchocerciasis control to all affected African countries. It further recognized that the efficacy of ivermectin in preventing onchocerciasis allowed for a control program based entirely on its mass distribution. At the launch of the program in 1995, the river blindness partnership was widened to include two important partners: nongovernmental organizations (now numbering more than 40), who help acquire and distribute the donated ivermectin, and local communities, whose ownership of the program is essential for the program's long-term sustainability. There are currently 57 projects under way in 12 countries, with 32 million people under annual ivermectin treatment. The program already reaches nearly 70 percent of the population targeted for treatment by 2007.

Resources

We have seen that there are serious inefficiencies in the allocation of resources for human development in Africa. Nevertheless, extra resources are needed now, for four reasons. First, some countries are so poor that they simply do not have sufficient domestic resources, regardless of efficiency considerations. These are generally the lowest-income countries, like Burundi and Guinea-Bissau.

More resources are needed to achieve goals for health and education

Second, many countries have embarked on structural reforms designed to reduce inefficiencies and reallocate resources, but the reforms will take time and often will be slow to yield savings. The adoption of *volontaire* primary school teachers, paid less than public service teachers, in many Sahel countries is a good example. Over time this reform will lower unit and total costs. But in the short term, by reducing the student-teacher ratio while not displacing existing teachers, it increases the teacher salary bill.

Third, new programs and service delivery mechanisms are needed to combat HIV/AIDS and malaria. Effective programs against HIV/AIDS may cost 1.5–2.0 percent of GDP a year in a typical African country, and more in those with high HIV infection rates. Malaria program costs may run 0.3–0.5 percent of GDP a year.

Finally, as service coverage increases, the unit costs of delivering services to the previously unserved are higher than those to the previously served. These beneficiaries tend to be the rural poor, the poorest of the poor, living in dispersed areas without good transport and other infrastructure. So, proportionately more resources are needed to achieve goals for health and universal primary education.

Moreover, an important barrier to serving such beneficiaries has been the need for them to pay for services. Though the poor are willing to pay for human development investments, their resources are limited. User fees have deterred primary school enrollment and health center use. Fees have been advocated because they generate revenue and increase allocative efficiency—and there is merit to both arguments. Anecdotally, modest user fees seem to improve the quality of health services. In Madagascar, for instance, the ability of health facilities to charge fees—and to retain them—has kept drugs in stock and increased patient demand because quality is perceived as having improved. But the effect of such fees on service use has likely been severely underestimated, especially in education, and most especially for the poor. In Uganda, for example, primary enrollments doubled in one year, from 2.6 million to 5.2 million, when parent-teacher association dues were eliminated (box 4.4).

Revenue generation can be effective when the revenues are held and used at the community level. The impact of fees on resource allocation has not been sufficiently studied for there to be clear results in Africa; we simply do not know if higher charges at hospitals than at health centers,

---

Box 4.4 Uganda's Commitment to Basic Education

DURING THE 1990S UGANDA EMBARKED ON A SWEEP-ing national program to achieve universal primary education. This program, probably the most ambitious in Africa, has the following elements:

Massive political commitment. Education was the principal electoral platform of President Yoweri Museveni in his successful 1996 campaign and is the most talked-about topic in Uganda today. Basic education is Uganda's top priority.

Elimination of barriers to access. Until 1996 education was not free. Fees were minor, but parent-teacher association dues amounted to $6–8 a child—a major burden for most Ugandan families. In 1997 free schooling was introduced for up to four children a household. Primary enrollments immediately doubled from 2.6 million to 5.2 million, and in 1999 reached 6.5 million.

Sustained budget commitment. The government has dramatically increased the share of the national budget going to education, from 22 percent in 1995 to 31 percent in 1999. Two-thirds of this goes to primary education, allocated to districts on a capitation basis. Waste has been eliminated with the elimination of ghost teachers, cutting payroll numbers by a third. Moreover, the government is committed to concentrating future increases in spending—including from the Heavily Indebted Poor Countries initiative—on education.

Decentralization with central support. All primary education is now run by Uganda's 45 districts. Each district deploys and pays teachers, though they remain centrally financed. Classroom construction is also managed at the district level using a community demand approach, which has resulted in faster and better construction. Multigrade teaching is being piloted in sparsely populated areas. Support to schools and teachers is provided by a cascading system linking teacher training colleges to district coordinating centers and then to schools. Nationally, 560 tutors are in place, each responsible for supporting 20 schools, a large but manageable responsibility. Schools select textbooks from a nationally approved list.

Accountability. Districts and schools are held accountable for results and funds are used transparently.

Curriculum reform. The curriculum has been modernized for the core subjects of mathematics, English, social science, and natural science. Books and materials have been developed and are being deployed. An assessment system is being put in place to measure student achievement.

Teacher support. Teacher pay has been increased to provide a living wage. Competency tests have been administered to all uncertified teachers, and an in-service training program introduced for those deemed trainable. There are still not enough teachers, given the massive increase in enrollments, but the government is committed to reducing student-teacher ratios from about 60:1 (and as high as 100:1 in the first two years of primary school) to 40:1 as soon as is financially feasible. Budget increases to fund more teachers and build classrooms are the government's spending priority for the next decade, and resources released through the Heavily Indebted Poor Countries initiative will be used for these purposes.

for instance, increase the portion of people initially seeking care at the centers. We do know that modest fees for drugs at health centers seem to improve both quality and use.

Sustained and specific political commitment is needed for effective investment in human development

The extra resources that are needed should be made available. Africa remains a principal beneficiary of much multilateral and bilateral aid and of the Heavily Indebted Poor Countries initiative (chapter 8). It will be necessary to finance fiscal deficits that may seem large in conventional GDP terms, but this will be justified so long as the macroeconomic consequences are funded by grants or highly concessional loans and so long as the programs the deficits finance expand access to and improve human development services. This may entail large deficits, with continued aid dependence over an extended period (chapter 8). But these funds need to enhance programs, not simply finance them. Special programs may be needed for countries not eligible for the Heavily Indebted Poor Countries initiative or for which the terms of the expanded initiative do not free significant resources.

Political Commitment

General political commitment to human development is already in place in most African countries. What is needed for effective investment in human development is sustained and specific political commitment. This involves focus, sustained resources, and active involvement.

Focus can come from a commitment to the poor, especially poor children. Poor children require political commitment because they are voiceless in society, even though those under 15 typically account for 45 percent of African populations—a portion unlike that anywhere else in the world. Children represent these societies' futures as well as half their present. A commitment to poor children is also a commitment to equity. Closing urban-rural and male-female gaps is a central challenge for human development, above all in education. Primary enrollment rates in Niamey (90 percent), Addis Ababa (85), and Bamako (80) are more than four times those in the rural areas of Niger, Ethiopia, and Mali (World Bank 1999c). Girls' enrollment rates lag boys' in most countries but can be increased rapidly with sustained political commitment, as happened in Guinea, Mauritania, and Uganda in the 1990s.

Resources for human development must be sustained over time, as with education in Uganda (see box 4.4) and nutrition in Madagascar (box 4.5). Commitment also involves continued involvement in human development by the political elite, as happened in both of these countries in a direct way, with education being a key topic of discussion throughout Uganda and child nutrition throughout poor areas of Madagascar.

A particular type of commitment is needed to combat HIV/AIDS, commitment of the sort seen in Senegal (see box 4.2). This commitment requires a readiness to openly discuss topics—including sex and sex workers—that are normally below the surface in Africa. Discussing such topics is not easy for political leaders anywhere. Many African countries have begun open discussions of these topics, but more must do so to reverse the epidemic.

A commitment to the poor requires a commitment above all to basics: basic nutrition, basic education, basic health, and basic protection against vulnerability. These basics have long been emphasized but have yet to be achieved. Moreover, a commitment to basics does not mean ignoring

Special commitment is needed to combat HIV/AIDS

Box 4.5 Improving Nutrition in Madagascar

THE MADAGASCAR FOOD SECURITY AND NUTRITION Project, recently completed and now being extended, reduced malnutrition among target populations by about 50 percent over four years. In Antananarivo malnutrition dropped from 43 to 18 percent, and in Toliary, from 26 to 13 percent.

The project had several key elements:
- Strong political support, as evidenced in the provision of new funding in a tight fiscal situation and in public support by the political elite.
- A social fund that financed income-generating activities.
- A food for work program.
- A nutrition program that worked through mothers groups, each organized by a community nutrition agent and supported by nongovernmental organizations.
- The universal iodization of salt.

The lessons from the project and other success stories—such as the Senegal Community Nutrition Project, the Benin Community-based Food Security Project, and the Mali Grassroots Initiatives to Fight Hunger and Poverty—are simple but important:

- Programs must be truly community-based—planned, managed, and implemented by local beneficiaries.
- Programs must be flexible and provide training to increase the capacity of communities to address challenges.
- Strong national political leadership is essential, so communication efforts are needed to keep government and people aware of the programs and to ensure that they support them.
- Collaboration and partnerships are also essential, especially with nongovernmental organizations that know how to work with community groups, donors, and United Nations agencies.
- Technological innovations must be applied, such as the use of micronutrients, as well as simple policies like salt iodization.
- Programs must be multisectoral. Targeting must focus on the malnourished, but interventions must be varied to meet the needs of the community (such as literacy classes, food for work programs, and microcredit for agriculture).

Source: World Bank; UN ACC/SCN 1997; UNICEF 1996.

other parts of the social system. Basic education, for example, can only be achieved through a direct commitment both to the basic level and to the balanced development of the education system as a whole.

Appropriate Service Delivery

Appropriate interventions vary according to the problem to be addressed

Human development service delivery in Africa should be based on two simple premises:

- Most problems have well-known, cost-effective interventions.
- Weak public institutions at the national level mean that effective delivery must be based on stronger community and private institutions.

Appropriate interventions vary according to the problem to be addressed. In education, for example, they involve removing barriers to access and providing books, materials, and trained and motivated teachers to children healthy and well-nourished enough to learn in schools close enough to their homes for them to attend (World Bank 1999c). In nutrition they include salt iodization, which reduced the African population at risk of iodine deficiency from 33 percent in 1994 to 23 percent in 1997, including in such countries as Kenya (100 percent iodization), Madagascar (100 percent; see box 4.5), and Nigeria (97 percent; UN ACC/SN 1997). In preventing HIV infection appropriate interventions involve public information and condoms, the use of which has resulted in a sharp decline in new HIV and sexually transmitted infections among sex workers in countries as diverse as the Democratic Republic of Congo and Thailand (World Bank 1999b). Indeed, the elements of a complete national program against HIV/AIDS are well-known, if not yet fully in place in any one African country (box 4.6). Implementing such programs could cost $15 billion a year for the continent as a whole.

Decentralized delivery focused on the community and the local school or health facility is the second key to effective service delivery. It characterizes successful programs for onchocerciasis in West Africa (see box 4.3), education in Uganda (see box 4.4), nutrition in Madagascar (see box 4.5), and safe motherhood in Chad (box 4.7)—all very different societies and economies, but all with weak national institutions.

Decentralized delivery can involve a range of mechanisms but is based on the simple concept of getting resources to where they are needed, and putting them more under the control of the immediate beneficiaries. This can include decentralization to the district level, decentralization to autonomous schools and health centers, and much greater reliance on nongovernmental organizations and other private organizations, including public funding of private service delivery. What is common to these approaches is their proximity to the beneficiaries, involving them in governance structures so that there is increased accountability and better service availability and quality.

Examples abound. Zimbabwe's Social Fund has enabled communities to mitigate the consequences of drought and economic stagnation, and even helped empower communities further. Community schools are growing rapidly in Chad and Mali, partly in response to the slow expansion of the formal system. Nutrition programs in Senegal rely on implementation through a contracted private agency, with payments directly related to actual results in terms of nutrition outcomes among the target population. Centers run by nongovernmental organizations are an important aspect of Zambia's health program. Public funds are being used to fund private schools in Cameroon.

Decentralized delivery is based on the simple concept of getting resources to where they are needed

Box 4.6 Elements of Successful HIV/AIDS Programs

SUCCESSFUL NATIONAL HIV/AIDS PROGRAMS SHARE a number of features:

- Government commitment at the highest level and multiple partnerships at all levels with civil society and the private sector.
- Early investment in prevention efforts.
- Cooperation and collaboration among many groups and sectors: those most affected by the epidemic, religious and community leaders, nongovernmental organizations, researchers and health professionals, and the private sector.
- Decentralized participatory approaches that bring prevention and care programs to a national scale.
- A response that is forward-looking, comprehensive, and multisectoral, addressing the socioeconomic determinants that make people vulnerable to infection and targeting prevention interventions, care, and treatment to support them.

- Community participation in government policy-making as well as in the design and implementation of programs, many implemented by nongovernmental organizations, civil society, the private sector, and people living with HIV/AIDS.
- Core interventions that include developing communication programs to reduce risky behavior, especially among youth; making the diagnosis and treatment of sexually transmitted infections readily available and affordable; treating opportunistic infections, including tuberculosis; making condoms affordable and widely accessible; ensuring a safe blood supply; making voluntary counseling and testing available and affordable; and preventing transmission from mother to child.

Few countries have all these elements in place. They may cost 1.5–2.0 percent of GDP.

Source: World Bank 1999b.

Decentralization is not a panacea, however. Nor can it be universal. Inappropriate or overly rapid decentralization can have negative effects, as has often been the case with that to district governments. With some notable exceptions, local government has had a checkered past in Africa. Newly independent governments, keen on strengthening a fragile sense of nationhood, were reluctant to devolve powers that might aggravate ethnic and tribal divisions. This anxiety was especially apparent in Nigeria and Uganda, where colonial rule was largely exercised through traditional authorities that retained considerable autonomy.

More generally, colonial rule, though often limited, was tightly retained at the center. Indeed, in francophone countries the metropolitan model was highly centralized. Few countries entering independence

Decentralization is not a panacea, however—nor can it be universal

---

Box 4.7 Chad's Health and Safe Motherhood Project

CHAD IS ONE OF THE WORLD'S POOREST COUNTRIES, and its demographic and health indicators lag behind those of most low-income countries. In 1998 life expectancy at birth was 50 years, one of the lowest in the region. Maternal mortality is estimated at 827 deaths per 100,000 live births, a staggering eight times the African average.

Despite difficult political and economic conditions, Chad's government increasingly committed itself to addressing these problems in the 1990s. It adopted a national health plan (1993–2000) whose central objective is to increase access to quality basic health care, focusing on the most vulnerable groups—children and women of childbearing age. The key instrument for this is decentralized service delivery at the district level, crucial given Chad's dispersed population.

Within this framework, the Health and Safe Motherhood Project supports the development and implementation of policies and investments designed to:
- Strengthen capacity to support regional health services.
- Provide assistance for health, nutrition, and family planning services by establishing a network of district health facilities.
- Support the development and implementation of a national drug policy.

Progress is already apparent. In 1994, 310 of the 656 responsibility zones and 24 of the 50 health districts were operational, covering 33 percent of the population. By 1998, 453 zones were operational, covering 71 percent of the population. By the end of the project 80 percent of the population is expected to be covered. And use is up: in Guera and Tandjile districts the rate of prenatal visits doubled from less than 15 to almost 30 percent in four years.

Government commitment is strong, to health in general and the project in particular. Ministry of Health outlays increased from 3.3 percent of government spending in 1994 to 7.1 percent in 1998. The government has also allocated funds to the project beyond those required in the project agreements—funds that were used to drill boreholes to provide water to health centers. Chad has passed a law allocating increased revenues to health (along with education, rural development, and transport), expected as the country develops its oil reserves. This should assure sustained continued increases in health coverage rates, lowering maternal mortality and increasing life expectancy in the near future.

had developed a tradition of local government. And central governments rarely had the personnel and machinery needed to monitor local governments' activities.

As a result governments in many districts, towns, and cities proved corrupt, inefficient, and unresponsive to local needs. In country after country in the 1970s and 1980s, locally elected councils were replaced by centrally appointed commissions that exercised limited independent authority over service delivery and the raising of revenues to finance it. More recently, there have been commendable attempts to revive local government, but the process will take considerable time as capacity is built. Thus decentralization is most likely to be effective when it is to communities and autonomous institutions, not just to lower levels of government, whose institutions may be just as weak as those of central government.

Some functions are not appropriate for decentralization. The most important is public budgeting, for two reasons. First, coherent public budgeting is essential for macroeconomic management. The variability of government revenues in Africa from year to year—reflecting the unpredictability of trade- and transaction-based tax revenues in small, open economies—leads sector ministries (of which education and health are usually among the largest) to engage in opportunistic behavior, especially with external aid. This tendency can be compounded if local governments are allowed to enter into relationships with external sources of funds. Second, even where some revenues are raised locally, national systems are needed to compensate for the different resources available throughout a country. This is usually carried out through transfers from the central government.

Certain nonbudget functions are also most appropriate for central government. In education, assessment systems must be national to permit comparisons of schools. And, as Uganda shows, support to teachers in decentralized schools can be provided most effectively through a centralized system linked to teacher training. Drug procurement can be inefficient if it is carried out entirely by local institutions; national procurement implies some national pharmaceutical storage capacity. Public information campaigns for HIV/AIDS should be delivered locally but require development at the national level.

The key to making decentralized delivery effective is the governance of the local systems. Such governance is most effective when communities are directly involved, formally through school and clinic boards, for

Decentralization is most likely to be effective when it is to communities and autonomous institutions, not just to lower levels of government

example, or less formally, as is much more common. Governance structures that support autonomy, transparency in the sources and uses of funds, and accountability are essential (chapter 2).

Increased International Cooperation

Some key aspects of human development in Africa must be tackled internationally

Some key aspects of human development in Africa must be tackled internationally. These fall into four categories:

- Providing resources—the international community must provide more resources, including those freed by debt relief (chapter 8).
- Reaping the benefits of economies of scale, given the small size of many African economies and populations. Many areas are ripe for regional and subregional cooperation, including higher education, social science research, distance education, and drought and disease early warning systems. Little has been done in these areas, but recently there has been a welcome resurgence of interest.
- Tackling diseases that recognize no borders. The successful approach followed with onchocerciasis provides an example for the international community as it marshals human and financial resources (see box 4.3). The same approach is needed for malaria, trypanosomiasis, and other endemic diseases, where concerted actions across countries are essential for sustained success. International cooperation is beginning in malaria, most notably with the World Health Organization's Roll Back Malaria program. But cooperation is still needed for other diseases.
- Funding research to develop vaccines and drugs to deal with diseases that are essentially African. Vaccines, for instance, are one of the most cost-effective interventions in health, and many African diseases are in principle preventable through vaccines. New genetically based vaccines hold great promise, though many potentially effective vaccines (such as for malaria) are still in the research and development phase and not yet operational. Past successes with vaccines and their use, notably against smallpox and polio, have been driven by the diseases' global nature. Major efforts are under way to develop vaccines against African diseases.[3] But much more is needed to encourage research, including commitments to purchase new vaccines for poor countries.

Notes

1. Surveys in Côte d'Ivoire Ghana, and Mauritania show potential losses of almost 6.4 percent of normal earnings from illness. Losses were 2.5 percent in Indonesia and the Philippines and averaged 3.2 percent in Bolivia, Jamaica, and Peru. Losses in the United States were 1.5 percent (Strauss 2000).

2. The other goals are to reduce extreme poverty by half, to implement a national strategy for sustainable development in every country by 2005, and to reverse trends in the loss of environmental resources by 2015 (OECD 1996).

3. These initiatives include various partnerships among the World Health Organization, United Nations Children's Fund, World Bank, pharmaceutical companies engaged in research and development, foundations, and nongovernmental organizations such as the Children's Vaccines Initiative, the International AIDS Vaccine Initiative, the International Vaccine Institute, and the Global Alliance for Vaccines and Immunisation.

CHAPTER 5

Lowering Infrastructure, Information, and Finance Barriers

Developing infrastructure is difficult in Africa due to its low population density and high number of small and landlocked countries

S ERVICES SUCH AS TELECOMMUNICATIONS, POWER, TRANS-portation, water, and sanitation—often called "hard" infra-structure—are vital for economic growth. But the financial sector—part of "soft" infrastructure—is just as important. Africa needs both types of infrastructure to develop com-petitive agriculture and manufacturing. And to make sure that development is broadly based, it is essential that as many people as possible have access to all these services.

One sector above all offers Africa a chance to leapfrog forward. If Africa can rapidly equip itself with an excellent information and communica-tions technology infrastructure, it will be able to exploit the gains offered by the emerging knowledge-based economy. This opportunity exists now, and it will not come again. If it is missed, information and communica-tions technology will become yet another sector in which Africa trails the rest of the world.

In developing infrastructure, Africa faces problems more severe than any other region. Vast distances and low population density make service provision costly. The division of Sub-Saharan Africa into 48 states, many of them landlocked, makes the barriers worse because small national mar-kets limit scale economies, reduce competition, and increase risk. Poor policies are also to blame. Weak states have taken a large role in these sec-tors—with disappointing results. State capacity has been overstretched or even undermined, and service provision has been inadequate. In their current state, infrastructure and the financial sector, rather than promot-ing development, are barriers to it.

This chapter examines these barriers and suggests ways to surmount them. It concludes that new ways of doing business are needed—from a more regional approach to infrastructure development to greater participation by the private sector and local communities, with the state concentrating on facilitation and regulation rather than direct provision.

Though Africa requires an estimated $18 billion a year in infrastructure investments, investment is not the whole story. Substantial benefits could be reaped from more effective operations and maintenance of existing facilities, from better regulations and policies, and from greater devolution of functions to the private sector and to lower tiers of government and communities. Such efforts have produced impressive results in several countries. Worldwide experience suggests, however, that development of appropriate regulation should precede privatization or liberalization. Widening access to infrastructure services, especially for rural populations, requires both more resources and innovative approaches. Community and user involvement in infrastructure construction, maintenance, and management—especially in water supply, irrigation, and rural roads—is an important way of improving services in rural areas.

Africa requires investment—as well as better policies, operations, and maintenance

The policy challenge posed by information and communications technology in Africa is to create mass awareness of how it works and what it can do, to foster indigenous capacity and research, and to identify ways to achieve universal access to service. Meeting this challenge requires education. In primary and secondary schools, this can be done through school networking programs. In universities, capacity must be enhanced in applying new technology for research, teaching, and learning. Lifelong learning must be offered through community centers and school and university networks that promote equal access to all.

Funding access to technology remains a major challenge, however. A growing number of African countries—Botswana, Mauritius, South Africa, Uganda—are adopting innovative approaches to fund mass access to information and communications technology, and other African countries could learn from them. Regional cooperation is urgently needed to develop strong system backbones and share resources and knowledge. Broader regional collaboration could also lead to bulk purchasing of capacity, capacity-building initiatives, and innovative financing, helping to achieve economies of scale and to lower costs.

The financial sector also poses policy challenges. In modern finance both the quantity and quality of capital matter greatly. On both counts Africa suffers huge deficits. Liberalization is incomplete, and the thinness of financial markets and gross inefficiencies need to be addressed. There is also an urgent need to expand access by offering financial instruments that serve the economically active poor and by developing closer relationships between the formal and informal sectors within an integrated financial market.

The most effective way to improve the quality, cost, accessibility, and quantity of capital is to build a market-based financial system. This requires that governments follow sound fiscal policies, that banks and firms be commercialized or privatized, and that governments not stifle markets. In many countries financial sector governance is a higher priority than further liberalization. Improving transparency, contract enforcement, payments systems, and other micro and institutional aspects of the financial system presents the biggest challenge for development. Regulation and supervision are particularly important, especially accounting standards, disclosure requirements, and contract law. As with hard infrastructure, better regulation should precede liberalization.

Banks dominate Africa's financial sectors. Greater emphasis should be given to developing nonbank financial institutions such as stock markets, contractual savings institutions, and leasing companies. In addition, Africa's financial markets are tiny. Regional pooling would diversify risk, promote competition, and generate economies of scale. A cross-border financial system requires improvement in commercial and financial law, contract enforcement, accounting standards, and prudential supervision, and their harmonization across countries.

Regional pooling would diversify risk, promote competition, and generate economies of scale

Catching Up on Infrastructure

ESPECIALLY WHEN SOUTH AFRICA IS EXCLUDED, AFRICA LAGS behind the rest of the world on almost all dimensions of infrastructure development—quantity, quality, cost, and equality of access (table 5.1). Moreover, over the past 15 years the gap between Africa and the rest of the world has widened.

In 1997 Africa (excluding South Africa) had 171,000 kilometers of paved roads, about 18 percent less than Poland. Africa also contains just 2 percent of the world's telephone mainlines. There are about 10 million telephones in Africa—less than in Brazil—and half are in South Africa. The other 5 million are so dispersed that most Africans live two hours from the nearest telephone. Even when Africa appears to be doing well, other measures highlight inadequate supply. For example, Africa fares better than East or South Asia on length of roads per capita but is at the bottom when it comes to road density per square kilometer of land area (figure 5.1)—meaning that most people are farther from a road in Africa. In Ethiopia 70 percent of the population has no access to all-weather roads.

War-affected economies in Africa are perhaps the hardest hit by the inadequate provision of infrastructure services. Physical infrastructure stocks—telecommunications, airports, ports, roads, bridges—are often key targets during war. Although some parts of these countries may not be directly affected by war, infrastructure maintenance is neglected during war, and capital spending is cut back in favor of military spending.

The quality of infrastructure also tends to be worse in Africa. The waiting time for a telephone connection averages 3.5 years. Only 16 percent of roads are paved. More than 80 percent of unpaved roads are only in fair condition, and 85 percent of rural feeder roads are in poor condition, with accessibility limited in most cases to the dry season. In many countries such roads have to carry a large portion of transported goods. These shortcomings are not simply a matter of limited investment. Inadequate maintenance and operating inefficiency have reduced the value of much of the investment that has taken place. One-third of the roads built in Sub-Saharan Africa in the past 20 years have eroded from lack of maintenance. Timely maintenance expenditures of $12 billion would have saved $45 billion in road reconstruction costs over 10 years (World Bank 1994c).

War-affected economies are perhaps the hardest hit by the inadequate provision of infrastructure services

Table 5.1 Infrastructure Indicators by Region

Country group/region	Electric power consumption per capita (kilowatt-hours), 1996	Telephone mainlines per 1,000 people, 1997	Paved roads (percentage of total roads), 1997	International telecommunications (dollar cost of three-minute call to the United States), 1997	Population with access to safe water (percent), 1995	Population with access to sanitation (percent), 1995
Low and middle income	851	60	30	6.22	75	—
East Asia and Pacific	624	50	10	5.60	77	—
Europe and Central Asia	2,788	204	83	4.33	—	—
Latin America and Caribbean	1,347	110	26	4.42	75	68
Middle East and North Africa	1,166	75	50	6.02	—	—
South Asia	313	18	41	—	81	20
Sub-Saharan Africa	439	16	16	8.11	47	47
Sub-Saharan Africa excl. South Africa	146	10	—	—	46	47

Source: World Bank 1999.

135

Figure 5.1 Road Density and Road Length Per Capita in Africa, Asia, and Latin America, 1997

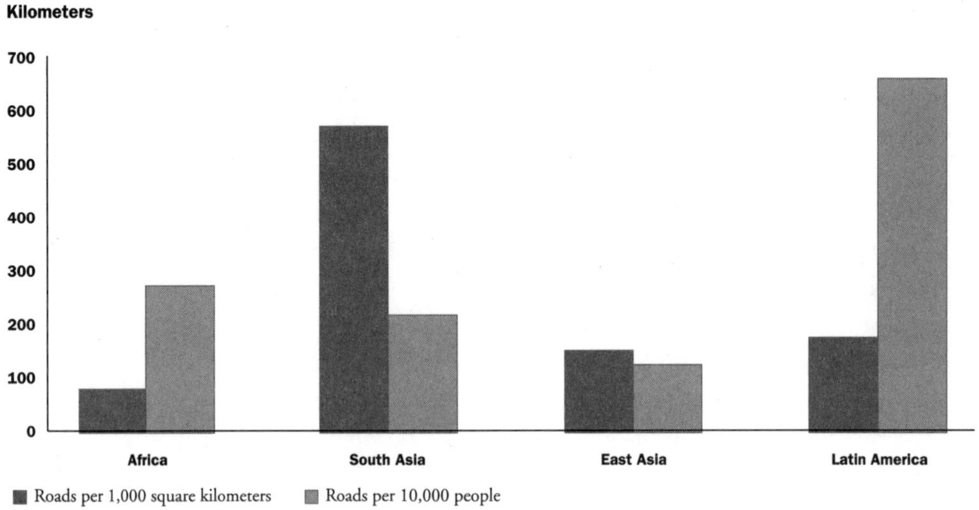
Kilometers
700
600
500
400
300
200
100
0
Africa
South Asia
East Asia
Latin America
Roads per 1,000 square kilometers
Roads per 10,000 people

Source: World Bank 1999.

Costs are also a problem—Africa's transport costs are the highest of any region. The continent is isolated from major maritime and air routes and is served by peripheral, high-cost routes. Freight costs for imports are 70 percent higher in East and West Africa than in developing Asia. For landlocked Africa costs are more than twice as high as in Asia. Air transport costs should be less affected by boundaries and distance from ports, but air transport costs across the continent are two to four times costs over the Atlantic. And in many West African countries air cargo transport is simply not available.

Internal transport costs are also high in Africa. For example, in the mid-1990s road transport costs in Côte d'Ivoire were two to three times those in Southeast Asia (UNCTAD 1999), and charges for moving agricultural produce were two to five times higher in Ghana and Zimbabwe than in a group of Asian economies (Mariki 1999). Higher costs in Africa result from lower road quality, higher fuel taxes, higher imported vehicle costs, and costly bureaucratic procedures. It is estimated that roadblocks and bribes paid to police raise the cost of road transport by one-third in parts of West Africa.

For other infrastructure services the picture is mixed. The cost of telephone calls between African countries can be 50–100 times the cost of calls within North America, but the average rate for a three-minute local call is lower in Africa ($0.09) than in Europe ($0.11). But averages are misleading. Electricity tariffs, for example, ranged from $0.001 per kilowatt-hour in Burundi and $0.022 in Ghana to $0.31 in Guinea-Bissau in the mid-1990s. (The typical cost in OECD countries is $0.06.) This variation reflects both real cost differences and policy differences. Ghana, for example, is blessed with one of the world's lowest-cost sources of hydropower. In other cases high charges may reflect much higher costs (or monopoly profits), while low charges may not cover costs. Paradoxically, very low electricity prices may be as undesirable as very high prices. If prices are low but costs are not, subsidies will be needed, creating macroeconomic imbalances, or the supplier will have less money to expand supply or improve quality—which may be more important than price for competitiveness or access.

Access to infrastructure services is more unequal in Africa than in any other part of the world. Less than one African in five has access to electricity, and less than half have access to sanitation or safe water. The distribution of services is skewed—urban areas receive more than 80 percent of services, while rural areas, with more than 70 percent of the population, get 20 percent. About two-thirds of rural Africa lacks access to adequate water supplies, and three-quarters is without proper sanitation facilities.

Access to infrastructure services is more unequal in Africa than in any other part of the world

Consequences of Lagging Infrastructure Development

Why does Africa's low infrastructure development matter? Production of all goods and services lags in Africa. Does infrastructure have a significance beyond that of any other type of production? Yes, because the value of infrastructure for growth and development lies in its consumption, not its production. Infrastructure is an input to all other production. This is clear in the case of economic infrastructure such as power and transport. But even social or household infrastructure, such as sanitation facilities, affects people's productivity and so indirectly affects production. Africa pays a high price for its inadequate infrastructure in lost opportunities for growth, for poverty reduction, and for access to services that could improve people's lives.

Low competitiveness. Poor infrastructure is one of the main causes of Africa's low competitiveness. This is not just a matter of inadequate quantity. Cost, quality, and access are all important determinants of competitiveness.

Infrastructure plays an important role in determining the destination and size of private capital flows

Africa's high transport costs are a major burden on competitiveness and growth. Amjadi and Yeats (1995) conclude that transport costs are a higher trade barrier than tariffs in Africa. Limão and Venables (1999) conclude that weak infrastructure accounts for most of Africa's poor trade performance. The volume of trade is very sensitive to transport costs—a 10 percent drop in transport costs increases trade by 25 percent. And transport costs are sensitive to the quality of infrastructure, as measured by such variables as the density of the road network, the paved road network, and the rail network, or the number of telephones per person. Improving a country's worldwide rank in infrastructure quality from the 75th percentile to the 50th (median) increases the volume of trade by 50 percent.

Unreliable service can be even more damaging to competitiveness than high costs. Production stoppages, missed delivery dates, or an inability to communicate reliably preclude the development of higher value-added products that depend on timely delivery. About 25 percent of the decline in Africa's share of world exports can be attributed to weak price competitiveness. The rest is due to nonprice factors, including infrastructure services and the flow of trade information (Oshikoya and others 1999). In newly industrialized countries successful exporters exhibit persistent export growth even in the face of falling world income. They are able to do so partly because they are in close contact with foreign customers, having established "insider" relationships with them. The quality of transactional infrastructure, as represented by the number of telephone lines per capita, is a statistically significant variable in explaining the success of insider countries (Mody and Yilmaz 1994).

Given its inadequate infrastructure and service levels, it is no surprise that Africa is considered a bad business address. This makes it hard for Africa to compete for private capital flows as public flows decline. Infrastructure plays an important role in determining the destination and size of private capital flows. African firms feel strongly about the importance of infrastructure in their business decisions and operations, ranking it high on their list of complaints (WEF and HIID 1998).

Not all African countries are badly placed. But even the better performers may be dragged down by bad neighbors. As much as 1 percentage point of Africa's lackluster growth performance may be due to neighborhood effects (Easterly and Levine 1997). In some cases this is merely reputational—guilt by association. But costly or unreliable infrastructure in neighboring countries can be nearly as important as a country's own (Limão and Venables 1999).

Weak market integration. Inadequate infrastructure also impedes the integration of domestic markets. Though less visible than the barrier to global competitiveness, the barrier to market integration is just as damaging to growth—and even worse for broadly based growth and poverty reduction. The lack of all-weather rural roads, in particular, condemns rural areas to isolation, subsistence production, and high risk.

High transport and other transactions costs, and the possibility of being cut off from markets and supply sources at critical times, limit the attractiveness of specializing in high-value crops (UNCTAD 1999). Though specialization might bring higher average returns in the long run, there would be no long run if there were one catastrophic year in the short run. Better roads and other infrastructure reduce risk and create opportunities for high-value production—including nonagricultural activities, the classic path out of poverty for rural households the world over. Falling transport costs also expand markets for urban production, lower food costs in urban areas, and create opportunities for people and investment to move back and forth between rural and urban areas. Deregulation of transport in Kenya in the 1970s, for example, set in motion a virtuous circle of growth between Nairobi and smallholder agricultural areas for 100 miles around (World Bank 1980).

Slower growth. Many studies have found a link between infrastructure development and growth. The World Bank's *Word Development Report 1994* found that a 1 percent increase in infrastructure stock was associated with a 1 percent increase in GDP. Easterly and Levine (1997) found that inadequate telecommunications infrastructure caused a 1 percentage point drop in Africa's growth rate.

What is harder to see is whether growth causes infrastructure or infrastructure causes growth. But it is generally recognized that the link works both ways. Despite the ambiguity about causality, it seems clear that inadequate infrastructure is a major barrier to growth and poverty reduction, particularly because it lessens competitiveness and impedes market integration.

Poverty and inequality. Some infrastructure services—such as sanitation and safe water—contribute directly to poverty reduction. But the provision of infrastructure services does not automatically reduce poverty. Poorly designed infrastructure could have more costs than benefits for poor people because of inadequate targeting or adverse social, health, financial, and environmental effects (DBSA 1998).

Inadequate infrastructure is a major barrier to growth and poverty reduction

In addition, infrastructure provision can widen the gap between the poor and the nonpoor where access is expensive or where services are not planned to meet the needs of the poor. Delivery can also be disempowering if it turns the poor into passive recipients of services rather than central actors in their own development. There is a presumption, however, that developing rural transport and water infrastructure will especially benefit women, because they bear the biggest transport burden in Africa (box 5.1).

Causes of Lagging Infrastructure Development

Africa's infrastructure development has lagged for many reasons, including structural features—geography, poverty, low urbanization, division into small states—inadequate investment, and poor policy.

Difficult geography. Africa is a vast continent with a sparse population mostly living far from the sea. This geography makes transport to and within the region expensive. Bloom and Sachs (1998) identify some spe-

> *Developing rural transport and water infrastructure will especially benefit women, because they bear the biggest transport burden*

Box 5.1 The Gender Impact of Infrastructure Provision

KENYAN WOMEN WORK AN AVERAGE OF 41 HOURS a week, compared with 26 hours for men. In Cameroon and Guinea-Bissau women's working days are twice as long as men's. In Uganda women produce 80 percent of food and provide 70 percent of agricultural labor.

Similarly, village surveys in Burkina Faso, Uganda, and Zambia have found that African women move, on average, 26 metric ton-kilometers a year (especially water and fuelwood) compared with less than 7 metric ton-kilometers for men. This, combined with women's contribution to agriculture, has led to rough estimates that women contribute about two-thirds of the total transport effort. Given these disparities, time savings in these activities will benefit women most. Improvements in rural infrastructure can also raise the incomes of the poor, particularly women, through several mechanisms:

- *Reducing the time spent collecting water and fuelwood.* The time freed can be used for leisure or for productive purposes such as education or agricul-

tural activities. There is evidence that a significant portion of time saved is used productively.

- *Increasing crop production.* Agricultural output can benefit, particularly where bulky, low-value crops are involved. For example, trucks can be hired to move bulk harvests, fertilizer can be moved to villages and stored in local facilities, and hired farm labor can move more readily to the fields.
- *Improving marketing opportunities.* Isolated rural communities have great difficulty marketing their crops. Crops can be moved in bulk by trucks, but also in smaller quantities by cart or bicycle if adequate roads or paths are available.
- *Expanding access to social services and nonagricultural income-generating activities.* These include health clinics, for which travel time can be reduced, and travel from periurban locations to work in services and construction in the urban informal sector.

Source: ADB 1999 based on Weiss 1998 and Barwell 1996; Hanmer and others 1997.

cific problems: Africa's distance from major markets in Europe and North America, the barrier imposed by the Sahara Desert, Africa's small coastline relative to total area, a shortage of natural ports along the coastline, the fact that only 19 percent of Africans live within 100 kilometers of the coast, the large proportion of landlocked states, and the small number of navigable rivers.

Widespread poverty and low urbanization. Large markets lower infrastructure costs by allowing economies of scale and by broadening competition. But infrastructure costs are also affected by per capita income and urbanization. Many indicators of lagging infrastructure development reflect low demand rather than inadequate supply. If basic household telephone service cost 5 percent of household income, for example, less than 10 percent of Tanzanian households could afford telephone service (Mariki 1999).

Africa's GNP is only slightly larger than that of Belgium, and it has less than one-fiftieth the per capita income and one-twelfth the population density. Even if Africa were a single market, this would not offset the disadvantages for infrastructure development of low income relative to area. In this respect it is interesting to compare Africa with India. Total and per capita GDP are comparable, but India has two important advantages when it comes to infrastructure development: it is a single country, and its population density is nearly 13 times that of Africa.

Small states. The division of Africa into many small states also affects infrastructure development. Sometimes there are physical incompatibilities between infrastructure systems: rail lines may be of different gauges or may not link up at borders. More generally, border crossings entail high transactions costs. Even if rail systems are compatible, coordination between independent systems entails long delays and high costs that lead to a disproportionate share of bulky items being transported by road rather than rail in East and Southern Africa.

For truck transport, border delays of 10 hours are common, while taxes, licenses, and insurance requirements raise the direct costs of transport. Protection of domestic transport and tour operators further raises costs, impedes the development of cross-border tourist circuits, and greatly reduces competition and service in air transport. Finally, and most important, potential sources of low-cost energy and water resources remain untapped because of the lack of regional cooperation. World-class, low-cost sources of hydropower have not been exploited because of the difficulties, rivalries, and uncertainties attached to producing energy in one country for consumption in another—often with transmission across a third.

Many indicators of lagging infrastructure development reflect low demand rather than inadequate supply

141

Institutions, incentives, and policies are the main barriers to the provision of infrastructure

More disturbing is the enormous amount of energy wasted through gas flaring, particularly in West Africa. Africa flares gas equivalent to 12 times the energy it uses. Because of the distances involved, not all this energy can be used commercially. But a significant amount could be harnessed, to the benefit of producers and consumers, if the countries with these resources demonstrated a commitment to developing regional solutions to energy shortages.

Inadequate investment. UNCTAD (1999) argues that Africa's poor infrastructure performance is mainly explained by a collapse in investment over the past 20 years. Most estimates suggest that Africa requires infrastructure investment of 5–6 percent of GDP a year, with most coming from the public sector. Yet total public investment more than halved in Africa between the early 1970s (12.6 percent of GDP) and the early 1990s (5.6 percent of GDP). Moreover, official development assistance fell in the 1990s, and the share going to infrastructure fell even more.

This decline has not been offset by higher domestic or foreign private investment in infrastructure except in Côte d'Ivoire and South Africa, which have attracted foreign private investment. This investment squeeze contributes to the deterioration in infrastructure, especially in road transport. Insufficient funding for maintenance has also been a binding constraint. In nine East African countries maintenance spending was sufficient for only 20 percent of current networks (Sylte 1996, cited in UNCTAD 1999).

Bad policies. While structural factors and low investment help explain the current state of infrastructure in Africa, institutions, incentives, and policies are the main barriers to its provision. Almost without exception, infrastructure services have been provided exclusively by governments, which own, finance, and manage nearly all infrastructure projects. Public provision typically leads to low efficiency and high costs, with more attention paid to creating jobs than to providing services. High subsidies to insolvent utilities undermine macroeconomic stability and growth. Although data for Africa are scanty, the World Bank recently estimated that energy subsidies for all developing countries total $100 billion a year, equivalent to two-thirds of sector investment requirements.

Governments have often controlled prices with little regard for commercial objectives, including cost recovery. Most prices are far below what is required to operate, maintain, and rehabilitate facilities. In response to the resulting supply shortages, many businesses and households resort to self-provision, often at high cost. In Nigeria as much as half of public electricity capacity may be inoperable at a given time, mostly because of inadequate maintenance of transmission and distribution networks. As a result more than 90 percent of manufacturing firms have bought their own generators. For firms with 50 or more employees, the extra cost of private power generation was 10 percent of the machinery and equipment budget. For smaller firms the burden was as high as 29 percent (Lee and Anas 1992).

Public policy toward the private sector also impedes infrastructure development. Licensing and other restrictions prevent private firms from competing with state firms and with each other. Restrictions on competition are often defended on the grounds that they conserve scarce capital because utilities are natural monopolies. More often, the effect is to raise the cost and lower the quality of service, thereby restricting growth.

More generally, administrative barriers and high taxes impede the provision and use of infrastructure by the private sector. The high transactions costs arising from government restrictions deter private sector development and breed corruption, further undermining development. Kickbacks on construction contracts, pilferage in ports, corruption in customs services, and organized extortion of truckers all raise the cost of doing business and reduce competitiveness.

Geography need not be destiny, and much can be done within existing constraints

The Way Forward

Geography and other structural factors impose constraints on what can be done to solve Africa's infrastructure problems. But geography need not be destiny, and much can be done within existing constraints. Countries elsewhere have overcome isolation and landlockedness. Moreover, new technology creates new opportunities for Africa—even the potential for leapfrogging stages of development. To move forward, Africa must boost investment, develop private-public partnerships, improve government credibility, increase cross-border and regional cooperation, and widen access.

Boost investment. There is no doubt that Africa's weak and often worsening infrastructure performance is linked to low spending on investment and maintenance. The question is the extent to which low spending is an independent cause or the consequence of other factors—bad policies, lack of regional cooperation, structural features of geography and poverty—that lower the rate of return and, hence, the incentive for investment. In particular, lack of accountability to communities and inadequate commercial orientation may have reduced the incentive to invest in infrastructure.

Africa requires $18 billion a year in infrastructure financing—about 6 percent of GDP (ADB 1999). But increased spending will not be effective, nor will the funds be forthcoming, unless efforts are made to improve policies, management, and regional cooperation. Moreover, difficult choices will have to be made between spending on infrastructure and spending on health and education. And within the infrastructure sector, choices must be made between spending in cities or in rural areas and between spending on new investment or on maintenance.

Spending on rehabilitation and maintenance will probably provide a bigger payoff than spending on new investment

Funding is not always the main obstacle, however:

- Africa has a fairly well-developed stock of ports, rail lines, and long-distance trunk roads to the outside world. But this stock needs to be rehabilitated and used more efficiently. Rehabilitating this infrastructure and filling in the gaps in East and Southern Africa would cost an estimated $400 million (about 0.25 percent of GDP).
- Urban power, water, sanitation, and telecommunications require large investments, even if efficiency is improved. But much of this funding can come from the private sector—indeed, privatization can be a source of revenue for cash-strapped governments.
- Inadequate rural infrastructure is the biggest barrier to market integration and the most difficult to address. It is costly—bringing 90 percent of Ethiopia's population within 20 kilometers of an all-weather road would cost $4 billion, or 75 percent of GDP. Simply catching up on deferred maintenance in Malawi would cost 2.5 percent of GDP.

Rural infrastructure will remain dependent on public funding, including donor-supported spending, for a long time. Nevertheless, new ways of providing small-scale infrastructure by the private sector and increased user and community involvement in projects are also needed to ensure that access increases.

Given the deterioration in infrastructure investment and severe capital constraints, spending on rehabilitation and maintenance will probably provide a bigger payoff than spending on new investment. The key question in such instances, however, is why the infrastructure has not been maintained in the first place. Before rehabilitation investment begins, policies should be examined to ensure that incentives are consistent with maintaining the rehabilitated infrastructure. It is also important to consider whether a facility should be rehabilitated to the same standard as its original construction. Some facilities were built to uneconomic standards, especially given today's resource-constrained circumstances. Zambia, for example, has decided to downgrade the standard of some trunk roads. At the extreme, economic conditions may have changed so much that an existing facility should not be rehabilitated or maintained.

There may still be instances, however, in which supply-led investment can attract productive investment—as with investment in an export processing zone or in an access road to a high-potential area. Not many generalities apply to all countries, but a few may be appropriate:

- Look first for quick-payoff changes that do not involve investment. Improving border crossings for freight and tourists and eliminating unofficial tolls are obvious examples.
- Develop appropriate regulations before preceding with privatization or liberalization.
- In the case of regional cooperation, bilateral projects may be easier to arrange than grander multilateral programs. Latecomers can often join after a project has been launched.
- If things are moving, the most urgent investment or next step will usually be obvious, driven by demand. If the economy is stagnant and there are no obvious infrastructure bottlenecks, there may be a case for carefully chosen supply-led investments in infrastructure.

One of the best ways to finance investment and increase efficiency is to increase private participation in infrastructure

Develop public-private partnerships. One of the best ways to finance investment and increase efficiency is to increase private participation in infrastructure. Complete reliance on public ownership and provision of infrastructure has created inefficiencies in management and put an undue financial and managerial burden on the state. With the right incentives and regulations, the private sector and other nonstate institutions can deliver services that satisfy the socioeconomic objectives of public goods, often more efficiently than the state.

Private investment in infrastructure varies widely across countries. Among industrial countries the United Kingdom has fully privatized telecommunications, power, and sewerage, while France and Germany retain almost total public ownership in these sectors (table 5.2). In developing countries private participation in infrastructure could reach 40–50 percent (DBSA 1998). Even though Côte d'Ivoire is one of Africa's leaders in attracting private investment, it lags behind many other countries. Private participation in infrastructure offers enormous scope for cutting budget costs (box 5.2).

Table 5.2 Private Investment in Infrastructure in Various Countries, 1995 (percentage of total)

Income group/country	Telecommunications	Power	Transport	Sewerage	Weighted private share
High income					
France	0	0	10	36	13
Germany	0	67	0	20	9
Japan	35	96	3	0	14
Netherlands	100	23	—	50	46
United Kingdom	100	100	21	100	71
United States	100	81	13	22	47
Middle and low income					
Chile	100	99	7	4	54
Côte d'Ivoire	0	30	0	25	10
Hungary	98	100	53	0	76
Philippines	87	49	25	0	32
Thailand	31	30	20	0	17

Source: DBSA 1998.

Public-private partnerships can take many forms. African countries have used a variety of approaches to attract private participation in railways, airports, and seaports (table 5.3). Introducing competition and private involvement in maritime transport in Côte d'Ivoire generated many benefits for consumers (box 5.3).

Improve government credibility. There are many obstacles to increasing private participation in African infrastructure. The main sources of capital are likely to be foreigners or local European, Asian, or other ethnic minorities, and many governments do not want to cede control to either group. Governments also worry about private investors exercising monopoly power in small markets. Privatization may lead to higher prices for basic services such as electricity and water.

Moreover, foreigners may be reluctant to invest. Political uncertainty is high in Africa, and in traditional utilities the capital costs are high, the expected lifetime of the investment is long, and returns will be in local rather than foreign currency. Thus investment appears quite risky, and if foreign investors are willing to invest at all, they may demand a high risk premium.

To attract foreign investment on acceptable terms, governments need to create a favorable climate for business by providing macroeconomic stability, competitive taxes, freedom to repatriate capital, and all the aspects of governance that affect willingness to invest—including contract enforcement, low corruption, and adherence to transparent rules,

---

Box 5.2 Harnessing the Potential of Telecommunications

TELECOMMUNICATIONS IS A STRIKING EXAMPLE OF how new ways of doing business could both cut budget costs and improve business services. Malawi, with very poor telecommunications services, illustrates the potential. There are 0.31 telephones per 100 people, compared with 0.5 in Sub-Saharan Africa and 50 in high-income countries. The average wait for a phone line exceeds 10 years. The new, single-provider cellular phone service is expensive ($1,000 to sign on) and has chronic service problems. Many services—data transmission, paging, Internet—are limited or nonexistent. And the monopoly public provider, Malawi Posts and Telecommunications Corporation, cannot afford investments that could improve service.

Telecommunications is the core of the information infrastructure needed for countries to compete in the global economy. With such poor and costly services,

Malawi has little chance of attracting foreign (or local) investment for export production. Worse, many other African countries have taken steps to attract foreign investment and technology that will lower their telecommunications costs and enhance their competitive advantage.

Malawi could attract new service providers and private investment that could increase the number of telephone lines sixfold within five years, vastly improve other services, and lower prices—and it could secure almost all of the required $300 million in financing from private sources. Without such a program, including regulatory and other changes, Malawi has little hope of financing the service improvements needed to compete with its neighbors.

Source: World Bank 1997.

---

including for privatization (Ayogu 1999). At the same time, to protect against exploitation of a monopoly position, governments should develop regulations that conform to international good practice for governance and pricing. An even better way to prevent abuse of monopoly power is to permit free entry and open competition where this is compatible with market size and technology. New technology such as cellular phones and small-scale generating plants offer new scope for competition. In brief, governments need to enhance their credibility and the rule of law to attract private finance and to protect both property rights and the public interest.

The appropriate form of public-private partnership depends on technology and market structure. The key to deciding the structure of ownership—whether a public-private partnership or full privatization—is whether the market can be made contestable, that is, potentially competitive even if only one firm is active. A starting point is the recognition that infrastructure services can often be unbundled into standalone services with distinct market structures.

The electric power sector, for example, can be unbundled into generation, transmission, and distribution. The technology for power gen-

Table 5.3 Selected Forms of Private Participation in Africa's Railways, Airports, and Seaports

Form	Sector	Country	Year
Management contract	Railways	Cameroon	Pre-1996
		Togo	Pre-1996
		Malawi	1993
		Burkina Faso	1997
		Congo, Dem. Rep.	1998
	Airports	Guinea	Pre-1996
		Madagascar	Pre-1996
		Togo	Pre-1996
	Seaports	Cameroon	Pre-1996
		Sierra Leone	Pre-1996
Lease	Railways	Côte d'Ivoire	Pre-1996
		Gabon	1997
		Cameroon	1998
	Airports	Mauritania	Pre-1996
		Côte d'Ivoire	1996
	Seaports	Mozambique	Pre-1996
		Zambia	1998
Concession/build-operate-transfer	Railways	Malawi	1993
		Mozambique	1998
	Airports	Senegal	1996
	Seaports	Mali	Pre-1996
Demonopolization/build-own-operate	Seaports	South Africa	Pre-1996
Divestiture	Airports	South Africa	1997

Source: ADB 1999.

Box 5.3 Private Involvement in Maritime Transport in Côte d'Ivoire

RESTRICTIVE PRACTICES FAVORING THE STATE-OWNED shipping line, SITRAM, resulted in high costs and poor services for Ivorian exporters of major crops and importers of essential goods. These restrictions were first eroded in 1993, when the banana-pineapple exporters association chartered its own vessels at much lower costs, halving freight rates for banana exports to Europe and cutting those for cocoa exports to the United States by one-quarter. Given the increased competitiveness of Ivorian products, the government agreed to liberalize maritime transport in stages.

In 1995 SITRAM was liquidated and a new carrier with majority private Ivorian ownership, COMARCO, was set up. COMARCO and other domestic shipping lines benefited from a reservation of 50 percent of bulk and refrigerated traffic for the three product groups that had been handled by SITRAM (bananas and pineapple, palm oil, wine) until December 1996, when all non-conference traffic was formally liberalized. These measures substantially lowered import prices for consumers and shipping costs for exporters, increasing the competitiveness of Ivorian exports

eration is diverse, ranging from small diesel generators to large hydro installations. Installed capacity can be varied to suit demand. Thus it is possible to rely on the market to deliver an efficient industry configuration—provided the transmission sector is capable of switching between generating plants. If switching capability is limited, competitive discipline is weakened and regulation will be needed to offset this handicap. In principle, however, power generation offers considerable scope for full privatization. Cross-border partnership can extend the range of options outside national boundaries.

Power transmission and distribution networks, on the other hand, are costly and uneconomic to duplicate. Thus territorial exclusivity is warranted. But public-private partnerships are possible through "competition for the market," in which competitors bid for the right to serve a territory—implying continued public ownership but private service provision. In a state with a credible rule of law, contracts can blend decisionmaking and control rights that confer the advantages traditionally associated with ownership.

In addition to financing, partnerships can involve institutional innovation. One promising institutional innovation has been road funds to improve road maintenance. Learning from mistakes made in earlier attempts, second-generation road funds are being used to contract out maintenance and are funded by user charges, normally a fuel levy plus vehicle licensing fees. The funds are overseen by public-private boards with broad representation, including road users, with an independent chairman and subject to external audit. Boards recommend charges to the legislature. Evidence suggests that users are willing to pay charges if these go toward efficient road maintenance. Well-managed road funds can increase private participation in road maintenance and boost the growth of business.

In Ghana the revenue mobilized for road maintenance doubled in real terms between 1995 and 1997, and the share of roads rated as good or fair rose from 41 to 80 percent between 1995 and 1998. Road funds have also been successful in Zambia. They work best when users can see that the charges they pay are spent on maintenance, and when governance mechanisms ensure that stakeholders have an adequate voice in management. There is a danger, however, that road funds will reduce fiscal flexibility. Thus they should be viewed as a provisional solution for underfunding of road maintenance, to eventually be replaced by reintegration into a reformed and well-functioning bud-

Well-managed road funds can increase private participation in road maintenance and boost the growth of business

get process or by a commercially operated road agency (Gwilliam and Shalizi 1999).

Increase cross-border and regional cooperation. Regional cooperation could also improve the infrastructure linking African states with each other and with the rest of the world. There are two approaches to regional cooperation: a program approach and a project approach. A recent example of the program approach is the Transport Protocol for Southern African, a promising effort to harmonize transport policies and procedures in the region. Another is a resolution from a November 1999 conference of air transport ministers in Yamoussoukro (Côte d'Ivoire) under which 23 states agreed to liberalize air transport in West and Central Africa within two years. The Yaounde Treaty of 1961 assigns to one company (Air Afrique) the traffic rights of 11 West and Central African countries and allows national carriers to service only local markets. Schedules are inconvenient, do not reflect market demand, and are changed for political reasons. Air safety and security are deficient. Prices are high and services limited—Burkinabe fruit and vegetable producers could sell more than 10 tons of produce a week to Gabon but are offered only 3 tons of capacity. And transport and handling charges total as much as 71 percent of costs for products sold on the Rungis market in Paris. It is hoped that liberalization will increase competition, lower air transport costs, modernize safety equipment and navigation systems, and promote tourism and trade.

An example of the project approach is the initiative to develop the Maputo Corridor between Mozambique and South Africa, with the full support of the Southern Africa Development Community. This effort combines cross-border cooperation with private participation to rehabilitate and upgrade transport infrastructure—including roads, rail lines, ports, and harbors—and promote broad economic development. The project also aims to streamline border crossings and involves large industrial investments, including a $1.4 billion aluminum smelter and a $2 billion steel plant using Mozambican gas. The project is an example of infrastructure leading rather than following growth, the rationale being that the uncertainties for such a cross-border project would simply be too great without the public sector taking a lead and, in this case, involving international organizations as well.

Regional cooperation could significantly cut the cost of power and water in some countries. By exchanging electricity with its neighbors, South Africa could save $80 million a year in operating costs. And with

Regional cooperation could improve the infrastructure linking African states with each other and with the rest of the world

coordinated construction rather than national plans, it could save $700 million in expansion costs over the next 20 years (Sparrow and Masters 1999). Such cooperation requires institutions or agreements that build trust—users have to abandon costly policies of self-sufficiency, and producers have to risk heavy investment for export production. International organizations and other outside agencies may be able to facilitate such agreements by providing finance or, just as important, by acting as mediators or guarantors of projects.

A successful example of this approach is the Lesotho Highlands Water Project, in which South Africa guaranteed repayment of a World Bank loan used to build a dam in Lesotho that provides water to South Africa. Another promising approach is the Southern Africa Power Pool, an association of national power companies that meets regularly to coordinate power system planning, including regional production. Though no new large regional project has been launched, the power pool is laying the groundwork. West Africa would benefit from a similar mechanism to export the natural gas now being flared (see above). Investment in a pipeline would be needed, but the potential return is high.

Widen access. Widening access to infrastructure services, especially for rural residents, requires more resources and more innovative approaches. Paradoxically, efforts to ensure equal access for rural and urban areas have often proven counterproductive. Rural residents are generally willing to pay considerably more than the actual costs for services such as electricity and clean water. Yet attempts to provide services below cost, along with political pressures not to collect fees, have limited funds for maintenance and expansion—creating a vicious circle of poor maintenance and low payments.

One promising way around this is being tried in Mozambique. Electricity can be produced from small diesel generators for about $0.18 a kilowatt-hour, excluding capital costs. This is more than twice the average price of electricity in urban areas, but still well below the $0.25–0.35 a kilowatt-hour that rural users are willing to pay for high-value uses of electricity. The government has set up utility companies using diesel generators that have then been sold to private investors below cost (a capital subsidy) for continued commercial operation. Innovative schemes such as this could greatly expand access to infrastructure services at modest public expense while providing incentives for efficient operations and maintenance—while also providing opportunities for small business to both provide and use the services.

Widening access to infrastructure services, especially for rural residents, requires more resources and more innovative approaches

**To be effective, local
participation should
incorporate all users of
infrastructure services**

Community and user involvement in infrastructure construction, maintenance, and management is the most effective way to improve and expand infrastructure services in rural areas. Infrastructure projects with user participation are generally more successful than those without—especially for rural roads and water supply, where an inability to exploit economies of scale and lower technical efficiency make implementation difficult. For example, water systems in Kenya built as part of self-help efforts proved far more reliable than those installed by the water ministry, which were hampered by lack of funds, poor organization, and failure to design according to community needs.

Many governments, usually in association with nongovernmental organizations or donors, have set up social funds to provide supplementary resources for small community projects. There are many variants, but most such schemes allow communities to choose projects (for example, road, water system, or school) and require a substantial community contribution to construction, maintenance, or both. Such participation increases efficiency, strengthens community ownership of projects, ensures transparency and accountability in project planning and implementation, and empowers the users or beneficiaries of the project. To be effective, local participation should incorporate all users of infrastructure services to ensure that the project meets local requirements, uses local materials and technology, and is provided and maintained at lower costs.

Faced with undersupplied and poorly maintained infrastructure services, many African governments have taken steps to devolve responsibility for management, especially in sectors with direct local benefits (water supply, irrigation, rural roads). In water supply, governments are devolving management and maintenance to water associations, which ensure that decisions on supply are consistent with the local environment and the requirements of farmers.

Decentralized planning and local participation requires that communities be granted greater autonomy and be held accountable, and that there be functioning channels of coordination. Greater autonomy can come by making central funds available to implement local priorities in education, health, welfare, and poverty reduction. Local implementing agencies should also be given some financial independence in charging and collecting fees for services. Greater autonomy should be complemented by a system of accountability that enables local governments and community groups monitor the implementation of projects.

Exploiting Information and Communications Technology

IN THE EMERGING KNOWLEDGE-BASED ECONOMY OF THE 21ST CEN-
tury, information and communications technology will likely assume
an importance that dwarfs other types of infrastructure. This shift
offers Africa a chance to leapfrog intermediate stages of development by
avoiding costly investments in time, resources, and the generation and
use of knowledge. Africa has a chance to benefit not only as a consumer
in the new knowledge economy, but also as a producer. It cannot afford
to miss this opportunity.

Politics and institutions, not technology or economics, are the biggest
hindrance to the development of Africa's information and communications technology. Africa's leaders must have a better understanding of the
benefits of information and communications technology in order to foster the political, legal, and institutional conditions under which it will
flourish. This involves developing the knowledge to apply the technology to local settings, improving relevant infrastructure, promoting equitable access, and creating enabling environments for the development
and flow of the necessary content and knowledge. Above all, African governments must promote a competitive telecommunications industry and
educate their people in information and communications technology.

*Politics and institutions
are the biggest hindrance
to the development of
Africa's information and
communications
technology*

Where Do Things Stand?

Broadcast infrastructure. Broadcast technology, mainly radio, is the dominant mass medium in Africa. In 1996 Africa had more than 104 million
radios, or 19.8 per 100 people, compared with 3.6 televisions and 0.3
personal computers per 100 people (Okigbo 1999). More than three in
five Africans can be reached by radio transmitter networks, while television coverage is largely confined to major towns. Most information
resources are widely shared—one copy of a newspaper may be read by
more than 10 people, and there are usually three users per Internet dialup
account. It is not uncommon to find most of a small village crowded
around the only television, which is often powered by a car battery or
small generator.

Broadcast technology will continue to dominate the region. Thus
African countries must integrate traditional broadcast technology with
new Internet tools in a way that meets social, economic, and political

153

needs. Africa requires both high-tech solutions such as satellites and low-tech solutions such as wind-up radios and low-cost community telecenters where poor people can make telephone calls and receive faxes or email.

Telecommunications infrastructure. Telecommunications is a core component of the economy, a primary form of infrastructure, and the basis for the development of the information society (Adam 1998). The International Telecommunication Union estimates that in 1998 global sales of telecommunications equipment and services exceeded $1 trillion—five to six times Africa's GNP. Africa has the world's least developed information and communications infrastructure, with just 2 percent of the world's telephones and fewer than 2 telephones per 100 inhabitants. On average there is one telephone line for every 200 people—and in Mali, Niger, and Zaire there is one line for every 1,000 people (Jensen 1999).

Some African countries, however, have made telecommunications a priority and are installing digital switches with fiber-optic intercity backbones and the newest cellular and mobile technology. For example, some of the world's most sophisticated national networks are in Botswana and Rwanda, where 100 percent of the mainlines are digital.

Mobile cellular telephony has grown rapidly in Africa, from reaching just 6 countries in the early 1990s to 42 countries serving more than 250,000 customers (excluding 2 million in South Africa). Although cellular phones are expensive, they are the only viable alternative to long waits for a standard phone—and more than 1 million Africans are on waiting lists for a phone. Operators provide access mainly in capital cities but also in some secondary towns and along major trunk routes.

The use of fiber-optic cable for international traffic is still in its infancy in Africa, and most international connections are carried by satellite. Although it is improving, Africa's terrestrial network is still analog in some countries and prone to faults caused by changing weather and poor maintenance. But the low base of the infrastructure is a blessing for the installation of digital circuits. In 1996 the portion of digital lines in Africa was 69 percent—close to the world average of 79 percent. Overall, however, the region averaged 116 faults a year per 100 lines, compared with a world average of 22 and a high-income country level of 7.

Although telecommunications infrastructure is spreading, few Africans can afford their own telephone. In 1996 the average business connection cost $112 to install, $6 a month to rent, and $0.11 for a three-minute local call. But installation charges were above $200 in some coun-

Although telecommunications infrastructure is spreading, few Africans can afford their own telephone

tries (Benin, Mauritania, Nigeria, Togo), line rentals ranged from $0.80 to $20 a month, and call charges varied from $0.60 an hour to more than $5 an hour. The cost of renting a connection averaged almost 20 percent of 1995 GDP per capita, compared with a world average of 9 percent and an average for high-income countries of just 1 percent.

There is a strong correlation between the liberalization of telecommunications, increased access, and lower costs. In Africa liberalization has promoted a bottom-up approach in the form of short-term, low-risk investment in cellular services, trunk radio technology, very small aperture terminals (VSATs), and other value added services (such as the Internet).

The need for universal service and increasingly complex technical standards, interconnectivity arrangements, and traffic and frequency management and monitoring have created pressure for better telecommunications regulation. For example, the proliferation of broadcast and communication applications has made radio spectrum scarce in Africa. New policies are required to develop national information systems and harmonize national and international frequency plans (Struzak 1997).

Many African governments have created regulatory bodies, drafted legislation, and sought technical assistance for telecommunications. But getting down to business has often been difficult. Some countries have established regulatory bodies simply to meet World Trade Organization or World Bank requirements. These bodies vary considerably in terms of scope, design, function, staffing, and separation from the parent ministry. Improving information and communications infrastructure, especially in deploying the Internet in rural areas, will require better training and equipment of these entities.

Internet infrastructure. Internet growth has been phenomenal in Africa, with the number of countries with access jumping from 4 in 1995 to 50 in 1999 (including North Africa). Similarly, Internet hosts grew from 316 in 1995 to 10,703 in January 1999. Although these numbers are impressive, access is unequal both between and within countries. Access is largely confined to capital cities, though a growing number of countries have providers in some secondary towns.

There is also a rapidly growing interest in kiosks, cybercafes, and other sites for public Internet access (schools, police stations, clinics) that can share the cost of equipment and access among many users. Many phone shops are adding Internet access to their services—even in remote towns where reaching the nearest dialup access point requires a long-distance

Improving information and communications infrastructure will require better training and equipment

155

call. In addition, a growing number of hotels and business centers are providing Internet access.

The cost of Internet access is a substantial barrier to its growth in the region. Charges vary between $10 and $100 a month. The average monthly cost of using a local dialup account for five hours is $60 (including usage fees and telephone time, but not telephone line rental). Twenty hours of Internet access costs $29 a month or less in the United States. Although European costs are higher than U.S. levels, most are far lower than African charges for comparable use. Moreover, industrial countries have per capita incomes at least 20 times the African average.

The greatest challenge for Africa's Internet connectivity is not access but content

Competition could cut Africa's costs dramatically. Most African capitals now have more than one Internet service provider, and there are more than 400 public providers across the region. Yet 20 countries have just one provider, most of which are run by public telephone operators. Other challenges include low-bandwidth access to international gateways, inadequate cooperation among local providers, poor strategies for managing domain names and Internet protocol (IP) addresses, insufficient regional cooperation, and the lack of a regional Internet backbone.

Still, the greatest challenge for Africa's Internet connectivity is not access but content. A recent survey found that Africa generates just 0.4 percent of global content. And when South Africa is excluded, Africa generates a paltry 0.02 percent. It is difficult to categorize content on Africa into meaningful subject areas. But a large portion can be broadly classified as business information—about institutional activities, products and services, and news. There is a dearth of scientific and technological information on Africa, from Africa.

Applications for Social and Economic Development

Despite the limitations, many Africans have embraced information and communications technology. Electronic mail, for example, has been adopted by almost every agency with international communication needs. Similarly, the Internet has become a cheap and effective means of exchanging information on and marketing African businesses, including for selling distinctive products abroad.

More than 6,000 correspondence course students all over Africa can now use email and the World Wide Web to obtain advice and reading materials from their tutors at the University of South Africa. The university offers its tens of thousands of students in South Africa electronic registration, downloading of study materials, and posting of exam results. Farmers are also starting to realize the benefits of information and communications technology. They have begun to search for the latest market quotations to negotiate better local prices for their crops, and many are exploring new avenues for international trade. A Kenyan farming cooperative has established a relationship with the U.S.-based Earth Marketplace to sell local produce directly to North American consumers, bypassing distributors. Independent newspapers and magazines in more than 40 African countries are now published on the Web, allowing remote users to obtain the latest news and analysis without waiting days or weeks for postal deliveries.

Though some projects show promise, the potential for dramatically boosting Africa's access to education and knowledge has barely been tapped

The potential of information and communications technology for social and economic development is demonstrated by school networks in the Eastern Cape in South Africa and by a regional network for exchanging information on malaria outbreaks operating from South Africa's University of Durban. To date these initiatives have been carried out as experiments, without sufficient human resources and tools. But access to information could stimulate change and create learning environments more meaningful and responsive to the localized and specific needs of learners. Teachers and learners could obtain material using new technology, transforming education and enabling people to develop new skills. The African Virtual University now brings top-quality scientific training and online reference materials to 13 countries in Africa. But the potential for dramatically boosting Africa's access to education and knowledge has barely been tapped.

Unlike earlier broadcast media, interactive information and communications technology can empower people. Such technology could, for example, play a decisive role in developing human capacity for food security in Africa, by providing people with the knowledge and skills they need to put agricultural science and production inputs to best use.

Information and communications technology could also improve health care. Many of the problems in Africa's health sector stem from a lack of information. Information and communications technology could provide health workers with rapid information exchange, conferencing, and distance learning, as well as immediate access to advice and diagnostic assistance (chapter 4). In Mozambique, for example, the Faculty of Medicine in Maputo is developing a local teleconsultation service that transfers images to doctors in other hospitals.

Better information and communications technology can also improve people's access to government, increasing participation in government decisionmaking and improving public services. New technology also offers benefits to government. Through a comprehensive database, South Africa's government can now reconcile housing applicants across regions, spotting double applications and reducing fraudulent housing claims. And government Websites are increasingly promoting tourism and culture to attract foreign investment and strengthen trade links.

Rapid changes in technology require constant awareness not only of new developments but also of what has been done in other countries

The Way Forward

Though information and communications technology offers enormous benefits for Africa, developing it will not be easy. What steps should Africa take?

Disseminate information on what is possible. Underdeveloped information and communications technology is often attributed to a lack of understanding of what is possible. Rapid changes in this technology require constant awareness not only of new developments but also of what has been done in other countries.

Many African countries have already developed a wealth of best practices that could be shared. Several countries have substantially privatized telecommunications. Mozambique has developed a national information and communications infrastructure. South Africa has established an agency for universal service and conducted a study of electronic commerce. Mauritius has set up an informatics park. And Senegal, South Africa, and Uganda have created community information and communications centers. All these efforts offer lessons for other countries. Thus there is a need to:

- Develop awareness-raising programs to improve government and public understanding of information technology applications as they are being used elsewhere.
- Establish "centers of specialization" that train policymakers and government and private users, and provide opportunities for advanced training at existing regional centers of excellence.
- Offer training that uses distance learning technology to introduce users and policymakers to the creative use of existing infrastructure.

Create an enabling environment. Although there is no universal model for liberalizing information and communications services, governments should favor competition, not monopoly, and promote private rather than public investment. In addition, policymakers should assess the demand for new technology and set clear objectives. The need for a better quality of life and equality of access makes universal service a mandatory objective.

A growing number of countries—Mauritius, South Africa, Uganda—have created universal service funds to which telecommunications operators contribute a small percentage of their revenues (0.16 percent in South Africa). The funds are then used to finance rural infrastructure development. Other countries use the license fees from telecommunications operators to finance rural telecommunications projects. In Botswana the government ensures that rural villages have access to telecommunications services by contracting the operator to build the necessary infrastructure.

Many policy issues could be tackled by developing clear and coordinated policies and guidelines through broad national participation, international consultation, and within regional and subregional discussions of national information and communications infrastructure plans. Such plans are in place in more than half of African countries. By themselves, however, these national strategies are no panacea. Increased government commitment and action, improved capacity of regulators to evaluate new technologies and projects, and innovative applications are just as essential. Policies should not only improve the governance of information and communications technology, but also use information and communications technology to improve governance.

Foster indigenous capacity and research. Africa will have trouble participating in the global information economy unless it increases the generation and flow of knowledge. Beyond building basic skills such as reading, writing, communications, and teamwork, Africa requires trained people—especially young people who can use technology, choose technology, and develop local applications. Making the next generation literate in information and communications technology will require progress in education, especially in integrating technology into primary and secondary schools through networking programs. It will require enhancing the capacity of African universities to apply new technology for research, teaching, and learning. And it will require creating opportunities for lifelong learning through community centers and school and university networks that promote equal access for all.

Africa will have trouble participating in the global information economy unless it increases the generation and flow of knowledge

159

Enhance national, regional, and international cooperation and partnerships.
Given Africa's small markets, regional and international collaboration is
key for achieving the economies of scale needed to lower costs and attract
sufficient private investment. Countries must collaborate to develop
strong system backbones and to share resources and knowledge on information and communications infrastructure. Regional and national collaboration that leads to the bulk purchasing of capacity, capacity-building
initiatives, and innovative financing arrangements—public offerings,
build-operate-transfer agreements, joint ventures, bond sales to users—
could also help achieve economies of scale and lower costs.

Some efforts have already been made. The Regional African Satellite
Communications initiative, which plans to launch Africa-based satellite
systems, has provided incentives for regional cooperation. In 1998 com-
munications ministers from more than 15 African countries agreed to
support an information and communications infrastructure known as the
Africa Connection, and development efforts are under way by the
Southern Africa Development Community, the Common Market for
Eastern and Southern Africa, and the Economic Community of West
African States. Kenya, Tanzania, and Uganda (together known as the East
African Community) have launched a multimillion-dollar telecommunications backbone project to improve access to advanced and reliable
communications. Regional cooperation could also help resolve common
issues such as Internet governance and encourage the creation of economic communities.

*Regional and
international
collaboration is key for
achieving the economies
of scale needed to lower
costs and attract private
investment in information
and communications
technology...*

Developing a Robust Financial Sector

A WELL-FUNCTIONING FINANCIAL SYSTEM IS ESSENTIAL FOR DEVEL-
opment. It should be able to mobilize foreign and domestic
resources and channel them to high-return investments, intermediate between savers and investors to reduce and allocate risk, and provide broad access to financial services, including for people on the
margins of the economy. In so doing, finance facilitates competition,
market integration, broadly based growth, and poverty reduction.

The quantity, quality, cost, and accessibility of finance are as important to development as those of more traditional forms of infrastructure. In addition, the financial sector performs a crucial function that

has no direct parallel with physical infrastructure—it provides a channel for macroeconomic policy, as an instrument for stabilization and growth.

How effective is the financial sector in promoting African development? Despite numerous reforms, not very. South Africa has one of the deepest, most sophisticated financial sectors outside OECD countries, and a few other African countries—Kenya, Mauritius, Zimbabwe—have relatively developed systems. But most of the region's financial systems are weak. Limited savings are mobilized from domestic or foreign sources. Credit to the private sector is modest and often costly. Financial sectors are dominated by banks providing a small range of services.

Harnessing finance for development will be a long process in Africa. Progress will require financial sector development as well as financial reform. Indeed, most African countries have introduced market-based reforms, but post-liberalization problems need to be addressed. Increased access to financial services is essential, and will require making borrowers more creditworthy (rather than lowering standards for formal sector credit), developing nonbank financial institutions (leasing companies, mutual funds, insurance companies), and strengthening links between formal and informal financial systems. These efforts will improve quality and access to services and increase competition. Financial sector governance—regulation and supervision, transparency, contract enforcement—will also require sustained attention. Given the small size and limited diversity of many African economies, a regional approach to financial sector development will be needed to increase competition, cut costs, and lower risks.

...just as a regional approach to financial sector development will be needed to increase competition, cut costs, and lower risks

Financial Sector Reforms and Their Legacies

After independence most African governments intervened heavily in the financial sector, nationalizing private banks, creating new state banks and nonbank financial institutions, setting interest rates for savings and lending, restricting the allocation of credit, and limiting external capital transactions. These policies were intended to increase savings and direct them to areas of high economic and social priority. The methods used were broadly in line with the development thinking of the time, and in many cases were supported (or at least not opposed) by international financial institutions and bilateral donors.

By the late 1980s, however, it became widely apparent that this approach was not working. Repressed financial systems failed to mobilize capital or steer investment to areas of growth, and the solvency and capacity of financial institutions were undermined. Controls encouraged politically motivated loans and corruption and diverted funds from intended purposes. Nonperforming loans increased alarmingly in many African countries, and a lack of sound savings alternatives contributed to capital flight.

While many countries now have stronger financial systems, reforms have often been less successful than expected

Financial sector reforms introduced in the 1990s tried to correct these problems. While the scope and pace of reforms differed across countries, they were based on two pillars: liberalization and balance sheet restructuring. Most reforms liberalized interest rates and removed ceilings and other controls on credit allocation. Though the details varied, the outcomes were similar (Soyibo 1997). Thus even though Ghana lifted restrictions on lending much faster than did Tanzania, interest rates followed the same pattern (Nissanke and Aryeetey 1998).

Weak standards for capital adequacy, lending, and accounting had led to excessive concentrations of risk, unrecognized loan losses, and inflated profit reports (Popiel 1994). Thus balance sheet restructuring and recapitalization of state banks were often among the first steps of reform. But as disillusionment with the results set in, efforts were directed toward increasing private participation in banks. Privatization of financial institutions usually began with governments seeking strategic buyers to assume majority ownership of large commercial banks. This approach was only partly successful: some publicly owned banks were divested, but in many cases the state remains dominant.

Other institutional reforms have been introduced in recent years. Licenses have increasingly been granted to new private banks—including foreign banks—and nonbank financial institutions, and efforts have been made to improve regulation and supervision. Stock markets have opened up in several countries. And an increasing range of nongovernmental organizations and other agents have entered the semiformal or microfinance sectors. But while many countries now have stronger financial systems, reforms have often been less successful than expected.

Costlier credit and wider spreads. Reform programs anticipated an initial increase in the spread between lending and deposit rates. But, more than a decade after reforms were started, the spread continues to widen in many countries, sometimes to high levels (table 5.4). And since liberalization, many financial systems have seen high real interest rates.

Little financial deepening. Liberalization was expected to encourage financial deepening, with a positive effect on savings mobilization and credit allocation. But for the most part ratios of money and credit to GDP have not increased since reforms. On both indicators, most African countries continue to lag behind their Asian comparators. In many countries banks have reduced commercial lending (including in rural areas) in favor of holding government securities.

Continued distress and limited competition. Governments are still reluctant to close distressed state banks. At the same time, small, undercapitalized institutions have mushroomed since liberalization. Many of these new institutions are not only weak, they have also failed to trigger competition in the banking sector. As a result market segmentation has emerged between foreign and domestic banks, solvent large private and public banks, and small private banks.

Limited development of money markets and capital markets. In some cases access to cheap credit through central bank discount facilities has made interbank borrowing and lending less attractive. In other cases issues of large quantities of high-yielding bills to meet fiscal requirements

Governments are still reluctant to close distressed state banks

Table 5.4 Inflation, Interest Rate Spreads, and Real Interest Rates in Africa and Asia, 1980–97 (percent)

Country	Inflation			Interest rate spread (lending rate minus deposit rate)			Real interest rate, 1997
	1980	1990	1997	1980	1990	1997	
Benin	—	—	3.5	8.3	9.0	—	—
Botswana	13.6	11.4	8.6	3.5	1.8	4.8	5.0
Cameroon	9.6	1.1	1.5	5.5	11.0	17.0	18.8
Côte d'Ivoire	14.7	−0.8	4.0	8.3	9.0	—	—
Ethiopia	4.5	5.2	−3.7	—	3.6	3.5	7.1
Ghana	50.1	37.3	27.9	7.5	—	—	—
Kenya	13.9	15.6	12.0	4.8	5.1	13.5	12.8
Malawi	—	11.8	9.1	8.8	8.9	18.0	13.0
Mozambique	—	47.0	5.5	—	—	—	—
Nigeria	10.0	7.4	8.2	3.2	5.5	13.1	8.9
Senegal	8.7	0.3	1.8	8.3	9.0	—	—
South Africa	13.9	14.4	8.6	4.0	2.1	4.6	11.2
Tanzania	30.2	35.8	16.1	7.5	—	21.4	8.3
Uganda	—	33.1	6.9	4.0	7.4	9.5	16.8
Zambia	—	107.0	24.8	2.5	9.5	12.2	16.5
Zimbabwe	5.4	17.4	18.7	14.0	2.9	13.9	14.2
Bangladesh	—	6.1	5.2	3.1	4.0	5.9	12.9
India	11.4	9.0	7.2	—	—	—	7.8
Malaysia	6.7	2.6	2.7	1.5	1.3	1.8	6.0
Philippines	18.2	13.2	5.9	1.8	4.6	6.1	9.7

Source: World Bank 1999.

163

*Financial reforms have
built on weak institutions
and have often been
poorly sequenced*

have deterred other capital market issues. Though Africa has about a
dozen stock markets, several of which opened in the 1990s, their mere
existence is inconsequential for economic growth and investment if
there are few opportunities for sharing risk, trading shares, and providing liquidity. Except in South Africa, the region's stock markets are
by far the smallest of any region, both in the number of listed companies and in market capitalization. They are also highly illiquid, which
seriously constrains their ability to contribute to economic growth
(Senbet 1997).

Why Have Reforms Been Disappointing?

A number of explanations have been offered for the lackluster results
of financial reforms.

Incorrect sequencing. Financial reform has often preceded macroeconomic stabilization. In particular, interest rates were often liberalized
before fiscal deficits were brought under control. When that happens,
higher interest rates can increase government debt, crowd out private
credit, and contribute to further macroeconomic imbalances—as well as
reduce incentives for banks to seek out new clients. Domestic public debt
has reached high levels in a number of countries, including Cape Verde,
Ghana, Kenya, and Zimbabwe. In Nigeria unstable political and economic conditions led to the collapse of the financial system, necessitating
policy reversals that undermined credibility (Soyibo 1996).

Incomplete reforms. Continued poor financial performance has reflected
a lack of progress on some reforms (World Bank 1994a). Financial systems have still been used to finance public activities. Restructuring balance sheets and recapitalizing banks were not sufficient · to change
behavior; that would only happen if banks were no longer publicly owned
and pressured to lend to loss-making public enterprises.

Weak institutions. To be fully effective, financial liberalization requires a
number of prerequisites (World Bank 1994b). In addition to a stable
macroeconomy and adequate regulation and supervision, there must be
reasonably sophisticated and solvent banking institutions operating in
contestable financial markets. Few African countries satisfied these conditions prior to liberalization and deregulation, limiting the possibility of
rapid gains.

A focus on national systems. Except in the West African monetary zones,
reforms have focused on small national systems. These offer little scope

for competition, economies of scale, or diversification of risk, particularly given the dependence of most African countries on a few primary products with variable prices.

Macroeconomic risks. Macroeconomic risks reflect poor coordination between fiscal and monetary policy. If tight monetary policy is maintained in the face of loose fiscal policy, interest rates will likely rise to unhealthy levels, and banks will retreat from developing new business in favor of holding public debt. Inconsistent policies (including overvalued exchange rates) and external shocks also contribute to uncertainty, again raising interest rates. High perceived macroeconomic risks can be inferred from the short-term maturities at which most African governments borrow. In some African countries these risks have been estimated to raise government borrowing costs by 6 percentage points.

Market risks. Market risks arise from capital market inefficiencies such as a lack of liquidity or severe interest rate volatility. For example, lack of a secondary market for treasury bills restricts liquidity and raises risks and the costs of borrowing. Poor liquidity management by governments is estimated to have added 0.5–3.0 percentage points to short-term borrowing costs in many African countries.

Microeconomic risks. Microeconomic risks are also affected by government policy, but tend to have a greater impact on capital costs for the private sector. The accuracy and reliability of financial information, including company accounts, affect the cost of capital, particularly in equity markets. A legal system that does not enforce financial contracts in a timely manner will reduce the supply of capital, increase its cost, and limit access to finance. A payments system that does not permit rapid and reliable transfer of funds for settlement of financial contracts will increase the cost of capital. A system for title transfer that is untimely or insecure will increase the cost of capital raised through debt securities by reducing transactional liquidity in the secondary market or by causing a risk premium to be built into secondary market rates.

To these risks should be added the risk entailed in lack of diversification in small markets, along with the higher costs of supervision and other overhead that raise the cost of capital. Lowering the cost of capital is not a simple matter of stabilization or a few macroeconomic or financial policy reforms. Rather, financial reform and development is a long process involving the development of trust and policy credibility, complex institutions, and complicated governance procedures within a framework of economic and financial integration (Wilton 1999).

Financial reform and development is a long process involving the development of trust and policy credibility, complex institutions, and complicated governance procedures

The Way Forward

Commercial microfinance institutions that serve the economically active poor are an encouraging recent development

Africa's financial systems face many challenges. The financial side of macroeconomic policy still requires strengthening—including by setting appropriate fiscal deficits, taking into account the arrangements for their financing. To a large extent, well-working financial markets are the result of sound government policy and its day to day operations. Money market development, for example, depends on such mundane factors as whether treasury bills are issued daily or weekly, and how these funding operations are coordinated with the central bank. Some priorities for financial sector development can be summarized in light of the preceding discussion.

Improve access to financial services. Increasing access to basic financial services—particularly savings facilities—is a major issue in Africa, where most people do not have access to the formal financial sector. As noted, the number of bankable clients should be increased by using innovative approaches rather than by lowering prudential standards and so increasing financial instability. One encouraging recent development has been the expansion of commercial microfinance institutions that serve the economically active poor (Robinson forthcoming). Leading examples include Bolivia's BancoSol and Bank Rakyat Indonesia.

The Kenya Rural Enterprise Programme, which is modeled on BancoSol, is Africa's best-known example. Commercial microfinance institutions typically offer savings and credit services on commercial terms to economically active households and enterprises that are too small to be served by large commercial banks. Well-structured commercial microfinance institutions have managed to sustain high loan recovery rates, cover costs, and make profits. Their lending rates are higher than those of commercial banks but lower than those of informal moneylenders, who are the main alternatives for their customers.

The growing financing needs of small borrowers can also be met by developing closer links between the formal and informal financial sectors. Such links can enable banks to lower the costs of information as well as develop innovative, community-based contract enforcement mechanisms. In Ghana, for example, there is potential for linking informal savings collectors (*susu*) to commercial banks in a way that increases the portion of susu savers with access to susu credit (Aryeetey and Steel 1995). Such links, where formal institutions mobilize deposits and allocate credit through informal and microfinance agents, could be encouraged by fiscal policies and regulation and supervision systems.

To share risk, informal and semiformal financial agents must be credible. Because it is difficult to regulate and supervise such agents, they should be given incentives for increasing formalization through stronger links with the formal sector. A possible approach is to develop rural banking based on cooperative arrangements that allow banks to regulate informal and semiformal lenders (Aryeetey 1997).

Strengthen financial sector governance. In many countries improving contract enforcement, transparency, payments systems, and other micro and institutional aspects of the financial system is a higher priority than further liberalization. While regulation and supervision have improved in some countries, further improvements will require, among other things, paying competitive salaries for skills that are in high demand in the private sector and outside Africa.

There is also a long way to go in ensuring that regulators are truly independent. External links may enhance independence and offer economies of scale. For example, regional supervisory agencies might be more credible than national ones. But accounting standards, disclosure requirements, and contract law will all require sustained attention to ensure the integrity and credibility of financial institutions. The issues involved in creating proper incentives for financial sector development go beyond financial institutions to much broader issues of governance, such as judicial independence. Without a political commitment to good governance, financial sector development will be difficult whatever the level of technical expertise in the sector.

Develop nonbank financial institutions. As noted, Africa's financial sectors are dominated by commercial banks. More emphasis needs to be placed on developing nonbank financial institutions, including those offering contractual savings and leasing services, as well as equity and debt markets. These can promote competition in different segments of the market. Africa's young and growing population suggests potential for contractual savings institutions such as pension funds and insurance companies, but in many countries this area of finance is underdeveloped and provides few attractive options to potential clients. Capital markets improve risk management, offer opportunities for price discovery, bolster corporate governance, and create possibilities for privatization and can be stimulated by it (Aryeetey and Senbet 1999; box 5.4). While a portfolio in any one African country might be risky, rates of return for groups of countries are far less volatile.

Pursue a regional approach to financial sector development. As noted, most African financial sectors are small, and most economies depend on a

Accounting standards, disclosure requirements, and contract law will require sustained attention to ensure the integrity and credibility of financial institutions

167

few primary products. A few large firms may represent a disproportionate share of the bankable demand for credit, and a few major banks may saturate the market, reducing the potential for competition and lowering incentives to develop new clients. In many countries, even well-intentioned efforts to strengthen national institutions will have a hard time overcoming these obstacles.

Africa's young and growing population suggests potential for contractual savings institutions such as pension funds and insurance companies

A regional approach offers many advantages. It enables institutions to operate over a wider area and diversify risk, and it offers potential for greater competition and economies of scale—especially important for spreading the high fixed costs of institutions such as stock markets and bank supervision agencies. But in the presence of capital controls and without a common currency, there are limits to what can be done regionally. And even with free movement of capital and a common currency, financial development will not occur unless other policies are in place. In the CFA zone during the 1980s, for example, banking systems were used to avoid the fiscal rigor required by the monetary union, leading to the buildup of arrears by public enterprises and subsequent financial distress. But a number of cross-border activities can be developed on a regional basis, including banking, bank supervision, and stock markets.

The basic building blocks for cross-border banking are improving and harmonizing commercial and financial law, contract enforcement, accounting standards, and prudential supervision. A number of regional organizations—the Southern Africa Development Community, the Central Bank of West African States, the Macroeconomic and Financial Management Institute of Eastern and Southern Africa—are working at the political and technical levels to improve and harmonize regional stan-

---

Box 5.4 Privatization Based on Capital Markets

CAPITAL MARKETS HAVE BEEN AN IMPORTANT VEHICLE for privatization in countries such as Chile and have, in turn, been stimulated by new issues stemming from divestiture. In Africa transactions such as the privatization of Kenya Airways and of major utilities also have potential for stimulating capital market development, deepening markets by increasing the supply of major listed companies. This is particularly welcome given the thinness of Africa's stock markets.

Capital market–based privatization also offers less obvious benefits. These markets can provide a monitoring mechanism to curtail inefficiencies resulting from mismanagement. They increase the likelihood that enterprises will be fairly priced and so can help depoliticize privatization. And privatization through local capital markets allows for local investor participation, diversifying ownership of the economy's resources and contributing to the credibility of privatization.

dards. Well-capitalized regional and international financial institutions are increasingly recognized as a means of providing a base of institutions with the ability to diversify risks within their aggregate balance sheet, and it is notable that Africa already has the highest penetration by foreign banks of any region.

Foreign banks have provided stability, know-how, and a range of services to African financial systems. But the marginal returns to further foreign entry may be lower than elsewhere. And if finance is confined to small countries, foreign entry will not solve the problem of banking concentration. In the next phase of financial sector development, greater gains may come from improving incentives and transparency in local markets and aligning policies and regulation to facilitate regional banking.

More broadly, pooling resources for regional capital market development would enhance the potential for mobilizing local and international finance for regional companies, while injecting more liquidity into the markets (Senbet 1998). Among the potential vehicles for financial integration are regional securities and exchange commissions, regional self-regulating organizations, regional committees to harmonize legal and regulatory systems, and coordinated monetary arrangements. Tax treatment of investments must be reviewed with a view to harmonization, because tax policy is an important incentive or disincentive for both issuers and investors. Clearance, settlement, and depository systems, along with regulation and accounting standards, should conform to international standards.

This discussion of regionalization is not taking place in a vacuum. Initiatives have already developed mechanisms for regional capital markets, anchored around the Abidjan (Côte d'Ivoire) Stock Exchange. There are also proposals in Southern Africa for developing stronger links between the Johannesburg (South Africa) exchange and the smaller exchanges of Botswana, Namibia, Swaziland, and Zimbabwe (Aryeetey and Senbet 1999). These efforts at regional capital market integration are positive examples for the rest of the region.

Pooling resources for regional capital market development would enhance the potential for mobilizing local and international finance

169

CHAPTER 6

Spurring Agricultural and Rural Development

Comprehensive improvements in policies, institutions, and investment could accelerate agricultural and rural growth to levels that would help reduce rural poverty

CENTURIES OF POOR POLICIES AND INSTITUTIONAL FAIL-ures are the primary cause of Africa's undercapitalized and uncompetitive agriculture. Adverse resource endowments have also had some direct effects, as well as indirect effects through their influence on policy. The lack of a prolonged period of favorable incentives, rural public investments, and institutional supports has limited the opportunities for African farmers and agroindustrialists.

As a result the potential of African agriculture remains latent—good reason for optimism. Indeed, modest policy improvements in the 1980s and 1990s triggered a significant response. Thus persistent and comprehensive improvements in policies, institutions, and public and private investment could accelerate agricultural and rural growth to levels that would help reduce rural poverty.

Indeed, the undercapitalization of agriculture will have to be addressed if Africa is to feed itself, compete in world markets, and reduce rural poverty. As the main source of rural livelihoods, agriculture dominates many African economies, accounting for about 35 percent of the region's GDP, 70 percent of employment, and 40 percent of exports (World Bank 1997a).

One often overlooked contribution of agriculture is the strength of backward and forward linkages within agriculture and with other sectors of the economy. Recent evidence from Africa suggests that the added growth and rural income from such linkages, especially from increases in farm incomes, has been underestimated (Delgado, Hopkins, and Kelly 1998).[1] Moreover, these linkages generally become stronger with development (Vogel 1994) and drive agriculture-led industrialization (Adelman 1984).

Indeed, few low-income countries have achieved rapid nonagricultural growth without rapid growth in agriculture. Thus agriculture cannot continue to be neglected.

Drawing on analysis of these issues, this chapter offers a "business plan" for agricultural and rural development in the 21st century—a strategy for capitalizing agriculture and increasing its competitiveness. In developing the elements of this strategy, several questions need to be answered:

Few low-income countries have achieved rapid nonagricultural growth without rapid growth in agriculture

- What are the main issues confronting African agriculture as it enters the 21st century?
- What should be done to address these issues?
- What should be the roles of African states, other stakeholders, and development partners?
- What is the likely impact of the proposed strategy on overall agricultural performance, food security, natural resources, and rural poverty?
- Where will the resources come from to finance the strategy, and how should they be used and allocated?
- What challenges lie ahead, and what can be learned from leading and emerging agricultural countries?

Explaining the Poor Performance of African Agriculture

DESPITE AGRICULTURE'S IMPORTANCE TO AFRICA, IT HAS remained below its potential—even backward relative to other developing regions. This is apparent in agriculture's extreme undercapitalization and lack of competitiveness in world markets (table 6.1; figure 6.1).

Less than 7 percent of cropped area in Africa is irrigated, and the use of purchased inputs and machines is limited. Cereal yields (a reflection of the productivity of land under cereal production) are less than half those in other developing regions.[2] Even for tubers and plantains, which have suitable agroecological conditions in Africa, yields are lower than in Asia and Latin America.[3] Agricultural labor productivity is low: historically, the marginal product of labor has been about the same as the average product, whereas in Asia and Latin America the average product of labor is much greater than the marginal product (Delgado and Ranade 1987). Africa's agricultural capital stock per hectare of agricultural land in 1988–92 was about one-sixth of that in Asia and less than one-quarter of that in Latin America (UNCTAD 1998).

Undercapitalization is associated with the lack of competitiveness of African products in world markets. And this position is made worse by high transactions costs (Ahmed and Rustagi 1987; Jaffee and Morton 1995), inadequate market infrastructure (Hayami and Platteau 1997), weak institutions and support services (Eicher 1999), inadequate diversification, and limited vertical integration (Delgado 1998b). As a result

Table 6.1 Agricultural Indicators for Africa, Asia, and Latin America

Indicator	Africa	Asia	Latin America
Agricultural GDP (millions of dollars), 1997	62,367	400,105	143,186
Agriculture/GDP (percent), 1995	30	25	10
Labor force/agriculture (percent), 1995	70	72	29
Agriculture/exports (percent), 1995	40	18	30
Agricultural production index (1961–64 = 100)			
1965–69	113	115	115
1975–79	135	154	153
1985–89	166	230	200
1995–98	221	338	253
Agricultural production per capita index (1961–64 = 100)			
1965–69	100	103	102
1975–79	92	110	106
1985–89	84	135	112
1995–98	87	169	120
Cereal yields (kilograms per hectare), 1994	1,230	2,943	2,477
Cereal output per capita (kilograms), 1993–96	133	285	256
Agricultural land/labor (hectares per worker), 1994	5.9	1.3	24.8
Fertilizer/arable land (kilograms per hectares of arable land), 1993–96	15	180	75
Irrigated area/arable land (percent), 1994	6.6	33.3	9.2
Tractors/arable land (number per 1,000 hectares), 1994	290	804	1,165
Road density (kilometers of road per square kilometer), 1995	0.06	0.37	0.16
Paved roads (percentage of total roads), 1995	15	29	25
Population density (people per square kilometer), 1995	25	146	24
Rural nonfarm income/total rural income (percent)	42	32	40
Nonagricultural/agricultural value added per worker, 1980–90	7.8	3.6	2.5

Source: World Bank 1997a, 1999a, 1999c; FAOSTAT 2000; UNCTAD 1998; Hayami and Platteau 1997; Reardon and others 1998; Larson and Mundlak 1997.

Figure 6.1 Africa's Share of World Trade for Its Main Export Crops, 1970 and 1997

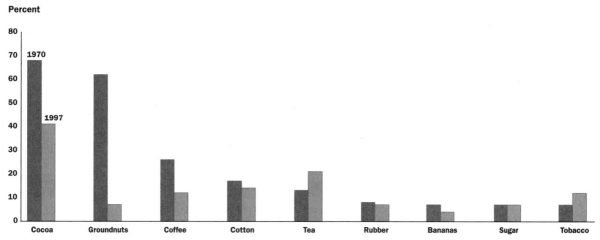

Percent

Source: FAOSTAT 2000.

African agriculture has been steadily marginalized in world trade (Ng and Yeats 1996). What caused these factors to occur?

History and Policy

African agriculture has been plagued by centuries of poor policies and institutional failures—and a record of heavy extraction and heavy taxation of rural areas (box 6.1). Although there were policy improvements between the mid-1950s and the late 1960s, these were temporary. Subsequent policy distortions—in the form of overvalued exchange rates and inward-looking industrialization policies—reversed the gains, particularly in crop exports.

Over the past few centuries private individuals and groups have had few opportunities to engage in free, competitive trade and investment in agriculture and agroindustry. Farmers have had little incentive to invest in cash or in kind in their farms and natural resources. There has been no extended period of active public investment for agricultural and rural development—and the programs that were implemented have suffered from severe public sector bias and excessive centralization. In most countries local populations have not been able to use local tax bases for their development—because tax bases were assigned, by design or default, to colonial or central governments or to monopolistic private or

173

state structures. Despite high taxes, public investment in rural services and infrastructure has been poor.[4] Indeed, if high taxes had been complemented with significant public investment in agriculture (as in Asia), the sector would not have fared so poorly.

Box 6.1 Centuries of Extraction from African Agriculture

Precolonial era. Extraction from rural Africa during the precolonial era occurred through the slave trade. Especially between 1650 and 1850, the slave trade disrupted Africa's demographic, social, institutional, and moral development (Fage 1977, Aplers 1977, Curto 1992). The political entities that conducted the slave raids were never able to reproduce themselves (Meillassoux 1981). They even failed to reproduce the population of captured slaves, depending on ever-widening geographic areas to capture new slaves from subsistence agricultural systems.

Colonial era. With the onset of colonialism, policies for extraction from rural areas changed. Several mechanisms were developed to ensure labor supplies for mines, plantations, settler farms, and public works (Binswanger, Deininger, and Feder 1993). Access to markets was restricted through cooperatives or monopoly marketing schemes that excluded peasant farmers or forced them to sell their crops at depressed and uncompetitive prices. In East and Southern Africa land for peasant agriculture was systematically reduced, confining these farmers to less fertile lands. In addition, access to agricultural public goods and services (roads, extension, credit) was limited to plantations or settlers. Such distortions were also used on other continents, but in Africa they persisted much longer and left policy and institutional remnants still visible today.

Between the mid-1950s and late 1960s, however, policy improvements, together with favorable world prices, bolstered the performance of African agriculture, and export cropping spread rapidly (Anthony and others 1979; Kamarck 1967; De Wilde 1967). Export crops induced technological change because they had different seasonal labor profiles from traditional crops, allowing farms constrained by seasonal labor bottlenecks to significantly expand cultivated land (Delgado and Ranade 1987). Market-oriented agriculture grew rapidly in many countries (Delgado 1998b). But this improved performance was halted by policy changes that shifted from export crop growth strategies toward import-substituting industrialization, partly induced by the 1973 oil shock. Real exchange rates became overvalued, and incentives shifted from agriculture to manufacturing.

Postcolonial era. The chance was missed to create a better policy environment for agriculture at the start of the postcolonial period. Policies continued to impose high explicit and implicit taxes on agriculture: pricing policies taxed agriculture about as much as the indirect tax resulting from industrial protection and macroeconomic policies (Schiff and Valdés 1992; Herrmann 1997). With help from donors, postcolonial regimes built on the institutional residues of colonial powers and increased public sector dominance over agricultural marketing and input supply systems, inhibiting the development of individual traders, private companies, and farmer cooperatives. In most countries output markets were dominated by marketing boards (World Bank 1994). In more than 60 percent of African countries, governments completely controlled the procurement and distribution of fertilizer and seeds (World Bank 1981), yet these systems were unreliable. Parallel trading or processing was inhibited. Controls on crop movements, particularly for grains (Jayne and Jones 1997), were common. And such marketing systems imposed huge fiscal costs.

More recently, particularly in the 1970s and 1980s, heavy taxes and constraints on private and collective initiatives continued to retard agricultural growth and rural development. Consider the limited opportunities of a dynamic rural entrepreneur in a typical African country around 1980. Private investment in agriculture and agroindustry was undermined by heavy taxation, and the space for private sector activity was severely limited by the dominant public sector. There was little potential for producer organizations and nongovernmental organizations to be involved in the development process. Local governments could not provide public services (roads, schools, health, agricultural services) because the authority and financing needed to do so were with centralized government agencies. Even if they wanted to raise revenues for local development, local governments did not have access to significant tax bases.

Economic policies and institutions in Africa have been characterized by urban bias and by centralized political, fiscal, and institutional systems

Economic policies and institutions in Africa have been characterized by urban bias and by centralized political, fiscal, and institutional systems (chapter 2). Both features have inhibited agricultural and rural development. And both have received increased attention in the literature.

The urban bias in services and prices persistently favored urban people over rural, harming efficiency and income distribution (Lipton 1977). By organizing, centralizing, and controlling political and economic power, elites have controlled policy and the distribution of resources. In many other countries pernicious political, administrative, and fiscal consequences have made urban bias unsustainable. But these pressures do not seem to have been strong enough in most of Africa, despite the continent's exceptionally high urban bias. Why? Because of the lack of open political systems and of well-articulated, competitive institutions in civil society (Lipton 1993).

Africa's postcolonial regimes had many reasons for establishing highly centralized political, fiscal, and institutional systems for rural development. These reasons included a desire for political integration of fragile nations and the dominance of state-led development and planning ideologies in the Western and Marxist development economics of the time (Manor 1999).

Recent World Bank research on decentralization and rural development developed scores for decisionmaking and resource allocation in six important areas of rural development: rural primary education, rural primary health care, rural road maintenance, agricultural extension, rural water supply, and forestry management.[5] The African countries in the

Figure 6.2 Levels of Decentralized Rural Service Delivery in Various Parts of the Developing World, 1990s

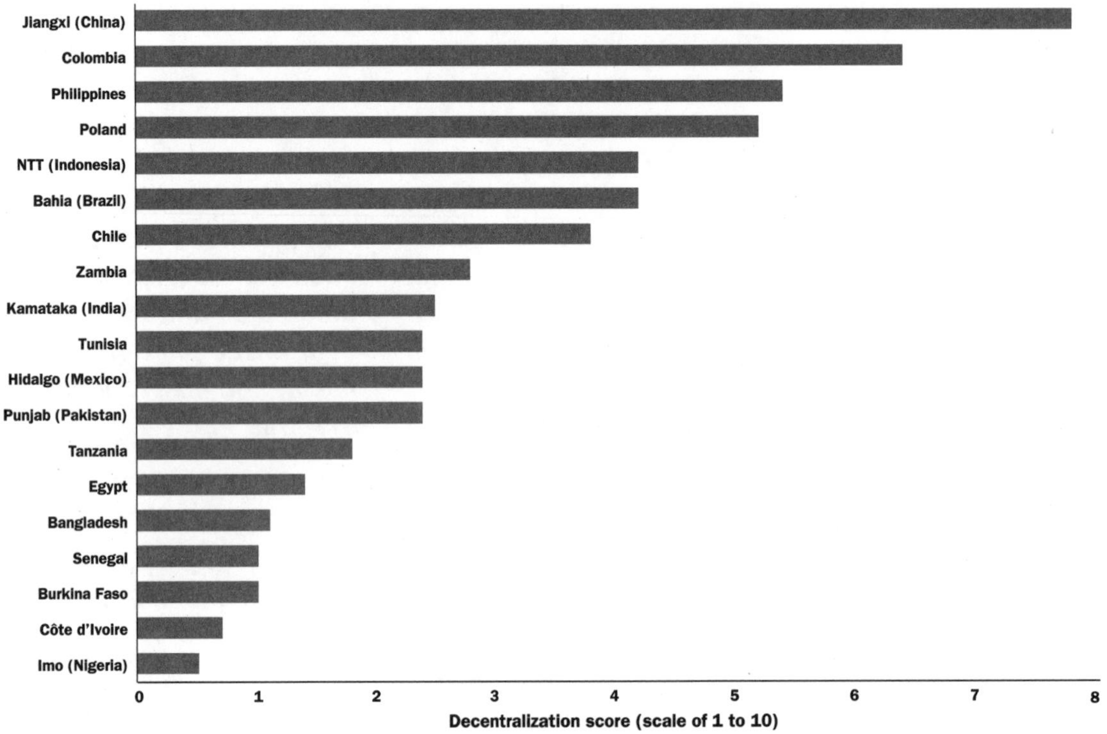

Source: McLean, Kerr, and Williams 1998.

Agricultural subsidies and market access restrictions in developed countries have limited Africa's agricultural export growth

sample had the most centralized institutions for rural development in the first half of the 1990s (figure 6.2). High centralization inhibited the development of local institutional capacity, limited local resource mobilization, undermined the accountability of development programs to local populations, and discouraged popular participation (McLean, Kerr, and Williams 1998; Parker 1995). Further inhibiting local initiatives was the lack of democracy in most countries—and the discouragement or even suppression of voluntary private associations.

In addition to Africa's poor policies and institutions, developed country policies and market access restrictions—prominent in the postcolonial period—have limited Africa's agricultural export growth (box 6.2). Several developing countries (Brazil, Thailand) have managed to penetrate developed country markets for some products despite such restrictions. But Africa, for the most part, has not. Indeed, poor domestic policies and institutional failures, as well as developed country policies limiting market access, have reduced incentives to invest in African agriculture.

Box 6.2 OECD Subsidies to Agriculture—Equal to Africa's GDP

TRANSFERS TO FARMS IN OECD COUNTRIES FROM TAX-payers and consumers—a result of the agricultural policies used by OECD members—have changed little in recent years. In 1996 these transfers were estimated at $300 billion (OECD 1997), about the same as Africa's GDP. These transfers are largest in the European Union, with Japan and the United States transferring income at just over half the EU level (Josling 1998).

Removing these supports would have significant benefits. Global trade in beverages, meat, and livestock products would increase significantly (Hertel, Anderson, and Francois 1999). Production patterns would shift, with agricultural production declining in Western Europe and increasing in developing countries. Meat production in Africa could increase 20 percent (Anderson and Strutt 1996).

The welfare cost to developing countries of OECD agricultural policies is well above that of OECD textile and clothing trade barriers. Not only are OECD countries' protection rates still very high, but "dirty" tariffs and the introduction of tariff rate quotas in the Uruguay Round mean that large commitments to bound tariff cuts, quota expansion, or both will be needed to significantly reduce agricultural protection (Anderson 1999).

What would happen if OECD countries reformed their agriculture policies?

- *World food prices would increase, but not by much.* Expected price increases are 4–6 percent for wheat, rice, and coarse grains (Valdés and Zietz 1995)—

and many of these commodities show a downward trend in real prices over time.

- *Commodity prices would become more stable.* The freer is world trade, the less volatile will world food prices become. Surpluses and deficits can be evened out more easily when there are more trading partners with different climate conditions for food crops (Bale and Lutz 1979; Zwart and Blandford 1989).

- *Real income in Africa and other poor regions would increase.* Annual per capita income would increase by $1 in South Asia, $4 in Southeast Asia, $6 in Africa, and $30 in Latin America. The average producer household in developing regions would gain from liberalization, while consumer households with a food deficit would incur losses. But the gains for producers would be larger than the losses for consumers and would have dynamic multiplier effects for rural areas and developing economies as a whole—so even consumers could benefit in the long run.

- *Welfare in OECD countries would increase as well.* OECD countries are incurring $63 billion a year in welfare losses from their distortionary policies (Anderson, Hoekman, and Strutt 1999). The main losers are consumers, who pay higher prices for such commodities as milk, sugar, and bananas. The main gainers are favored producers, who will likely be strongly opposed to the needed liberalization.

Source: Adapted from Binswanger and Lutz 2000.

Geography and Resource Endowments

Africa's natural adversities have often been used to explain agriculture's poor performance. Indeed, many studies have highlighted Africa's adverse conditions: landlockedness (Bloom and Sachs 1998; Collier and Gunning 1997), poor land quality (Voortman, Sonneveld, and Keyzer 1998; Donovan and Casey 1998), endemic livestock diseases (Coetzer, Thomson, and Tustin 1994), and human diseases (Bloom and Sachs

1998)—the most devastating being malaria, tuberculosis, and AIDS (chapter 4; UNAIDS 1998). UNCTAD (1998) suggests that almost half of Africa's land is unsuitable for direct rainfed cultivation because the growing period is too short, mainly due to aridity. In addition, there is a high risk of drought on 60 percent of African land.

In discussing endowment effects, a distinction needs to be made between the direct effects of adverse endowments on agricultural development and their possible indirect effects as codeterminants of poor policies for agricultural and rural development.

Bloom and Sachs (1998) focus on the direct effects, discussing the consequences of Africa's climate, soils, topography, and disease ecology on agricultural productivity. In addition, they suggest that the isolation of African agriculture from major global markets renders it noncompetitive because, with a few exceptions, it is concentrated in the deep hinterlands and supported by a low-density, widely dispersed rural population. These factors retard agricultural development directly by increasing transportation costs, inhibiting technology adoption, raising the costs of agricultural and social services, and suppressing competitive product, factor, and credit markets (Hayami and Platteau 1997). The direct effects of adverse endowments, not just adverse policies, therefore explain many of the institutional and market failures holding agriculture back.

While there is little doubt that adverse endowments and physical conditions continue to be a negative factor in African agricultural development, it is not clear how important they are relative to adverse policies and institutions. As Udry (1998) points out, the low productivity of African agriculture cannot be attributed exclusively to bad technology or bad geography; it has clearly also been the result of policy failures. There is much evidence that farmers and rural nonfarm entrepreneurs respond to incentives (box 6.3). Conversely, there are many examples of well-endowed and well-connected regions and countries—Ghana, Guinea, Madagascar—whose performance has deteriorated rapidly as a consequence of worsening policies in the postcolonial period. Indeed, some of the areas with the strongest agricultural resource base are among the least developed on the continent—Angola, Central African Republic, Democratic Republic of Congo, Republic of Congo, Gabon, Guinea-Bissau, Liberia, Sierra Leone, and Sudan.

In many countries agricultural performance over the past 25 years has been inhibited by civil war and conflict (chapter 2). Sudan has huge potential, but its current phase of civil war has lasted 16 years, about

The low productivity of African agriculture cannot be attributed exclusively to bad technology or bad geography—it also reflects unfavorable legacies, including policy failures

2.5 million people have lost their lives, and the country has the largest number of internally displaced people in the world—hardly an environment conducive to sustained agricultural growth. Conflict also continues in Angola, Burundi, Democratic Republic of Congo, and Somalia, and has recently occurred in Guinea-Bissau, Liberia, and Sierra Leone. The benefits to agriculture from a cessation of conflict have recently been illustrated by Mozambique (luckily the main agricultural production regions have not been widely affected by the recent massive flooding).

Countries that emerge from conflict can reap benefits for agriculture

Political Economy

A growing literature suggests that there are indirect causal links between low population density, remoteness from markets, and abundance of natural resources on the one hand, and conflict and adverse policies and institutions on the other (Brenner 1977; North 1989; Tilly 1990; Rueschemeyer, Stephens, and Stephens 1992; Collier and Binswanger 1999, chapter 2). Binswanger and Deininger (1997) summarize the key arguments for population density as follows:

- Low-density economies are subsistence-oriented, with little specialization.
- As a result few economic transactions can be taxed. Neither a profit

---

Box 6.3 Do African Farmers Respond to Price Incentives?

AFRICAN FARMERS, LIKE THEIR COUNTERPARTS ELSE-where, respond significantly to both price and nonprice policy reforms. The level of this response has generally been found to be lower in the short than in the long run, for perennial than for annual crops, and for aggregate than for individual crop output (Bond 1983; Oyejide 1986; Tshibaka 1986; Binswanger 1989; Elamin and Mak 1997). There is also a high degree of complementarity between pricing policies and investments in public goods (Schiff and Montenegro 1997).

This relationship suggests that the removal of price distortions (due to both direct and indirect government interventions) through macroeconomic and sec-tor policy reforms will have only a limited impact on farmers' supply response if market infrastructure, institutions, and support services are undeveloped (Kwanashie, Ajilima, and Garba 1998; Elamin and Mak 1997; Tshibaka 1997; Killick 1990; Oyejide 1990; Binswanger 1989). In these situations transactions costs will be high and farmers are at a double disadvantage because of high input costs and low output prices. Similarly, the removal of structural and institutional constraints alone will have only a limited impact on farmers' response if price distortions remain significant. Thus African farmers do respond. But they also face both price and nonprice constraints.

nor an income tax can be used. Land has little or no value and cannot be a tax base.

■ Extraction of a surplus therefore has to be based on one or more of the following: coercion through slavery, servitude, or tribute; head or hut taxes to force the local population to supply cheap labor to large estates of the ruling elite or in mines and public works; discriminatory interventions in product and factor markets—whether limitations on economic opportunities, restrictions on spatial or occupational mobility, or overt discrimination; and taxation of export commodities by the state, parastatal bodies, or monopolies (see box 6.1).

■ All these policies and institutions for extracting an economic surplus undermine the incentives of the poor to produce and invest—and so have a much higher deadweight loss than modern forms of taxation.

Rural public investment has typically been low, and subsidies have usually benefited large farmers and other members of the rural elite

Throughout history and across continents, a mix of such policies was often used in low-density areas. Clearly, it is not simply low population density that significantly retards agricultural development. Rather, it is the inability of sparse agricultural populations to organize themselves to have political voice.

The negative effects of heavy taxation and extraction on agricultural growth could also have been mitigated if the ruling elite set taxes low enough and invested some of the surplus in rural public services and infrastructure. Indeed, East Asia provides some 20th century examples of relatively high extraction from rural areas. But this extraction was combined with substantial public investment in smallholder agricultural and rural development (Karshenas 1998).

In Africa rural public investment has typically been low, and subsidies for fertilizer and credit have usually benefited large farmers and other members of the rural elite. The persistence of these policies is the result of the much greater capacity of the rural and especially the urban elite to organize relative to small farmers. The elite are therefore able to control policies, institutions, and the distribution of public resources. As noted, lack of open political systems and of well-articulated, competitive institutions in civil society have characterized these systems (chapter 2).

If policies and institutions are endogenous, and if a particular configuration of resource endowments—such as low population density and high mineral wealth—is an adverse codeterminant of policies, how can poor policies and institutions be corrected? The power of external actors is real but limited, as shown by the increasing evidence on the effect of conditions tied to external loans and grants. Conditionality has only been effective in bringing about lasting reform when there has been a strong domestic movement for change (World Bank 1998).

Over time increasing population density and market access, and the associated increase in economic specialization and growth, could help improve policies. But that would be a painfully slow evolution. Surely no one would advocate increasing Africa's population growth to get there faster. Instead the focus will have to be on helping poor rural populations organize themselves more effectively through education, training, and direct support to their economic and social organizations, and allowing them to build coalitions with internal and external allies that support policy and institutional change. Such an approach can only succeed if political systems become more open and competitive, and if there is freedom to organize for economic, social, and political purposes.

Thus African agricultural growth requires more than just reforming policies and institutions and increasing rural public investment. It also requires developing open political systems in which organizations of the poor can thrive and creating political coalitions that help improve policies and keep in place the gains already achieved (chapter 2).

Macroeconomic and agricultural reforms have begun to make agriculture more competitive

Assessing the Impact of Agricultural Policy Reforms

DESPITE ADVERSE RESOURCE ENDOWMENTS, IN RECENT YEARS macroeconomic and agricultural reforms have begun to improve the competitiveness of the sector, though the effect on capitalization of agriculture and rural areas has been limited (chapter 1). The analysis in this section covers factors influencing the incentives facing agriculture (recent macroeconomic and pricing reforms as well as the evolution of real prices for commodity exports) and a range of reforms in other areas influencing agricultural supply (transactions costs, entry barriers, investment and agricultural technology).

Macroeconomic Policy Has Improved, but New Challenges Have Emerged

The exchange rate overvaluations of the 1970s and 1980s have been reduced, and inflation and budget deficits have been lowered. Trade

Reforms have focused on improving agricultural incentives by reducing domestic market distortions

policies still raise import prices (chapter 7), but the antiexport bias has been eased. But while macroeconomic stability has generally improved, in many countries it remains fragile. Financial sectors, a key area for improvement, need development (chapter 5). And institutions and rules are weaker than in other regions, diminishing investor confidence (Brunetti, Kinsunko, and Weder 1998).

Further, in some countries there is still a danger that short-term capital inflows triggered by high interest rates could lead to exchange rate overvaluation (Elbadawi 1998; Asea and Rinehart 1995). To keep price incentives stable, despite current low capital inflows, African governments need to develop suitable approaches to global financial markets and consider the capital account effects of domestic fiscal and monetary policies.

Export Crop Policy Has Improved, but Reforms Need to Be Consolidated

Africa's agricultural reforms over the past decade have focused on improving agricultural incentives by reducing domestic market distortions through open trade policies. Emphasis has been placed on moving domestic prices to border parity levels and reducing overvalued exchange rates (Meerman 1997). As a result price incentives for export crops have generally improved.

Between 1990 and 1997 real domestic producer prices for agricultural exports increased in 15 of 19 African countries; in the 1980s only 9 of these countries experienced price increases (figure 6.3).[6] This favorable trend is due to both higher world prices and better policies (Townsend 1999). In the 1980s real world commodity prices declined significantly. While world prices were falling, macroeconomic policies improved considerably, with sharp declines in overvalued exchange rates. But in many countries this barely offset the large declines in world prices. Over the same period the nominal protection coefficient for agriculture barely changed, indicating that changes in sector policies did little to raise farm-level prices.

The situation changed in the 1990s. Real world commodity prices were more favorable in 1990–97, and sector policies contributed to higher domestic prices. Macroeconomic policies continued to improve, though these changes were less dramatic than in the 1980s because the space for further improvement was limited. Even so, the changes improved price

Figure 6.3 Changes in Real Producer Prices of African Agricultural Exports, 1981–97

Between 1981–83 and 1989–91

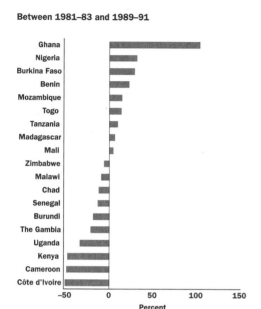

Between 1989–91 and 1995–97

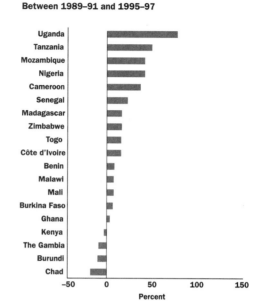

Source: World Bank 1994; Townsend 1999.

incentives. For the 15 countries experiencing real producer price increases in 1990–97 (see figure 6.3), the increase due to real exchange rate devaluation was more than twice the increase due to improvements in domestic policy. The decline in real domestic prices in Burundi, Chad, The Gambia, and Kenya is explained by the large decline in the producer's share of the border price—suggesting that sector policies were the main cause of the price declines. Indeed, in a few countries agricultural policies have continued to erode the price benefits from higher world prices and inhibited the pass-through of exchange rate depreciations to producer prices. So for some countries, even basic agricultural policy reforms are not yet complete. Real world prices became less favorable in the later half of the 1990s, declining from 1996–97 onward. [7]

Marketing boards and price stabilization funds (*Caisse de Stabilization*) were common export crop interventions across Africa, with the state controlling pricing, distribution, and marketing. Marketing boards typically set fixed prices that applied throughout the year in all growing areas, and controlled the physical handling of crops. Under the Caisse system, common in West Africa, prices were determined administratively—with purchasing and selling prices set at each stage of internal commercialization (as with cocoa in Côte d'Ivoire). Most of these state interventions have been or (as with cocoa) are being removed.

West Africa's cotton sector continues to be controlled by cotton parastatals (Pursell and Diop 1998). Under this scheme a single producer price for seed cotton is established each year before planting, and the guaranteed price applies throughout the year in all growing areas.[8] Although prices have been more stable, the benefits have been outweighed by the low share of the border price that farmers receive. These countries did not fare as well as other African countries in terms of real producer price increases between 1990 and 1997 (see figure 6.3).

Active support may be required to encourage producer organizations or private firms to enter output and input markets

Wide adoption of market liberalization policies was fueled by the idea that the private sector performs marketing functions more efficiently and competitively than the state. While there have been successes of private entry into markets after marketing boards have withdrawn (as with coffee in Uganda and cotton in Zimbabwe), in some countries the liberalization of domestic markets has not yet lowered the transactions costs involved in marketing export commodities (UNCTAD 1998). Privatization has reduced the role of marketing boards, but it has often not yet managed to improve marketing arrangements for inputs and products, provide access to credit and storage, and increase competition. This suggests that reforms need to be further consolidated, keeping in place gains already made. In some cases collateral reforms needed to facilitate private entry may not have been completed. In other cases active support may be required to encourage producer organizations or private firms to enter output and input markets.

Real Prices for Commodity Exports Are on a Secular Decline

Between 1990 and 1997 several export crops—coffee, rubber, cocoa, groundnuts—experienced large world price increases that converted into more favorable terms of trade for many African countries. This was a welcome upturn after significant price drops in the 1970s and 1980s. But in the last few years many of these favorable cyclical (short-term) trends fell to the downturn of the world market.

The declines hurt African economies, whose agricultural exports continue to be dominated by a few crops. (Since the 1970s nine crops have accounted for about 70 percent of agricultural exports.) Moreover, secular (long-term) price trends toward lower prices for traditional African export crops appear firmly set in place. This suggests that Africa needs both to diversify and to produce agricultural commodities at lower cost—using new technologies—if its position in world markets is not to erode further.

In sum: macroeconomic reform and liberalization of export crop sectors began only in the mid-1980s, and in some places was fairly notional until the early 1990s. In most cases real world export prices for agriculture fell from the mid-1980s to the early 1990s, rose from the early 1990s to 1997, and fell sharply thereafter. A few generalizations can be made:

- Where true export liberalization and macroeconomic reform occurred together in the mid-1980s, export crop incentives were favorable despite falling world prices.
- Where true export crop liberalization did not occur, price incentives remained poor.
- Where governments went backward on macroeconomic reform in the first half of the 1990s, exports started to slow down despite improving world prices.

Africa needs to diversify and to produce agricultural commodities at lower cost if its position in world markets is not to erode further

Further Reductions in Food Costs Require Fewer Market Entry Barriers

State intervention in Africa's food markets has been sharply reduced. Marketing boards have been dismantled, and in most countries market forces now determine prices. East and Southern African governments have generally intervened more in food markets than their West African counterparts, with several countries continuing to set floor prices (Malawi) or ceiling prices on foods (maize meal in Zimbabwe). Food security concerns, still high on the agenda of many African governments, are usually the reason for continuing intervention in these markets. There are high risks of drought, and many domestic food staples (millet, cassava, plantains, sorghum, yams, white maize) are nontradable at current prices and transfer costs (Delgado 1992).

Several factors led to initial market reforms in East and Southern Africa. Grain marketing board costs had escalated to unsustainable levels. The system of input delivery and crop payments had become increasingly unreliable. Parallel markets had developed due to pan-territorial pricing. Increased instability in marketing board purchases and sales added to fiscal demands. And smallholders had limited market access (Jayne and Jones 1997). The common reform package for marketing maize, a dominant

*The greatest
beneficiaries of food crop
reforms appear to have
been consumers—with
smaller marketing
margins and lower food
costs*

staple, included moving farmgate prices toward export or import parity, announcing administered prices closer to the planting times of crops on farms, speeding up payments to farmers, eventually liberalizing prices altogether, relaxing maize movement controls and other restrictions on trade, and restructuring parastatal maize marketing companies (Donovan 1996).

The reforms have had observable impacts, the most apparent being a reduction in the huge fiscal costs incurred by marketing boards. Another impact is a reduction in the cost of marketing food to grain-deficit rural areas, primarily by expanding small trading and milling networks to fulfill the residual grain needs of rural households (Jayne and Jones 1997). In many countries (Kenya, Mali, Zambia, Zimbabwe) opening grain markets to private traders has increased competition and lowered costs in food marketing and processing, reducing marketing margins and food prices (Jayne and others 1995). But some mobility barriers—such as access to capital, energy, and spare parts, as well as political risk—continue to constrain trader entry into market niches (Barrett 1997). The greatest beneficiaries of these reforms appear to have been consumers—with substantially lower food costs.

With the reduction of state production subsidies, producer prices have fallen for many food crops (UNCTAD 1998). Lower producer prices, higher fertilizer prices, the focus on export crop promotion, and the removal of marketing boards have raised considerable debate on food security. Studies on a range of countries (Kenya, Mali, Mozambique, Senegal, Zimbabwe) have demonstrated synergies between cash crop investment and food crop production (Strasberg and others 1999). Still, ensuring an increase in the level and reliability of food staples supplied will require improving food production policies (for example, raising productivity) in some countries and lowering the costs and risks of importing (for example, by lowering transportation and other marketing costs) in others (Delgado 1992).

Fertilizer Policy Reforms: A Mixed Bag

Fertilizer application rates in Africa remain low—on average, one-fifth the rates in Latin America and one-twelfth the level in Asia (see table 6.1). Much of this difference is due to the dominance of rainfed agriculture and the characteristics of the land in Africa (Voortman, Sonneveld, and Keyzer 1998). This average application rate masks great contrasts in fertilizer use across countries, with some (Mauritius, Swaziland, commercial agriculture in South Africa and Zimbabwe) applying fertilizer at the same rate as other developing or even developed regions.

In the late 1970s and early 1980s almost all countries in the region adopted fertilizer subsidies, distorting prices and leading to an unreliable, high-cost marketing and distribution system with a limited choice of basic fertilizers (Lele, Chistiansen, and Kadiresan 1989).[9] Most of the gains from these subsidies went to better-off farmers and intermediaries. Fertilizer reforms began in the 1980s with the removal of these subsidies in nearly all African countries. This, together with currency devaluations and world price increases, caused fertilizer prices to rise, sometimes by 200–300 percent. These high costs have led several countries to backslide on previous reforms, reintroducing fertilizer subsidies.

A key issue in the reform process, one that is not always considered, is the sequencing of subsidy removal. Eliminating subsidies at the same time as major macroeconomic reforms (such as currency devaluation) will exacerbate fertilizer price increases and inhibit the entry of the private sector to fulfill the role of parastatals. Alternatively, removing subsidies at the same time as a reduction in fertilizer import duties would mitigate some of the price increases from subsidy removals.

The private sector has responded weakly to fertilizer market liberalization. A few large private firms dominate the market. Trade restrictions are still widespread, with tariff and nontariff barriers. Some countries impose restrictions on the types of fertilizer that can be imported, along with stringent clearance requirements for imports and specifications for who can import (Gisselquist 1994). Many countries also rely almost exclusively on fertilizer aid to meet their domestic requirements, causing uncertainties in supply, limiting product choice, and disrupting domestic fertilizer markets. In addition, the mechanisms used to deliver fertilizer aid inhibit the development of sustainable private supply systems for agricultural inputs (box 6.4).

The mechanisms used to deliver fertilizer aid inhibit the development of sustainable private supply systems for agricultural inputs

Exploiting the Synergy between Price and Nonprice Factors

RECENT REFORMS HAVE IMPROVED AGRICULTURAL PRICE INCENTIVES. But they have not done as well at addressing other structural and institutional constraints, including rural infrastructure (irrigation,

Box 6.4 The 2KR Aid Program

JAPANESE GRANT AID FOR THE INCREASE OF FOOD Production, also known as the 2KR aid program, provides grant aid tied to the purchase of fertilizer, machinery, and chemicals. In 1996 the 2KR program provided 58 countries with these inputs. Twenty-six African countries received this aid, accounting for about 40 percent of the annual 2KR budget of $260 million. The process of supplying inputs under the program is similar to programs of other donors. Formal requests are made to the government of the donor country, discussions are held to assess the merits of the request and the ability of the donor country to supply the goods, the donor opens a restricted tender for the requested goods, an award is made to the lowest bidder, and counterpart funds are deposited by the recipient country into a designated domestic account upon sale of the goods. The 2KR program has been a significant source of agricultural inputs for the poorest African countries, but several concerns have been raised.

The procurement process has often resulted in a disconnect between the inputs acquired under the program (for example, the types of fertilizer, machinery, and chemicals) and the inputs needed by recipient countries. Inputs acquired through the program typically arrive too late for effective use. Recipient country governments usually distort the domestic markets for inputs received under the program, inhibiting private sector involvement in input (particularly fertilizer) importation, distribution, and storage. In particular, 2KR fertilizers have not been well integrated with the domestic market, being distributed through government channels with the exclusion of the private sector.

Competition in 2KR tendering and procurement is limited. Restrictions on who can participate in the program were most prevalent in the 1980s, when aid was tied exclusively to Japanese products procured through Japanese trading companies. Even today the tendering process appears to be insufficiently competitive, as indicated by the high price of 2KR inputs relative to the cost in competitive markets. Some countries even have difficulties setting up counterpart funds, which vary between one-half and two-thirds of the value of the aid (depending on recipient country conditions). Where these funds have been set up, they have often been used counterproductively.

Changes to the program must ensure the emergence of strong private networks for input delivery and should offer greater transparency and consistency as well as faster delivery.

Source: Tobin 1996; Adachi and Townsend 1998.

roads, power, telecommunications), agricultural research and extension, and farmer education and health—factors that impede agricultural productivity and output (Binswanger 1989). Removing these impediments would require substantial increases in both public and private investments in rural areas. Not only is there a direct effect of public investments, there is also complementarity between public and private investments.

Public Investments in Agriculture: Too Few and Too Inefficient

Data on public spending and investment in African agriculture are hard to come by, but the available evidence suggests that since the 1960s the level of public resources allocated to agriculture has been consistently low relative to the sector's size and contribution to the economy. In most African countries the sector receives less than 10 percent of public (recurrent and investment) spending but accounts for 30–80 percent of gross domestic output.

Moreover, the direct and indirect transfers of income from agriculture to government and the rest of the economy have been larger than the public resources allocated to the sector. Inadequate public resources have constrained the development of rural public goods (infrastructure, institutions, human capital, support services) and the ability of the private sector to develop. In turn, these policies have stifled economic development by forfeiting the strong linkage effects of high agricultural growth on the rest of the economy.

Spending on agricultural research has a potentially high payoff in Africa

Moreover, where public investments in African agriculture have been high, as in a number of countries in the postcolonial period, they have often been misallocated. Or the recurrent budgets to maintain these investments have been low (box 6.5)

African countries that have maintained strong price incentives and developed rural public capital goods and services have enjoyed faster growth—price and nonprice incentives are complementary (see box 6.3). That makes it imperative for policymakers to enhance the price incentives facing farmers and other economic agents in agricultural activities. Policymakers also have to promote rural public goods and services and stimulate private agricultural investments.

Despite High Returns, Research and Extension Remain a Low Priority

We know a little more about public spending on agricultural research, for which donors have typically contributed about 40 percent of the funds (Pardey, Roseboom, and Beintema 1997). These investments have a potentially high payoff in Africa: a recent study finds a median internal rate of return on research spending of 37 percent (table 6.2). But after increasing from $256 million in 1961 to $701 million in 1981, agricultural research spending in Africa dropped to $684 million in 1991.

The consistently high returns achieved in research stations and demonstration plots suggest that such research could contribute greatly to agricultural growth and development. Research continues by international and national agricultural research stations, though with shrinking budgets. But many constraints, including those discussed above, prevent farmers from adopting and internalizing these technologies.

Box 6.5 Problems with Public Investment in African Agriculture

Low public investment in Nigeria. The size and structure of public spending on agriculture have been grossly inadequate in Nigeria, with weak government commitment to agricultural funding worsening after structural adjustment. The share of agriculture in government spending was 1.9 percent during the boom period (1972–80), 3.0 percent during the crisis period (1981–87), and 1.1 percent after structural adjustment (1988–92) (Olomola 1998). Agriculture accounts for about 30 percent of GDP.

Misallocation of public investment in Senegal. An analysis of 79 agricultural projects and programs implemented in Senegal in 1990–95, costing about 3 percent of GDP, provides a good illustration. About 75 percent of the resources were allocated to crops, 15 percent to forests and other natural resources, 6 percent to fisheries, and 3 percent to livestock. For crops the overwhelming share went to irrigated rice. Factors such as agroecological potential, natural constraints, infrastructure development, human resources, institutions, demographics, and an area's contribution to GDP do not seem to have been considered in the regional allocation of public resources—the case in most of Africa.

Maintenance failures in Chad, Ghana, and Senegal. Africa's capital investments are often not matched by adequate recurrent budgets, limiting the maintenance and management of these public goods. Examples abound for roads, irrigation infrastructure, and other public structures. Even where significant investments developed public agricultural capital goods, governments have often not provided resources to maintain them and achieve high standards of management and use.

Irrigation infrastructure suffering from poor management and use is so widespread that it deserves mention. In Ghana, of 18,000 hectares developed, only 33 percent is cultivated; the rest requires rehabilitation to be effectively cropped. In Chad, of 12,000 hectares developed, only 25 percent is used effectively. In Senegal, where large investments were made to develop irrigation infrastructure in the north, the experience is the same.

Why do most African governments put such a low priority on investments in such a key sector? Simple benefit-cost analyses often grossly underestimate the benefits of rural investments, particularly in rural infrastructure (Lipton 1987). For example, rate of return calculations for building new roads usually ignore both the multipliers and upsurge of economic activity that come from resource movement following new road development. But even when there is ample evidence of high returns, as in agricultural research, government commitment is hard to obtain. Political economy issues are a major determinant of government spending—widely dispersed smallholders have a hard time organizing themselves for economic, social, and political purposes. Given the tight budget constraints facing most African governments, expenditures that are not defended by a well-organized constituency will likely be squeezed out, no matter what is known about high returns.

Better Policies Have Stimulated Agricultural Growth

Agriculture has become more competitive as better policies have improved incentives. But it remains undercapitalized. In 1990–97, 25 countries had real agricultural GDP growth rates over 2 percent, with 12 over 4 percent (Benin, Cameroon, Chad, Guinea, Guinea-Bissau, Equatorial Guinea, Lesotho, Malawi, Mauritania, Mozambique, Namibia, Togo).[10] In 1993–97 five more countries joined this group (Côte d'Ivoire, Ethiopia, Mali, South Africa, Zimbabwe). This is a big

Table 6.2 Internal Rates of Return on Agricultural Research and Extension Spending by Region

	Applied research		Extension	
Region	Number of studies reviewed	Median return (percent)	Number of studies reviewed	Median return (percent)
Africa	44	37	10	27
Asia	120	67	21	47
Latin America	80	47	23	46
OECD	146	40	19	50

Source: Evenson forthcoming.

There is still much to be gained from yield improvements in every African country

improvement over the 1980s, when only three countries (Benin, Guinea-Bissau, Togo) had annual agricultural growth rates exceeding 4 percent.

Though Still Low, Land Productivity Is Rising

Between 1980 and 1995 cereal production increased by 3.4 percent a year, mostly from area expansion. Cereal yields improved in 24 countries, and 9 countries had growth of more than 2 percent a year (Benin, Burkina Faso, Cameroon, Central African Republic, Ghana, Guinea, Guinea-Bissau, Mauritania, Mauritius). But there is still much to be gained from yield improvements in every African country. Continuing growth through area expansion is possible in only a few countries, because institutional and economic constraints generally limit access to land.

Labor Productivity Has Increased, Particularly in West Africa

In 19 of 31 African countries agricultural value added per worker increased between 1979–81 and 1995–97 (World Bank 1999c). Agricultural labor productivity in West Africa showed a particularly strong improvement after 1983 (UNCTAD 1998). The use of bovine animal traction has spread in the cotton-maize zones of West Africa, in northern Benin (Brüntrup 1997) and Mali in particular. This was in response to the need for a power source for the profitable cotton-maize technologies being extended. For Africa as a whole there was a dramatic decline in agricultural labor productivity in 1975–84, then a temporary improvement in the mid-1980s followed by fluctuating but generally stagnant levels (UNCTAD 1998).

Export Shares of Several Crops Have Grown, and Diversification Is Starting

Since 1970 Africa has suffered losses in its world market share for agricultural exports—55 percentage points for groundnuts, 27 points for cocoa, and 14 points for coffee (see figure 6.1). But recent trends have been more favorable (table 6.3). The export shares for five of the region's nine main crops (bananas, cotton, sugar, tea, tobacco) rose between 1980–89 and 1990–97, though some increases were small. In addition, many countries in East and Southern Africa (Kenya, Tanzania, Zambia, Zimbabwe) as well as in West Africa (Burkina Faso) have expanded into nontraditional export crops such as horticulture and floriculture.

Policies clearly matter, even where there are serious physical constraints

A Business Plan for Agriculture in the 21st Century

POLICIES CLEARLY MATTER, EVEN WHERE THERE ARE SERIOUS PHYSical constraints. That policies in Africa were poor for several centuries suggests huge unrealized opportunities for further growth in agriculture. Even limited and incomplete improvements have had significant effects. Yet many countries have not completed policy and institutional reforms or are experiencing second-generation problems

Table 6.3 Africa's Share of and Change in World Trade for Its Main Export Crops, 1970–97 (percent)

	Share			Annual change,
Crop	*1970–79*	*1980–89*	*1990–97*	*1970–97*
Bananas	6	3	4	−3.3
Cocoa	59	45	40	−2.0
Coffee	28	22	14	−3.1
Cotton	13	11	12	−0.2
Groundnuts	40	8	5	−10.2
Rubber	6	6	5	−0.5
Sugar	6	6	8	−0.2
Tea	15	15	19	1.3
Tobacco	8	9	12	1.7

Source: FAOSTAT 2000.

associated with the implementation of policy reforms. Private agents have not sufficiently entered input, output, and rural financial markets, and market development and competition remain low. Tariff and non-tariff barriers to agricultural and agroindustrial trade continue to be high, and access to OECD markets is still limited. Public spending in rural areas remains inadequate. The privatization of agricultural parastatals is well advanced, but the decentralization of public agricultural and rural development services is proceeding slowly in most countries, with fiscal decentralization still lagging badly.

All stakeholders need to take part in developing the vision for rural development and agricultural transformation

This section elaborates on key elements of the proposed agenda to capitalize African agriculture, increase its competitiveness, and harness the potential of agricultural growth and rural development. The agenda and business plan must address three key questions: What are the best ways to capitalize agriculture and the rural sector? Where can resources be found to do this? And how can the use of these resources be made more efficient?

Some of the proposed measures consolidate and expand the traditional domestic reform agenda. Others deal with emerging national, regional, and global developments. Many can be undertaken by African countries on their own. Others will have to be taken by their development partners, or in association with them.

All stakeholders need to take part in developing the vision for rural development and agricultural transformation and the broad outlines of the business plan. Roles for the public and private sectors and priorities for public action need to be further clarified through a consultative process. The need for consultation and for dealing with development constraints outside agriculture that could have profound impacts on the sector has been vividly emphasized by the Organization of African Unity in a recent position paper on food security and agricultural development (OAU 1996). The OAU states that the actions to be taken for implementation of this position must "ensure the participation of all segments of society in civil life through participatory and stable political institutions" and "mobilize national, regional and international initiatives to prevent conflicts and to resolve emergency crises" (p. 5). The OAU also suggests that to accelerate agricultural and rural development, the objectives must be "(a) to expand the effective participation of farmers and producers in the agricultural and rural development process; (b) to improve self-reliant food security throughout rural areas through increasing rural incomes; and (c) to promote and facilitate broad-based and more self-reliant rural development, including improvements in infrastructure, better marketing arrangements, access to improved technologies and supporting services and inputs, and more secure land tenure arrangements" (p. 14).

Any business plan for agricultural and rural development must address complex issues. How to strike the appropriate balance between a central vision and detailed, decentralized implementation? How to strengthen capacity and institutions? How to ensure that macroeconomic and agricultural policies do not work at cross-purposes and to devise the appropriate sequencing of reforms? How to implement and finance the plan, dividing responsibilities among development partners (public sector, private sector, producers, and donors)? How to allocate resources within and among sectors and regions, between production types (upstream and downstream), and between economic agents?

Moreover, implementation of a business plan should be continuously monitored and evaluated, and adjusted based on the findings. The assessment should analyze the plan's impact on three sets of impact indicators: agricultural performance (production, productivity, costs, competitiveness, diversification, vertical integration), welfare (food security, nutritional status, poverty reduction, food consumption, consumption of nonfood products, education, health), and sustainability of natural resources (preservation of farmlands, forests, and water). For a recent example of a comprehensive national strategy, consider the development of a framework to modernize agriculture in Uganda (box 6.6).

Huge Investments Are Needed to Capitalize Agriculture

Huge investments will be required to accelerate agricultural growth and rural development. Both the private and public sectors will have to make on-farm, agroindustrial, and infrastructure investments as well as investments in agricultural research, extension, and education (Thirtle, Hadley, and Townsend 1995; Vyas and Casley 1988).[11] Women must be assured access to productive assets and services if the growth potential of these investments is to be realized (box 6.7). On-farm investments include agricultural inputs, livestock, tree capital, soil improvements, irrigation, farm machinery, housing, and human capital. Agroindustrial investments are required for plants, equipment, skills, operating systems, and market development.

Huge investments will be required to accelerate agricultural growth and rural development

Investments will also be required to reverse natural resource and environmental degradation. Agricultural land is becoming extensively degraded, and desertification is on the rise. Soils are continuously being decapitalized. Insufficient investment in soil improvement has led to excessive nutrient extraction through crop production (Scherr 1999). Since World War II degraded soils have caused a 25 percent drop in Africa's cropland productivity (Oldeman 1998). In many countries overgrazing has led to a decline in rangeland quality (Cleaver and Schreiber 1994). In addition, water resources are being depleted and degraded while deforestation continues unabated—with two-thirds of Africa's wildlife habitat already lost (Scheer 1999; Drenge 1990; Sharma and others 1996; World Bank 1996).

Why are these phenomena occurring? Many blame Africa's rapid population growth, combined with the slow adoption of more environmen-

Investments will also be required to reverse natural resource and environmental degradation

---

Box 6.6 Developing Uganda's Framework for Modernizing Agriculture

UGANDA IS DEVELOPING A SECTORWIDE FRAMEWORK to modernize agriculture. The process has involved workshops held throughout the country to hear from all stakeholders: government ministers, members of parliament, government officials, farmer organizations, training institutions, and district officials. In implementing the plan, the government will:

■ Make poverty eradication the overriding objective of agricultural development.

■ Transform smallholder farmers from subsistence to producing for the market.

■ Reduce public sector activities to the extent possible, and support private sector development in all commercial activities.

■ Deepen decentralization of public service provision.

■ Support the spread of profound technological change throughout agriculture.

■ Address food security issues through trade rather than self-sufficiency.

■ Give priority to agriculture as the engine for economic growth and poverty reduction.

■ Improve access to productive assets for women and

youth and empower them to undertake income-generating economic activities.

The plan for modernizing agriculture has been set within the government's medium-term economic policy framework, which aims at maintaining macroeconomic stability with low inflation, rapid and broadly based economic growth, and a viable external balance of payments. This should lengthen planning horizons for savers and investors, create a climate of trust and enthusiasm in the private business sector, and protect the poor against real income losses that would otherwise result from inflation.

The explicit framework identifies priority actions for the public and private sectors and maps out a five-year plan within the overall macroeconomic framework. A joint product of the Ministry of Agriculture, Animal Industry, and Fisheries and the Ministry of Finance, Planning, and Economic Development, the document not only provides Uganda with a framework for action, it also serves as a useful tool for coordinating donor activities.

Source: Government of the Republic of Uganda 1998.

Box 6.7 Ensuring Gender Equality in Access to Productive Assets and Services

WOMEN PLAY A BIG ROLE IN AFRICA'S AGRICULTURAL production, performing 90 percent of the work of processing food crops and providing household water and fuelwood, 80 percent of the work of food storage and transport from farm to village, 90 percent of the work of hoeing and weeding, and 60 percent of the work of harvesting and marketing (Quisumbing and others 1995). Despite their importance in agricultural production, women face disadvantages in accessing land and financial, research, extension, education, and health services. This lack of access has inhibited opportunities for agricultural investment, growth, and income (chapter 1).

For example, giving women farmers the same agricultural inputs and education as men could increase women's yields by more than 20 percent in Kenya (Saito, Mekonnen, and Spurling 1994). And if Zambian women enjoyed the same level of capital investment in agricultural inputs, including land, as their male counterparts, output could increase by 15 percent (Saito 1992).

Thus more must be done to ensure gender equality in access to productive assets and services. Efforts could include providing clean, accessible water to reduce the time burden of domestic work, investing in girls' education, ensuring gender-neutral land policy and legislation, and building women's skills and capabilities to reduce their "political deficit."

Source: Blackden and Bhanu 1999.

---

tally friendly technologies and farming practices. The resulting degradation of soils constrains agricultural growth. Lagging agricultural growth perpetuates rural poverty and food insecurity, impeding the onset of the demographic transition to lower fertility rates (Cleaver and Schreiber 1994, p. 198).

Why aren't farmers adopting new technologies and investing in their soils? Why are the normal intensification processes described by Boserup (1965) and Ruthenberg (1980) not occurring, or not occurring fast enough? Farmers will only make these investments and adopt more productive and environmentally benign farming technologies and practices if it is profitable to do so. The central thesis of this chapter is that poor policies and institutional failures have undermined this required profitability. Under favorable policies and institutions, farmers protect natural resources—Kenya's Machakos district is a well-documented example (Monitimore and Tiffen 1994).

In addition to removing poor agricultural and macroeconomic policies, higher profitability will require increasing investments in notoriously weak transportation and communications infrastructure, as well as in food storage and processing facilities. Farmers will have more incentives to invest if input markets are made more efficient, property rights are strengthened (including formal and informal land tenure arrangements; box 6.8), and investments are made in their education and health and in agricultural research and extension (Crosson and Anderson 1995).

HIV/AIDS presents another significant challenge for African agriculture (chapter 4). The disease not only affects the rural population (primarily through increased deaths, lower labor productivity, and higher dependency ratios) but also the trained human capital needed to plan, design, and implement the business plan for agriculture and rural development. This makes the need for action against AIDS all the more urgent (World Bank 1999b).

Box 6.8 Do Indigenous Land Rights Constrain Agricultural Investment and Productivity?

MOST AFRICAN FARMERS STILL HOLD THEIR LAND UNder indigenous, customary, or communal land tenure systems (not to be confused with open access systems or collective farming). In the past these land tenure systems were alleged to provide insufficient tenure security to induce farmers to make necessary investments in land (World Bank 1974; Harrison 1987). Thus it was thought that the systems contribute to land degradation. But research has shown that such systems tend to allocate secure, inheritable land use rights to families and individuals.

Evidence from rainfed cropping areas suggests that indigenous tenure systems have been flexible and responsive to changing economic circumstances (Place and Hazell 1993; Bruce and Migot-Adholla 1994). Where population pressure and commercialization have increased, indigenous systems have evolved from a system of communal property rights toward one of individualized rights (Migot-Adholla and others 1991).

Individualized rights secured by formal title make farmers more creditworthy and so enhance their chances of receiving credit from formal institutions. So why not short-cut the process and replace customary tenure with freehold tenure, combined with large-scale land registration programs providing title to individual holdings? One reason is that modern land administration using formal title is costly to set up and maintain. Moreover, titling does not always result in secure tenure (depending on the quality of the title and respect for law), because national legislation for tenure reform has limited capacity to change behavior where indigenous values on land persist (Bruce, Migot-Adholla, and Atherton 1994).

Migot-Adholla and others (1991) highlight some circumstances where titling may be worthwhile:
- Where indigenous tenure systems are absent or weak. This is often the case in land settlement areas, but it can also occur after major economic or political upheaval, particularly if traditional lines of authority have been severed.
- Where land disputes are common. This may occur in areas where large numbers of migrants have laid claim to land owned by indigenous groups.
- Where major project interventions are planned that require full privatization of land rights for their success or are likely to weaken the land rights of vulnerable groups. Some irrigation and tree crop projects provide good examples.
- Where population growth and market access have led to an intensification of the farming system, to an individualization of communal tenure, and to high demand for credit from existing credit institutions that could be supported through land title (for example, periurban agriculture).

Where Will Resources for These Investments Be Found?

Most of the needed investments will have to be financed from rural incomes

Foreign aid has declined, and most African countries are not considered creditworthy in international capital markets. Rural financial and credit markets are poorly developed and difficult to establish (box 6.9). Even if such markets were well developed, credit cannot finance the constant and prolonged stream of investment required to capitalize Africa's farmers.[12] And central governments all over Africa are overextended and have to concentrate on absolutely essential public services. Central and local governments already partly or fully finance many investments, including transport infrastructure, water supply, electrification and communications, agricultural research and services, and human capital. But as noted, these investments are insufficient. So, where will the additional resources come from? In addition to removing the urban bias in public investment, most will have to come from rural incomes. But development partners should also reverse declining aid levels.

Box 6.9 Poorly Developed Financial Systems and Limited Credit Systems

A WELL-FUNCTIONING RURAL FINANCIAL SYSTEM CAN help manage the savings and the liquidity constraints of agricultural households and of the wider rural economy. But even with successful financial sector reform, creating viable rural financial systems will take a long time in Africa. The difficulty is particularly severe in low-density areas that practice low-intensity rainfed agriculture and where market penetration is limited by high transport costs (Hayami and Platteau 1997). In such areas rural financial systems face high transactions costs and high seasonality in the supply of deposits and demand for credit, as well as covariant risks in their lending portfolios. This suggests that, even with good financial sector policies, the expansion of the formal financial system into rural areas will be concentrated in areas with high population density and high potential. (Chapter 5 provides more discussion on improving access to financial services such as savings and credit.)

In some areas with well-developed cash crops, a credit system, rather than a full financial system, can be supported by linking or interlocking the supply of inputs and the provision and recovery of credit to agricultural marketing (Dorward, Kydd, and Poulton 1998). Most well-performing formal and informal providers of credit in Africa (and many other developing countries) use this approach. These lenders enter a formal or informal contractual arrangement ensuring that they can recover the credit by subtracting it from the payment due to the farmer at the delivery of the harvest. Examples include the cotton parastatals in francophone African countries, contract farming systems in cotton, tea, and many other export commodities, farmer cooperatives in Kenya, tobacco auctioning systems in Malawi and Zimbabwe, and the credit recovery practices of many informal lenders. But such systems usually cannot be applied to food crops, where the farmer has many alternative ways to market the crop, and contract enforcement is difficult for anyone but the local informal lender.

Most resources will have to come from rural agricultural and agroindustrial incomes. Most investment will have to be financed from the savings of rural populations and entrepreneurs, from cost recovery for services, from taxes levied by decentralized local governments and the central government, and from foreign direct investment. When incentives are favorable, even poor farmers are eager to save (Morduch 1999). Most of these savings take place in the form of applying labor to in-kind investments in land improvements, small-scale irrigation and drainage, growing of tree and livestock capital, and building of housing, storage facilities, and other farm structures. In addition, small farmers will use financial savings opportunities if they are available in or close to their villages. Many of the world's well-functioning rural microfinance schemes mobilize far more savings than they provide in credit to their members.

But farmers and other rural people will not be able to save, pay for services, or pay taxes to local and central governments unless they have high agricultural profits, wage incomes, or other incomes from rural nonfarm activities. Since rural nonfarm activities are driven largely by demands from agricultural enterprises and households, they will thrive only if agricultural incomes and profits are high. And domestic and foreign entrepreneurs will invest in agroindustrial enterprises only if the potential profit from such activities is high.

This is why the business plan to make agriculture and agroindustry more profitable must be pursued relentlessly—through further policy and institutional reforms in input and output markets and better access of agricultural and agroindustrial products to both African and OECD markets. Strengthening tenure security—under customary or modern forms of tenure—will also enhance agricultural investment and productivity (see box 6.8). Agriculture cannot be capitalized without getting tradable agriculture moving, and agricultural and agroindustrial growth cannot occur if producers are confined to narrow local or domestic markets. Only by exporting an increasingly diversified mix of raw and transformed products to cities, neighboring countries, and overseas can producers move beyond the low local demand for basic agricultural commodities.

Implicit taxation of agriculture should be reduced. Macroeconomic and trade policies should seek to reduce implicit taxation from currency overvaluations and high tariff and nontariff barriers to improve agricultural production and investment incentives. Despite reforms, import taxes are still high, levying an implicit tax on agricultural and agroindustrial exports

The business plan to make agriculture and agroindustry more profitable must be pursued relentlessly

(Ng and Yeats 1996, 1998). The threat of higher tariffs is also present. Though actual tariffs are much lower, under Uruguay Round commitments most tariffs are bound at 50–100 percent (Ingco and Townsend 1998). This raises risks for investors.

Strategic public investments can crowd in private business

Reducing the implicit taxation of agricultural commodities and the taxation of nonagricultural imports poses a fiscal dilemma because many African countries depend on these revenues. Agriculture remains the dominant sector in most African economies and so will have to continue to contribute to government revenues. The question is, how? The key principles when formulating agriculture taxes should be nondiscrimination, minimization of efficiency losses, effectiveness of fiscal capture, and capacity to implement (box 6.10).

Public investments should stimulate public-private partnerships. Governments can increase private sector activity by providing public goods. Investments in roads (both quantity and quality) will benefit the private sector in all areas of agriculture (export crops, food crops, fertilizers) through better access and lower costs. Providing electricity to rural areas may encourage private millers and processors (Barrett 1997). Providing key market information (prices, volumes) will also encourage faster responses from the private sector (Badiane and others 1997).

Box 6.10 How Should Agriculture Be Taxed?

FOUR KEY PRINCIPLES SHOULD GUIDE AGRICULTURE TAXES.

Nondiscrimination. Agriculture taxes should not be higher than those for other sectors, and should be integrated with general value added, profit, income, and wealth taxes.

Minimization of efficiency losses. Output and input taxes should be minimized. Land taxes have been suggested as a way to minimize efficiency losses. Although such taxes do not exist in many African countries, agricultural land is growing in value and should gradually be included in real estate taxation. Land or real estate taxes should be assigned to local governments (in the context of decentralization). Only local governments have the detailed information on local land ownership and values needed for effective taxation, and only they have a strong incentive to collect the tax. Commodity export taxes can be replaced by consumption taxes (sales or value added taxes) in countries with sufficient administrative capacity.

Effectiveness of fiscal capture. Income and value added taxes are problematic because millions of small farmers do not have the accounting systems or capabilities to comply with reporting requirements. Land taxes require careful design and local government capacity building. Nevertheless, these forms of taxation will become more important.

Capacity to implement. In many African countries the capacity to implement these new systems will have to be built over many years, during which little revenue will be generated. It may therefore be necessary to continue to rely partly on commodity and input taxes for revenue generation. But tax rates should be lower than in the past.

The financing and implementation of many of these services can be enhanced by public-private partnerships involving central, regional, and local governments. Such partnerships should go beyond private individuals and corporations to include producer organizations, as in the case of agricultural services. They can use many mechanisms—ranging from the privatization of some services and investments (including some agricultural research and extension) to formal partnerships, delegation of execution, and contracting, with full or partial cost recovery.

Development partners should increase aid and improve market access. Recent declines in donor assistance need to be reversed to provide resources for key investments. Given the importance of agriculture to African economies, the decline in research and extension, so central to the green revolution, is particularly disturbing. The decline has been fueled by four factors that suggest a fundamental misunderstanding of the importance of investing in agriculture (Delgado 1996). First, declining world cereal prices have created complacency about food availability. Second, large declines in real prices for Africa's agricultural commodities have cooled enthusiasm for agriculture-led growth strategies. Third, there is fatigue from the lack of a visible green revolution in Africa. Fourth, some think that extensive market reforms in many African countries will somehow solve the problems without further attention from public authorities. These perceptions are misguided. Moreover, aid needs to be provided in the form of program or budget support rather than as balkanized project intervention.

Development partners must also move beyond just providing aid— and improve the access of African countries to OECD markets. OECD and other developed countries have perpetuated trading arrangements that are particularly harmful to African countries, both for exports and imports. These barriers have huge costs (see box 6.2).

OECD countries could take a number of steps to improve market access:

Africa needs better access to OECD agricultural markets as well as development assistance

- Vigorously pursuing agricultural reforms and reducing tariffs, nontariff barriers, and export subsidies.
- Reducing tariff escalation, which has seriously hampered vertical and horizontal integration of African agricultural export systems.
- Including agricultural and agroindustrial commodities in future preferential trade agreements with Southern and West Africa.
- Streamlining phytosanitary and sanitary requirements and refraining from their abuse as market barriers.

201

- Providing technical assistance to public and private sectors in Africa to improve their capacity to apply World Trade Organization regulations and phytosanitary requirements and to strengthen their negotiating skills. African countries must know their rights and defend themselves against external attack. Most African countries cannot afford to take action on unfair trade practices in the World Trade Organization because it is simply too costly. These costs need to be reduced.
- Encouraging foreign direct investment in agriculture and related activities to promote technology and knowledge transfers and make the sector more competitive.

Much attention has to be given to creating representative institutions and transparent financial and political accountability mechanisms

How Can Resources Be Used More Efficiently?

Public investment will continue to be crucial for agricultural and rural development. Poor service delivery and public investment in rural areas have been explained by the urban bias in public spending and by the excessive centralization of the government and parastatal entities responsible for their provision. Many countries (Ethiopia, Ghana, Guinea, Tanzania, Uganda, Zimbabwe) have reintroduced elected councils at local levels. But these local governments need larger budgets for effective decentralized rural service delivery and public investment. The deconcentration of administrative and implementation responsibilities has become a feature of many sector investment programs. But progress in decentralizing and devolving resources and responsibilities remains limited.

Decentralize resources and responsibilities. Improving the fiscal capacity of local governments will require a mix of instruments: the transfer of more elastic tax bases to these jurisdictions, the creation of revenue-sharing funds that transfer funds from better-off to poorer regions and local governments, and the use of cofinancing funds to favor specific investments or groups, such as the very poor. Much of the resource flow should be unified—rather than in the form of balkanized projects—so that local committees and elected councils can allocate among services and investments. For this to work, much attention has to be given to creating representative institutions and transparent financial and political accountability mechanisms.

Improve services for agriculture. Better services are needed for research, extension, transportation, and information on new markets and products—to spur the growth of nontraditional export crops (such as horticulture) and the expansion of exports of value-added products. Some nontraditional exports require focusing on niche markets where timeliness, freshness, and quality are essential. Removing remaining restrictions on air transport could facilitate this process (chapter 5). Even food staples like cassava, yams, and plantains could become major export commodities if efforts are made to develop market niches in industrial countries. This diversification is essential to deal with the secular decline in world commodity prices. Although real prices for nontraditional export crops have declined, their rate of decline has been slower than that for traditional exports.

Reduce trade barriers and seek regional approaches to research and development. African countries need to work together to remove trade barriers and consolidate economic, monetary, and trade areas.[13] (Several such areas are already developing.) Doing so can lead to the pooling of their small markets. It can enable more bulk production and purchase of raw materials. And it can facilitate the realization of other economies of scale.

Moreover, large-scale infrastructure development is often a regional affair in Africa. Regional bargaining power is more powerful than that of any single country, and a good regional reputation can attract more foreign investment. The prevention and containment of livestock disease, so prevalent in African countries, is also a regional affair (box 6.11).

The research capacity of African countries differs widely. Some countries (South Africa) have sophisticated research facilities, while others are just starting to develop limited capacity. As with other enterprises, there are significant economies of scale associated with research and technology development. Most African countries are small, and agricultural production is usually not valuable enough to sustain large agricultural research programs. But many African countries face similar constraints and use similar technologies. Thus it would be useful to develop regional and subregional agricultural research partnerships or institutes.

Current regional efforts at cross-border collaboration, spearheaded by regional research organizations and by the Special Program for Agricultural Research, include the Association for Strengthening Agricultural Research in East and Central Africa, the Southern African Centre for Cooperation in Agricultural and Natural Resources Research and Training, and the West and Central African Council for Research and Development. There has been some debate on who will benefit from these regional partnerships—with concerns about losing market share to other African countries—but the regional benefits will likely outweigh the small compromises that some countries have to make. The

Regional and subregional agricultural research partnerships can provide significant benefits

Box 6.11 Regional Vigilance against Livestock Disease

LIVESTOCK IS PROMINENT IN MANY RURAL AFRICAN economies—Botswana, Burkina Faso, Cameroon, Chad, Ethiopia, Kenya, Lesotho, Madagascar, Mali, Namibia, Nigeria, Senegal, Somalia, Sudan, Tanzania, Zambia. But diseases continue to threaten livestock production systems and rural incomes. Africa has a much broader spectrum of infectious disease among animals than any other region (Coetzer, Thomson, and Tustin 1994). These diseases can be separated into two broad groups: erosive diseases (such as tick-borne disease) and more serious epizootic or transboundary diseases (such as foot and mouth disease, rift valley fever, lumpy skin disease, rinderpest, and contagious bovine pleuropneumonia, known as CBPP).

Epizootic or transboundary diseases are far more important in terms of threatening large numbers of livestock and thereby livelihoods over wide geographic areas. An outbreak of these diseases can result in explosive losses. Examples include the 1995 CBPP outbreak in Botswana, which spread rapidly throughout the Ngamiland area—resulting in about 300,000 cattle being slaughtered as part of the eradication strategy. CBPP affects 27 African countries, causing losses of up to $2 billion a year (Geering, Roeder, and Obi 1999). Foot and mouth disease outbreaks in Angola, Mozambique, South Africa, and Zimbabwe have caused major production losses through the loss of meat and milk production and draught power. Export revenues have also been lost because markets in Europe, North Africa, and the Pacific Rim are hesitant to import animal products from regions where contagious diseases are prevalent.

The most devastating disease impact in Africa was the rinderpest outbreak in the late 19th century. It spread over almost the entire continent within 10 years, killing an estimated 10 million cattle (Geering, Roeder, and Obi 1999). In South Africa the livestock losses from this disease disrupted agricultural production and transportation. Human malnutrition was widespread and, combined with high levels of malaria, caused thousands of deaths. The effect on the social structures of some rural communities was devastating (Vogel and Heyne 1996).

While earlier outbreaks of epizootic diseases have been contained and in some cases eradicated in Africa, their prevalence and distribution remain a serious concern. Cross-border movements of livestock are common and have caused disease outbreaks in many countries. For example, the 1995 CBPP outbreak in Botswana was said to have come from the cross-border movement of Namibian cattle. Transboundary livestock diseases are thus a regional issue requiring regional cooperation and vigilance.

Consultative Group on International Agricultural Research must also continue to play a significant role in improving agricultural technology in Africa (Anderson and Dalrymple 1999). Finally, biotechnology will inevitably become more important globally, and to maximize the benefits African countries will need to build their capacity to identify opportunities, access appropriate technologies, and evaluate the risks associated with their use (Byerlee and Gregory 1999).

Review procedures that discourage a competitive private supply of agroindustrial inputs. Although input markets are subject to fewer constraints than a decade ago, regulatory problems remain—and the commitment of African governments to stay out of markets is not yet credible. So, private firms are still reluctant to gear up for major investments.

Private intermediaries have been slow to enter the field vacated by parastatals, possibly because of the entry barriers that characterize the business climate more generally. In a recent study 60 percent of African entrepreneurs reported that unpredictable rules and policies have seriously affected their business (Brunetti, Kisunko, and Weder 1997), surely inhibiting private sector development. To attract private investment and foster competition, institutional arrangements need to be developed to foster responsiveness, accountability, and the rule of law. As stressed by the World Bank's *World Development Report 1997* (p. 38), "countries need markets to grow, but they need capable institutions to grow markets."

Unpredictable rules and policies are barriers to private sector development

While there is a lot of potential for agricultural and rural development, realizing it will require learning from failed approaches and building on successes (see Delgado 1998a and Cleaver 1997). African countries must develop and own the agenda and take primary responsibility for conceptualization and implementation. Government commitment to implementing a business plan for agriculture is a prerequisite for its success.

Notes

1. Delgado, Hopkins, and Kelly (1998) add consumption-side linkages that arise from the stimulation of demand-constrained nontradables, finding that they surpass production-side linkages by a ratio of about nine to one. The authors find that growth in household incomes resulting from increased agricultural production is largely spent on nontradable items such as services, perishable foods, and locally produced nonfarm goods. Overall the study finds that adding $1 of new farm income potentially increases total income in the local economy beyond the initial $1 by an additional $1, by stimulating local products and services that would otherwise not have a market.

2. There are exceptions: for example, maize and wheat yields on commercial farms in Zimbabwe are much higher than in the United States.

3. Average yields for cereals, cassava, and plantains are 1.2, 8.2, and 5.4 tons a hectare in Africa—while in Asia they are 2.9, 13.1, and 10.1 tons a hectare and in Latin America they are 2.6, 12.3, and 8.2 tons a hectare (FAOSTAT 2000).

4. Agricultural taxes in African and other developing countries were calculated by Schiff and Valdés (1992). In Côte d'Ivoire, Ghana, and Zambia from the 1960s to early 1980s the average direct taxation was 23.0 percent, indirect taxation was 28.6 percent, and total taxation was 51.6 percent. The indirect component includes the effects of overvalued exchange rates (39.4 percent) and tariffs (25.7 percent). In other developing countries direct taxation was 12.0 percent, indirect taxation was 24.4 percent, and total taxation was 36.4 percent.

Assessing individual commodities and including more African countries, these high taxation rates were corroborated by Nikolaus, Herrmann, and Günther (1996) for cocoa, Herrmann (1997) for coffee, and Pursell and Diop (1998) for cotton.

5. Because these scores are based on analysis of decisionmaking powers at different administrative levels (school, district, administrative region, state, central government), they are free of biases associated with country size.

6. Data for each country are based on the percentage change in the real producer price of export crops. The aggregate price changes were derived as a weighted average of the major export crops. World Bank (1994) included other countries in its analysis, but reliable price data for these other countries were not readily available for 1989–91 to 1995–97.

7. These price trends are largely consistent with those in UNCTAD (1998). The period used by that report in a similar representation of prices (chart 20, p. 164) is from 1981–83 to 1992–94 for individual (mainly food) crops. Much of that report's discussion is based on price trends in three groups of countries: "newly liberalized," "continued intervention," and "continued liberalization." The groupings were based on country status in 1992. Trends in export crop prices are examined for each group from 1970. Interpretation of these trends is difficult because the implicit assumption used is that countries have remained in their 1992 status for more than 20 years, which is not the case. A more instructive method would be to take trends in prices before reforms and after reforms on a country by country basis—a method used by Gardner (1995).

8. A second payment is made based on the difference in weight at purchase and factory, and on primary marketing activities performed by farmer organizations. In recent years additional payments have been made in some countries based on the actual lint export price, or if the parastatal's profits were higher than expected for the season.

9. Explicit fertilizer subsidies were widespread—25 percent in Malawi, 46 percent in Senegal, 50 percent in Cameroon, 60 percent in Tanzania, and 85 percent in Nigeria (in 1982/83 prices; Lele, Christiansen, and Kadiresan 1989). Implicit subsidies were also prevalent because almost all countries had an overvalued currency. The magnitude of these subsides placed huge direct pressure on government budgets.

10. Some of these growth rates may be overestimated due to the extensive drought in 1991/92, which had a significant impact on output, especially in Southern Africa. Agricultural output was thus increasing from a low base.

11. Thirtle, Hadley, and Townsend (1995) show that these investments are significant determinants of output and productivity growth in Africa. Vyas and Casley (1988) suggest the need to also develop technologies, institutions, and

marketing structures appropriate to the development of intensive agricultural production systems.

12. First, in a risky sector such as agriculture, debt-equity ratios have to be quite low, implying substantial investment out of savings. Second, credit has to be repaid, making a strategy based on credit, rather than savings, unattractive given the high real interest rates likely to prevail in most African countries for the foreseeable future.

13. Noxious cereal export bans—slapped on at will by local authorities—are an example of these trade barriers. Such bans are retarding growth in many high-potential but remote areas that have a natural market in another country (Mali, Mozambique, Tanzania, Zambia).

Diversifying Exports, Reorienting Trade Policy, and Pursuing Regional Integration

Africa has huge potential for more diversified production and exports, including in agroprocessing, manufacturing, and services

TO SUCCEED IN THE 21ST CENTURY, AFRICA HAS TO become a full partner in the global economy. The region accounts for barely 1 percent of global GDP and about 2 percent of world trade. Its share of global manufactured exports is almost zero. Over the past 30 years it has lost market shares in global trade—even in traditional primary goods—and failed to diversify on any scale. Africa thus remains almost totally dependent on its traditional export commodities—despite their low income elasticity and declining and volatile terms of trade. Continuing concentration on these traditional exports would have adverse consequences for income and employment, even more so given the speed of rural-urban migration (chapter 1). Had Africa maintained the share of world trade it had in the late 1960s, its exports and income would be some $70 billion higher today.

But Africa has huge potential for more diversified production and exports, including in agroprocessing, manufacturing, and services. The more successful African economies have already begun to diversify and make themselves more attractive business addresses. For some, nontraditional exports—including floriculture, other nontraditional agricultural goods, and nontraditional industrial products—have been growing by 30 percent a year since the mid-1990s, albeit from a low base. Tourism has also grown rapidly. And better-managed economies have been attracting higher foreign direct investment.

The challenge: to sustain the momentum of diversification in some cases and to initiate it in others. Given the region's tiny and fragmented economies—with a median GDP of barely $2 billion—the issue is not whether Africa should be quickly integrated, both regionally and with the global economy. The question is how, for much still needs to be done to make African economies competitive (see Helleiner forthcoming and Collier 1997, 1998). Trade reforms are important, but much more is needed. The six most pressing policy actions:

- *Anchor export orientation on competitive and stable real currencies.* Africa's comparative advantage in exports should be based on sustained real exchange rate competitiveness until economies are sufficiently developed to support a productivity-induced real currency appreciation.

- *Make trade reforms credible and effective.* This would require eliminating the most damaging aspects of the remaining antiexport bias—by administering effective compensating mechanisms to exporters, cutting red tape, and ensuring best practice customs clearance.

- *Integrate further trade policy reforms with national "business plans" for economic diversification.* For many countries that means further moderating tariff peaks, rationalizing exemptions, and taking other steps to ensure effective supply responses. The business plans should cover infrastructure, public service delivery, human capital development, stable and competitive exchange rates, and investment strategies—especially for small and medium-size enterprises. They should also broaden the domestic fiscal base away from trade taxes, so that reform is not destabilizing in macroeconomic terms.

- *Mainstream regionalism in a new way.* Open regionalism would enlarge economic space and lock in trade and other reforms to boost their credibility—and regional convergence criteria would be negotiated for macroeconomic, regulatory, and infrastructure reforms.

- *Create a platform for effective African participation in multilateral forums such as the World Trade Organization.* Such forums are essential for underpinning the credibility of reforms and for enforcing "appropriate" global standards, which are becoming prerequisites for accessing markets in developed countries.[1] But African countries also need to help shape these standards.

- *Base all this on consultative processes.* Underlying many of these actions are the relations between business and government and between labor and government. Too few governments have forged a supportive and consultative relationship with the private sector—one in which the government is accountable for service standards, and business for per-

Given the region's tiny and fragmented economies, the issue is not whether Africa should be integrated—but how

formance. In the same vein, the cooperation and support of the labor movement have always been critical to successful and sustainable development policy. In many countries closer consultation with labor will be needed in the new era of globalization, democracy, and participatory politics.

Why Should Africa Diversify?

Without broad and growing markets, investment will not be attracted to Africa

THE NEED TO DIVERSIFY AFRICA'S ECONOMIES, PARTICULARLY TO increase the weight of industry, has preoccupied the region's governments for many years. Diversification is indeed a valid concern. Africa's urban population will triple by 2025. Urban growth and agglomeration create opportunities for new types of economic activity by lowering transactions costs, concentrating consumer power and skilled labor, and facilitating dense producer networks. But providing employment for rapidly growing urban population will be an enormous challenge—as will creating a productive urban economic base to support the infrastructure investment needed to make cities attractive places to live and invest.

Export diversification has received less attention but is equally vital for two reasons. First, export receipts are needed to finance imports of consumer, intermediate, and capital goods. But receipts have been limited by lost trade shares for traditional products and by concentration on a few primary commodities with low demand elasticity. The prices of these staples, though volatile, are expected to continue their long-run decline. Second, given Africa's small economies, it is hard to imagine a successful diversification drive based solely on domestic markets. For the same reason, exports—especially of industrial and nontraditional products—provide the best avenue for attracting high and productive investment. As the experiences of other developing regions suggest, the virtuous circle begins with investment, which triggers higher and sustained growth, increased voluntary savings, and further investment (UNCTAD 1998; Helleiner forthcoming; Rodrik 1996; Agosin 1997). But without broad and growing markets, investment will not be attracted to Africa.

African countries are not just small—they also have a history of high trade restrictions and low domestic competition, and are far behind on global technology (chapter 5). This suggests that African firms are even more likely to see productivity gains from exporting than firms in other regions:

- In many lines of activity the minimum efficient plant size is large relative to the domestic market. Thus exporting can make plants more productive by raising capacity use.
- Competition has historically been low in African markets. Exporters are likely to be exposed to greater competitive pressures than producers for the domestic market—and so are likely to be more efficient.
- Exporters learn from their buyers. Exporters of basic products gain by learning to process large orders, meet quality standards, and make timely deliveries. Even though this transfer of technology may not be at the upper end of the scale, it allows producers to establish reputations with buyers that lead to transfers of technology, product, and management knowledge.

Exporters in Africa are typically about 20 percent more productive than nonexporters

Firm-level studies provide support for these propositions—exporters in Africa are typically about 20 percent more productive than nonexporters (box 7.1). But most analyses of export diversification assume a sizable manufacturing base, true for only a limited part of Africa. South Africa's strong manufacturing base, created through import-substituting and strategic industrialization, is shifting toward a more competitive, export-oriented focus. Côte d'Ivoire, Ghana, Kenya, and Zimbabwe have

---

Box 7.1 Gains from Exporting in Africa

ARE AFRICAN EXPORTERS MORE PRODUCTIVE THAN nonexporters? The answer seems to be yes. Bigsten and others (1998) find that among manufacturing firms in Cameroon, Ghana, Kenya, and Zimbabwe, exporters have much higher technical efficiency. Exporting also increases efficiency over time. Small local markets and technological backwardness appear to make the export experience more advantageous; it is not simply the case that exporting firms are the most efficient firms to start with.

Mengistae and Pattillo (1999) find other differences between exporters and nonexporters. The aver-

age exporting firm is not much older than the average nonexporter, but it has almost three times as many employees. Thus it seems that exporting allows firms to break the scale barriers imposed by small markets. Capacity use is also higher for exporters. And external links through ownership or trade, though generally low among African manufacturers, are significantly stronger for exporters. At 20 percent, the average share of foreign ownership for exporters is three times higher. An exporting firm is also about twice as likely to hold a foreign license and almost three times as likely to have a foreign technical assistance contract.

manufacturing bases that need consolidation and expansion. Many other countries still need to create the essentials.

Will an open trade regime with an export-oriented strategy increase investment in manufacturing without focused government support? And who will invest in African industry lacking a base of strong small and medium-size enterprises? Such questions concern policymakers as they assess strategies for raising output (Rodrik 1996).

Africa can diversify and be competitive across a broad range of products—if policies are improved and transactions costs lowered

The Debate on Africa's Diversification Potential

CREATING A BASE FOR COMPETITIVE INDUSTRIALIZATION IN AFRICA will not be easy. Efforts to replicate the success of industrializers in Asia and Latin America face some daunting challenges, including landlocked states, high transport costs, low economic density, geographic isolation from high-growth clusters, and limited skills and technology (box 7.2). But there are enough examples to show that Africa can diversify and be competitive across a broad range of products—if policies are improved and transactions costs lowered. This is starting to

---

Box 7.2 Challenges for Competitive Industrialization in Low-income Africa

- Africa's comparative advantage lies chiefly in low labor costs (and sometimes low raw materials and energy costs). But with global competition, these lower-order comparative advantages have become less important.
- Africa's main competitive strengths are in industries where demand growth is slowest and where international competition—especially from low-cost Asian suppliers—is intense.
- The region's economies are not part of a cluster, so there is no Hong Kong (China), Japan, or Singapore to undertake foreign direct investment on the scale seen in East or Southeast Asia.
- African countries are at a serious disadvantage in infrastructure costs, especially for transport.
- They are at the bottom of the global league in

industrial sophistication and technology.
- The private sector is weak, dominated by a few multinational corporations at one extreme and by a mass of small enterprises at the other. The middle layer of medium-size indigenous firms is missing.
- "Technological terms of trade" have shifted against late-starters. The cost of acquiring new technology has risen both in money and, more important, in the skills of operators, technicians, and managers.
- The importance of labor quality in attracting foreign direct investment counts against Africa.
- The region has become excessively and unsustainably dependent on external support, including that for foreign technology and expatriate skills.

Source: UNIDO 1996.

212

happen in Africa's better-managed economies, and evidence suggests that reforms can have substantial catch-up effects. Still, can Africa expect to have a comparative advantage in labor-intensive products, including manufactures, rather than resource-based primary products?

The Resource-based Thesis

Adrian Wood and his research associates (Wood 1997; Wood and Mayer 1998; Wood and Berge 1997) argue that in an era of globalization and integrated capital markets, physical investment is likely to be an outcome rather than a cause of comparative advantage. Instead, natural resources and human capital are likely to be the main determinants of comparative advantage. Africa is richer in natural resources—but poorer in human capital—than any other region, with ratios corresponding to those of Latin America in the 1940s or 1950s.

Africa is richer in natural resources—but poorer in human capital—than any other region

This analysis predicts that Africa will find it hard to acquire a strong comparative advantage in processed primary exports and harder still to develop manufactured exports. Even with more education, improved infrastructure, and better policies, the share of manufactures in exports will remain far lower in Africa than in Asia, where natural resources per capita are far lower. Thus the way forward for Africa in the medium term is mainly to raise primary exports, both processed and unprocessed. Even so, one-third of African countries have considerable potential for manufactured exports.

But the resource-based thesis has been challenged by several scholars:

- *Resources are poorer than believed.* Bloom and Sachs (1998) argue that Africa's resource base is weaker than supposed. In their view specialization in agriculture is not a viable development strategy. The implication is that labor-intensive manufactures will provide the best poverty-reducing growth strategy if Africa takes steps to reduce the constraints of adverse geography, especially by improving transport infrastructure.
- *High transactions costs shape Africa's economies.* Collier (1997, 1998) observes that the resource-based thesis must operate by making African labor noncompetitive for manufacturing. But Collier argues that evidence does not support this. Africa's extensive natural resources have not translated into higher labor costs. Instead, Africa is poor, undercapitalized, and uncompetitive in transactions-intensive activi-

ties such as manufacturing. Poor policies and weak institutions have led to exorbitant transactions costs, while repeated policy failures and reversals have led to high risk. These, rather than resource wealth, are the key constraints to growth and diversification.

- *Overvalued and unstable real currencies remain a threat.* Williamson (1997) and Elbadawi and Helleiner (forthcoming) argue that a real exchange rate–led export diversification strategy remains relevant for different reasons than in the pre-1980s, when real exchange rates became overvalued due to controls and unsustainable and expansive macroeconomic policies. Because most African countries depend on official development assistance and few are poised to tap global capital markets, the region's economies will be increasingly susceptible to real currency overvaluation and instability. While these flows are essential to support investment and diversification (Collier 1997), their effects on economywide competitiveness can be damaging without an explicit strategy for protecting the real exchange rate. As Chile's recent experience makes clear, such a strategy is essential for successful export orientation (Williamson 1997; Hernandez and Schmidt-Hebbel 1999).

Even while increasing traditional exports, African countries should have considerable scope to diversify

What can be learned from this debate? Even if geography and climate limit African agriculture, the region is still performing well below its potential in this area (chapter 6). And there is no reason Africa should not fully exploit its comparative advantage in agriculture and minerals while also diversifying into (and deepening) other labor-intensive exports. A careful review of the debate suggests a broad consensus that, even while increasing traditional exports, African countries should have considerable scope to diversify. Many are poised, in the medium to long run, to significantly widen their comparative advantage—if they address the policy distortions (including those associated with uncompetitive or unstable real exchange rates), poor infrastructure services, and high risks and high transactions costs (including those due to corruption) that inhibit competitiveness. Indeed, business surveys carried out in 1996–97 for a large number of African countries indicate that in most cases these factors, rather than excessive wages or labor market rigidities, are seen as the prime barriers. (South Africa is a notable exception.) But the above studies also suggest that in many countries Africa's industrialization is likely to be closely linked to natural resource endowments rather than simply composed of "footloose" industries.

Recent Evidence

These conclusions are buttressed by recent trends in export diversification. The performance of nontraditional exports in eight African countries in 1994–98 suggests three encouraging patterns (table 7.1). First, in most cases the range of the new exports is quite wide. It includes diverse processed primary products, a few new agricultural exports, manufactures, and, in Uganda, gold.

Second, though starting from small bases, growth of nontraditional exports has been quite rapid in most of the eight countries. Even with gold exports excluded, nontraditional exports from Uganda grew by more than 70 percent a year, accounting for 22 percent of exports by 1998. Nontraditional exports from Ghana, Madagascar, and Mozambique have also shown impressive growth. In Ghana and Mozambique nontraditional exports now account for nearly one-fifth of exports. Most important, the growth in Ghana was mainly accounted for by exports of processed and semiprocessed products. In Madagascar the share of nontraditional exports soared to 86 percent. Côte d'Ivoire, Zambia, and to a lesser extent Senegal have also seen considerable export diversification, notably in product lines related to their natural resource bases.

Many African countries have seen rapid growth in nontraditional exports

Table 7.1 Nontraditional Exports from Selected African Countries, 1994–98 (percent)

Country	Share of total exports		Average annual growth (in current dollars)
	1994	*1998*	
Côte d' Ivoire	13.5	17.4	16.4
Excluding processed cocoa, coffee	6.9	8.8	16.2
Ghana	9.7	19.2	35.5
Processed and semiprocessed	6.3	15.2	42.1
Madagascar	64.1	86.1	11.9
Export processing zone	14.3	37.4	32.2
Mauritius[a]			
Export processing zone	67.2	68.9	2.9
Mozambique	5.6	17.8	50.3
Excluding processed cashews	3.5	10.1	47.1
Senegal	11.5	13.3	9.3
Uganda[a]	5.6	34.9	101.5
Excluding gold	5.6	21.6	72.2
Zambia[b]	14.7	33.0	16.5

a. Data are for 1994–97.
b. Nonmetal exports.
Source: World Bank data.

African countries can attract labor-intensive manufactures

With better policies and an improved economic environment, Africa's comparative advantage in natural resources and diverse cultures has started to pay dividends in terms of new commodity and services exports. For example, horticulture exports from several African countries have jumped to more than $2 billion a year (chapter 6), while tourist arrivals have been increasing at rates well above world averages (box 7.3). The potential of tourism is suggested by its 20 percent annual growth in Tanzania.

Third, there is evidence that African countries can attract labor-intensive manufactures. With rising labor costs, Mauritius has probably approached its limit in terms of textile exports (see table 7.1). But there is good news: Mauritian firms are trying to surmount this problem by investing in poorer African countries (box 7.4).

This is significant for Africa because a powerful force in East Asia's development has been the "flying geese" phenomenon—as leading countries have advanced on the technology and wage scale, labor-intensive activities such as garments and toys have moved to poorer countries. Mauritius shows that the geese can fly in Africa too. Confirming business surveys, recent international comparisons suggest that high labor costs are

---

Box 7.3 Chances and Challenges for Tourism

WITH ITS WIDE SPACES, SPECTACULAR WILDLIFE AND natural resources, and rich and varied cultures, Africa has tremendous potential for tourism. Moreover, indigenous ownership of tourism facilities is quite high. But according to the World Tourism Organization, Africa attracted less than 4 percent of the world's tourists and accounted for just 2 percent of international tourism receipts in 1997. Only South Africa was among the 40 top tourism destinations in 1998.

The region is gaining momentum, however. In 1988–97 world tourism grew 5 percent a year—but Africa's growth was 7.2 percent, second only to East Asia and the Pacific. And in 1997 Africa had the fastest growth in tourist arrivals (8.1 percent). The World Travel and Tourism Council estimates that travel and tourism accounted for more than 11 percent of Africa's GDP in 1999 and projects growth of more than 5 per-

cent a year (in real terms) over the next 10 years, outstripping global tourism growth of 3 percent.

Africa can do even better if governments and the private sector cooperate to eliminate impediments to tourism. Though largely a private activity, tourism needs public support through security, infrastructure development, and efficient visa and immigration procedures. For European and North American tourists, Africa remains the most expensive place to fly, largely because of a highly regulated and inefficient air transport system. In many countries visa processing and immigration formalities are a nightmare. Regional cooperation could help—at some borders, tourists and their luggage are forced to change buses because of protection of the local travel industry. And does it make sense for a tourist wishing to visit West Africa to secure separate visas for each of the region's 16 small countries?

no longer a major problem in most African countries, suggesting that more "flying geese" may be landing in Africa in the future. In Kenya, for example, labor productivity in multinational firms is comparable to that in non-African countries—but nominal wages are lower (Biggs and others 1996). Efforts to develop and upgrade skills are critical, but in many countries labor would be relatively competitive if other obstacles to business were reduced. And after a slow start, developments in Africa's subregions stand to intensify intraregional investment.

After a slow start, developments in Africa's subregions stand to intensify intraregional investment

A Simulation Exercise

The discussion here suggests that the factors inhibiting diversification into exports of nontraditional commodities and services are similar to those explaining Africa's low growth. They include human resources (including healthy and skilled workers), factors that affect transactions costs (including governance and infrastructure services), policies that ensure a stable and competitive macroeconomic environment, and geographic factors. Some of the geographic factors, such as being landlocked or having a low population density, are most damaging when they inter-

Box 7.4 Are the Geese Flying in Africa?

THE MAURITIAN EXPORT PROCESSING ZONE EXPORTS more than $1 billion a year in textiles and apparel. Its firms are 75 percent owned by local capital. Floreal, the largest textile maker, has gone from a labor-intensive knitting company in 1971 to an integrated spinning, knitting, dyeing, and finishing company with showrooms in Paris, London, New York, and Hong Kong (China). In 1989 Floreal started shifting labor-intensive parts of its business to continental Africa, first manufacturing knitwear in Madagascar—where the export processing zone, dominated by textiles, has created more than 55,000 jobs—then opening plants in Mozambique. With 17,000 workers, Floreal is assessing opportunities for expansion elsewhere in Africa.

With pay levels three times those in poor countries, Mauritius must position itself to become a center for capital- and skill-intensive operations such as design,

marketing, and logistics, complementing such "software" with the "hardware" from emerging African exporters. Just as Hong Kong needed China to grow, so Mauritius needs such countries to widen its economic space and keep its industries globally competitive. East Asia's development was spread and accelerated by the "flying geese" pattern, involving similar transfers of labor-intensive stages of production from richer to poorer neighbors. Africa can attract labor-intensive activities and make the geese fly.

But investors still see the usual obstacles. Heightening the urgency of strengthening African competitiveness in textiles is the abolition of the Multi-Fiber Arrangement on 1 January 2005. Guaranteed access to major markets, including through a renewed Lomé Convention and a liberal U.S. Africa Growth and Opportunity Bill, would help Africa compete.

Figure 7.1 Simulated Annual Values of Industrial and Processed Exports by a Median Africa Country

Billions of dollars

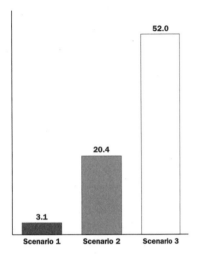

Note: Scenario 1 shows results if the median African country were to achieve East Asian exchange rate policies and transactions costs. Scenario 2 shows results if the median African country were to achieve East Asian exchange rate policies, transactions costs, and investment and education levels. Scenario 3 (directly attainable only by African coastal countries) predicts potential coastal Africa's industrial and processed export values if it achieved scenario 2 as well as East Asian population density along the coast.

Source: Elbadawi and Soludo 1999.

act with other variables—being far from the sea, for example, is a bigger problem if transport services are poor.

Elbadawi and Soludo (1999) estimate the relative effects of these variables across 32 developing countries—22 of them in Africa—to account for country shares of a broad range of industrial and processed exports relative to total exports of the same type of products by the 32 countries (figure 7.1). The export shares are assumed to be explained by four sets of variables:

- Geography and natural endowments, proxied by the percentage of land in the tropics and an interaction term combining the percentage of land on the coast and the population density at the coast. This term measures the potential for facilitating trade through ports.
- Development variables—capital and skilled labor endowments, with investment and primary education used as proxies.
- Two important policy indicators: the misalignment of the real exchange rate and its variability.
- Transactions costs are proxied by three indicators: paved road density as an indicator of infrastructure, the average cost of telephone calls to a global economic center (the United States) to gauge ease of communications, and a corruption index to capture the quality of public services.

The results confirm that geography affects the share of industrial and processed exports. Tropical location reduces the share, while a large, densely populated coast increases it. But other factors matter a lot, and reduce the role of geography. Higher investment and greater primary school enrollment are associated with higher industrial and processed export shares, as are better infrastructure and communications (roads and telephones). Corruption is associated with a smaller share of industrial exports. Consistent with international evidence (Helleiner forthcoming), real exchange rate overvaluation and variability can also lower industrial and processed exports.

Given the constraints of geography, what are the prospects for Africa to increase its market share in industrial and processed exports? To answer this question, Elbadawi and Soludo (1999) generate three illustrative scenarios. First, if the median African country were to adopt East Asian exchange rate policy and attain that region's transactions costs, its annual industrial exports would reach $3 billion (see figure 7.1). This would be a significant jump from the minuscule $28 million in industrial and processed products now being exported by the median African country. Moreover, it should be possible to attain the simulated levels of exports in a relatively short period given that a better macroeconomic environment and lower transactions costs could be achieved fairly quickly.

Second, should the median African country also attain East Asian investment and education levels, its industrial and processed exports would reach $20 billion a year in the medium to long run. Geography does not seem to be an insurmountable obstacle to diversification—the catch-up effects unleashed by sound policies, especially when augmented by strategies to retain and attract investment and invest in people, seem very strong.

Third, the simulations suggest that coastal countries have more options because of their more favorable location. Were it to benchmark policies and development variables on East Asian levels and achieve East Asian coastal densities (an unlikely outcome), the median African country would achieve industrial exports of $52 billion (figure 7.2).

True, any such estimates can only be taken as illustrative. But the central point of the simulations is that despite the constraints of geography, a lot can be done. And with appropriate integration, the dynamic spillover effects from big coastal countries could shorten the catch-up time for the median African country. The results also define the challenges facing policymakers in Africa. With knowledge of what is possible, countries need to design and implement national policies and regional cooperative arrangements to achieve their goals.

Figure 7.2 Aspects of Africa's Geography

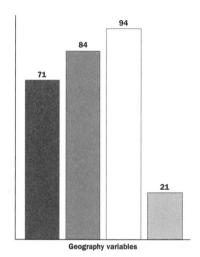

Percent

Geography variables

■ Population in African countries with coastal land/African population
▨ GDP of African countries with coastal land/African GDP
☐ Average density of population within 100 kilometers of the sea (people per square kilometer)
▨ Coastal population density in Africa/coastal population density in East Asia

Source: Elbadawi and Soludo 1999.

A Business Plan for Export Diversification

HAVING POTENTIAL IS ONE THING. REALIZING IT IS ANOTHER. Realizing Africa's export potential requires actions on several fronts—appropriate and stable real exchange rates and other policies to foster openness and economywide competitiveness, complementary measures to strengthen the supply response and raise international competitiveness, and measures to widen economic space through open regionalism and multilateralism. These measures go well beyond trade, but trade policy is the focus here.

Sustaining Competitive and Stable Real Exchange Rates

Real exchange rates are central to the business plan for diversifying exports. International evidence suggests that the real exchange rate is even

Chile's model of real exchange rate–led export promotion offers important lessons for Africa

more powerful for export growth than trade policy (Rodrik 1997; Helleiner forthcoming; Elbadawi 1998). Successful trade policy reforms have usually been accompanied by liberalized foreign exchange rates, drastically reducing real exchange rate overvaluations or parallel market premiums. Recently, however, some countries have seen a surge of speculative and short-term capital inflows, mainly driven by high real interest rates. The outcome has been increased real exchangerate instability.

Africa will have to attract much higher private capital flows in the future. Thus it cannot afford to reimpose sweeping capital account restrictions and so miss out on tapping global capital markets to finance future investment. Maintaining exchange rate stability and competitiveness on the one hand, and creating a hospitable and attractive environment for foreign capital on the other, promises to be one of the key challenges for export diversification and competitiveness.

Malawi and Chile illustrate the challenges and options facing many African countries. Malawi's real exchange rate turbulence is among the highest in Africa. Much of this instability can be attributed to fiscal crises and to pegging the exchange rate at levels that become unsustainable. Two structural elements make matters worse: the seasonality of the country's exports (70 percent are tobacco, mostly exported by three companies) and the difficulty of predicting concessional donor flows (which account for half of foreign exchange receipts). Countries like Malawi could do several things to create more stable incentives for trade: implement a medium-term budget framework to reduce fiscal crises, adjust the nominal exchange rate more often to prevent massive fluctuations, foster competition in the foreign exchange market by easing controls, and work toward diversifying exports, particularly by encouraging manufacturing exports. (World Bank 1999a).

Chile's recent experience suggests that economic competitiveness need not come at the cost of adequate integration with the global capital market. The Chilean model of real exchange rate–led export promotion offers important lessons for Africa, especially for countries with more advanced financial and capital markets. Chile has indirectly influenced both the type and size of private capital inflows in the context of an essentially open capital account. Long-term capital was encouraged while short-term and speculative capital flows were discouraged, holding aggregate capital inflows closer to sustainable levels.

Despite high capital inflows in the 1990s, Chile did not experience major declines in competitiveness. And unlike many emerging markets, it managed to avoid devastating financial and currency crises. In addition to strong macroeconomic fundamentals, genuine central bank independence has been important for Chile's success in managing capital flows. The Central Bank of Chile, which is responsible for exchange rate policy, has an explicit target for the current account: over the medium term it should be in deficit by 3–4 percent of GDP. This approach has allowed Chile to maintain a competitive real exchange rate that supports rapid growth and export diversification. It has also allowed Chile to avoid financial crisis despite the temptation of massive capital inflows (Williamson 1997).

Africa has come a long way on trade reform—but more needs to be done

Making Trade Policy Work for Diversification

> *There is actually a fair bit of consensus on what constitutes a reasonable trade strategy for countries of Africa. The consensus can be crudely expressed in terms of a number of do's and don'ts: de-monopolize trade; streamline the import regime, reduce red tape and implement transparent customs procedures; replace quantitative restrictions with tariffs; avoid extreme variation in tariff rates and excessively high rates of effective protection; allow exporters duty-free access to imported inputs; refrain from large doses of anti-export bias; do not tax exports too highly.*
> —Rodrik 1997, p. 2

How far have Africa's trade reforms come? Measured against these criteria, quite a long way. Quantitative restrictions, once widespread, have been replaced by tariffs. These tariffs have been steadily lowered in most countries, and their dispersion reduced. By 1998 trade-weighted tariffs in Uganda averaged 10 percent, with the countries of the West African Economic and Monetary Union not far behind. In most countries foreign exchange regimes have been liberalized for current transactions. And there have been significant moves to rationalize exemptions in most countries. What remains as the unfinished agenda?

Policies still discourage exports. African trade taxes and restrictions are still higher than in other developing regions, and antiexport bias is still considerable in most countries. Especially because of the small size of their economies and the importance of imported inputs, this has considerable impact. But countries typically depend on trade taxes for about one-third of government revenue, with half or more coming from tariffs on inter-

Liberalization has been uneven across the region—country–based, and not always compatible with regional coordination

mediate and capital goods. For countries where tariff collection approaches the average statutory rate, reducing tariffs is likely to mean losing fiscal revenue—trade liberalization is unlikely to be self-financing because exports will not expand sufficiently in the short run to permit a large increase in imports. Thus efforts to reduce trade taxes cannot proceed independently of measures to strengthen other sources of fiscal revenues.

Liberalization is not locked in. Liberalization is not yet anchored in an ideology, such as export promotion. This is because reforms have been spurred by adjustment programs negotiated with international financial institutions rather than by voluntary multilateral negotiations underpinned by strong national ownership. Donor-driven liberalization is subject to reversal—for example, in response to chronic fiscal and foreign exchange shocks. In addition, African tariffs are bound at high levels under the Uruguay Round. These features make private agents less certain of the credibility and sustainability of reforms. An emerging policy issue is therefore how trade reform can be "locked in" for credibility (Gunning 1998).

Reforms have been country-based, not regional. Perhaps for similar reasons, liberalization has been uneven across the region. Even within such subregional groups as the Southern Africa Development Community, wide variations in tariffs and other regulations make it hard to enlarge the economic space for private enterprise. Country-based reforms are therefore not always compatible with regional coordination.

Compensatory mechanisms for exporters often do not work. Africa is rich in export processing zones, duty drawbacks, exemption schemes, and value added tax rebates, to compensate exporters for tariffs on inputs. But except in Mauritius, these have not worked well. In West and East Africa incentives often leak to nonexporters, while rebates to exporters arrive late or not at all. In addition, key services—such as customs—often operate inefficiently, taking weeks to clear consignments and imposing additional costs on business.

The global frontier is moving rapidly in such areas, with normal clearance times down to as little as 15 minutes in some industrial countries. In other regions where trade restrictions are no lower than in Africa, export processing zones are well established and appear to operate more effectively. One example is Central America, where customs clearance is far faster and service standards are higher. An important reason appears to be the strength of powerful exporters and their ability to hold governments accountable for good services. Exporters are not yet a strong pressure group in most African countries. But governments will need to act as though they were if economies are to diversify.

Completing Africa's trade agenda requires embedding second-generation reforms in an overall export promotion strategy that includes widening economic space and working within—and influencing—the evolving rules of the global trading system. Three measures are important:

- Eliminate further antiexport bias. Because of fiscal constraints, this cannot be done by sharply cutting tariffs across the board. Thus there is no alternative but to focus on getting compensatory mechanisms to work efficiently. Aggressive export promotion also requires attention to service standards in key areas, especially for activities requiring imported inputs.
- Sequence further cuts in import tariffs and broaden the fiscal revenue base away from trade taxes.
- Deepen regional integration, not only to enlarge economic space but also to help lock in reforms. For many countries policy reforms will continue to lack credibility without a lock-in mechanism. This is possible through enhanced use of World Trade Organization bindings, by concluding reciprocal free trade agreements with countries outside Africa, and by harmonizing trade and investment policies along subregional lines.

Attracting substantial investment is the fundamental challenge for export promotion

Introducing Complementary Measures beyond Trade Policy

Trade reforms need to be accompanied by measures that lay a stable base for investment and production. These include effective and noncorrupt tax administration, honest customs administration, working commercial courts, reliable infrastructure (including air transport), and a working financial system (chapter 5). Failure to effect these measures has blunted the investment response to first-generation trade reforms in most African countries.

Lowering costs and risks. Attracting substantial investment to the export sector is the fundamental challenge for export promotion. But with Africa ranked among the world's riskiest place to do business, even retaining domestic savings becomes a challenge. So, the first order of business is for African governments to provide a safe and profitable environment to convince their citizens to invest at home. Investment booms everywhere have been led by domestic capital, including capital repatriated from abroad. In 1990 flight capital accounted for almost 40 percent of private wealth in Africa, compared with just 6 percent in East Asia and 10 percent in Latin America (see table 1.3). Capital flight from Africa and other regions has been caused by factors similar to those that discourage private investment: exchange rate overvaluation, a high-risk environment, and high external debt (Collier, Hoeffler, and Pattillo 1999). Foreign capital follows domestic capital. As noted, high costs for transaction-intensive activities, particularly in manufacturing, and high perceived risks have been among the main constraints to investment and diversification (Collier and Gunning 1999).

Business surveys confirm the high costs of operating in Africa. To some extent this reflects Africa's economic sparseness and the distance of much of its production from the sea. But weak business services, including infrastructure and regulation, are also major impediments to growth in countries that have advanced on macroeconomic and structural reforms (box 7.5).

Box 7.5 Why the Cost of Doing Business Is High in Africa

Local transport. An efficient Nacala rail line and port could save Malawi 3 percent of GDP. A survey in Uganda found that transport and other costs raised the cost of capital goods by 50 percent in 1997; it required 8 or 9 days for intermediate inputs to clear customs after a 30-day journey from Mombasa. Road transport may be twice as costly as in Asia, in some cases reflecting unofficial tolls. Delays at checkpoints in Southern Africa often last as long as a day.

International transport. International transport and insurance charges are higher than necessary for African countries because of restrictive agreements. Air transport is particularly vital given Africa's economic sparseness, the prevalence of landlocked countries, the high costs of road transport, and the promise of new high-value exports such as horticulture. Yet schedules are often inconvenient, and tariffs and handling charges can be twice those for comparable flights in other regions.

Communications. International telephone charges and Internet connections are among the world's most costly. Despite higher investment than in the past, telecommunications reach only a tiny fraction of the population, and waiting times for connections are the longest of any region.

Power outages , bribes, and violence. Ugandan firms lose an average of 91 days a year because of power outages. In addition, the median firm pays bribes equiva-

lent to 3 percent of gross sales or 28 percent of investment in plants and equipment, and bears a similar cost from theft and security charges. Crime and violence raise costs in many countries: a study for South Africa put the effect at 6 percent of GDP in 1996, comparable to estimates for Latin America (Bourguignon 1999).

Trade and tax policies. Despite reforms, tariffs in most African countries are still higher than in more outward-oriented developing countries. And they embody a significant antiexport bias, both for primary products (where the sum of export taxes and import tariffs can exceed 30 percent) and for manufactures (due to high taxes on intermediate inputs and capital goods). Duty drawback mechanisms have proven ineffective except in a few countries, and value added tax rebates are often slow. The effect is a high tax on potential exporters requiring imported inputs.

Slow regional integration. Regional integration has been slow to integrate markets and stimulate internal trade. Some countries belong to more than one regional association and are torn between conflicting obligations.

Restrictions everywhere. In many countries restrictive regulations and practices, often aimed at generating rents for officials and favored groups, constrain business activity, affecting both agriculture and industry.

Even better-managed African countries tend to rank lower on international risk ratings than their policies would warrant. Some countries, such as Mauritius and Uganda, have steadily improved their risk ratings. But others, including Kenya and Zimbabwe, have seen sharp declines in ratings, offsetting gains for the region as a whole. High perceived risks have several causes (box 7.6).

Increasing consultations with business and labor. Any business plan requires developing a supportive, mutually accountable relationship among business, labor, and government. Strong business associations and labor movements can help in this. Some dynamic relationships are starting to evolve in Africa (box 7.7). Much of East Asia's success has been attributed to active interactions between the state and business. The state provided incentives and services, while businesses delivered performance. Close interaction ensures effective feedback and continuing pressure on both parties.

A skilled and supportive workforce is also critical to diversification. Labor needs to be well educated about the pains and gains of reforms, and special efforts need to be made to carry labor unions along. Cooperation and higher productivity are more likely when a consultative process ensures the effective participation of labor in policy formulation, or at least its full understanding of the benefits.

Any business plan requires developing a supportive, mutually accountable relationship among business, labor, and government

---

Box 7.6 Why Risks Are Perceived As Being High

PERCEPTIONS OF RISK IN AFRICA INVOLVE FACTORS beyond political and social stability. On the macroeconomic side, many countries liberalized before containing fiscal deficits, and in some cases this placed greater stress on fiscal management. Many countries have been prone to policy reversals—increasingly associated with elections—and to external shocks. And real exchange rates, real interest rates, growth rates, and fiscal revenues have been unstable through the period of opening to markets (Guillamont and others 1999).

Aid dependence and high indebtedness also increase uncertainty. Large debt service obligations make countries more vulnerable. This is accentuated by "stop-go" patterns of quick-disbursing aid, where big cuts in financing can be triggered by a failure to meet governance standards or structural benchmarks (such as the privatization of a given company by a certain date) rather than by a loss of macroeconomic control.

Surveys of firms also highlight the risks of policy reversals. In contrast to other regions, Africa's trade reforms have been formulated as part of structural adjustment programs negotiated with the World Bank and the International Monetary Fund rather than as part of multilateral negotiations with trading partners. This has meant weaker commitment and higher perceived risk of reversal and incomplete reform.

Box 7.7 Listening to Business

POOR COMMUNICATIONS BETWEEN GOVERNMENT AND business limit growth in many African countries. Laws, rules, and institutions are often inimical to private sector interests. Governments that lack policy credibility have less influence on economic behavior. And a climate of uncertainty and mutual suspicion generates little private investment. There is a bias toward short investment horizons, and economic activity is pushed into the informal sector.

Enterprise networks are growing in West, East, and Southern Africa, providing a voice for emerging African businesses. Several African countries are adopting public-private consultative bodies to facilitate communication, some formal, some informal. These entities enable participants to take joint responsibility for policy choices, and the repetitive nature of the collaboration constrains self-interested behavior. This also helps establish credibility—private participants believe that cheating and reneging are less likely. Politically, these groups serve as proto-democratic institutions, providing direct channels to government for business, labor, and academia. As important, the rules established by the councils cannot be altered arbi-

trarily. As a result members can concentrate on business and not worry about others trying to curry special favors from the government.

Ghana's consultative group was among the first. Early initiatives led to a private foundation as an umbrella organization for business associations. Hostility and suspicion between government and business have been reduced and communications improved. Madagascar, Senegal, and Uganda have set up similar foundations. Cameroon, Côte d'Ivoire, and Senegal have set up competitiveness commissions, with public and private representation.

Consultative groups work best where there is urgency (a deadline) and a well-focused agenda. The focus should first be on policies and regulations that affect the entire private sector. The initial stages of this type of consultation are fragile and require moral and financial support. Open and public consultations increase public involvement and enhance the accountability of group members. These organizations can also act as "agencies of restraint" on government behavior, forming lobbying organizations to ensure support for pro-export policies.

Widening the Economic Space: Regionalism and Multilateralism

Despite past failures and the lackluster implementation of existing schemes, the case for Africa's economic integration remains compelling. There appears to be a widely held view within Africa that African unity could help stem its political and economic marginalization, create new structures out of its colonial heritage, and protect its interests in international political and economic negotiations. These political motivations, supported by the realization that integrated markets are needed for small African economies to develop, explain the continued support for integration in Africa. The promise of pan-Africanism has kept alive the ideals of the Lagos Plan of Action despite serious lapses in implementation.[2] More recently, continental African integration agendas have reflected the desire for even more ambitious economic and political integration—well beyond the Lagos Plan of Action.[3]

Thus the relevant policy question for the next century should not be whether regional integration will be on Africa's economic and political agenda. Rather, it should be how regionalism can help achieve Africa's development goals in a globalized economy. The starting point would be to identify the reasons for the region's rather disappointing record on regionalism.

Why has regionalism failed? Despite a multitude of subregional schemes and the strong political rhetoric supporting them, the results of integration remain modest. Progress on the 1991 Abuja Treaty—which envisions an African economic community—has been mostly subregional. The main schemes are the Common Market for Eastern and Southern Africa and the Southern Africa Development Community in the east and south, the Economic Community of Central African States in the center, and the West African Economic and Monetary Union and the Economic Community of West African States in the west. These arrangements are sometimes overlapping, with countries subject to conflicting obligations. There have also been wide variations in the nature and speed of integration (box 7.8).

Regional integration was conceived as an inward-looking instrument of industrial development—a way to increase intraregional trade and aggregate small national economies into regional markets. But this approach was stalled by several shortcomings, including institutional and political constraints (Oyejide, Elbadawi, and Yeo 1999; McCarthy 1999). First, though regional economies are larger than individual economies, the combined market was still not big enough to support industrial transformation through import substitution.

Second, the inward-looking strategy of industrial substitution had two unintended consequences that undermined regional integration. At the macroeconomic level, policies resulted in overvalued currencies and foreign exchange shortages, forcing a preference for trading partners who offered the best credit facilities. Given that most of these partners are from industrial countries, national industrialization strategies continued to support the hub-and-spoke pattern of trade (Kasekende, Ng'eno, and Lipumba 1999). Moreover, the trade protectionism associated with national industrial strategies led to powerful lobbies and "economic nationalism" that also undermined regional development.

Third, the design and objectives of regional integration schemes have been driven by a preference for formal trade and factor market integration rather than by basic policy coordination and collaboration in regional projects. This has resulted in rather ambitious models of regional integration.

Despite a strong political impetus for integration, integration efforts have had modest results

But Africa's unfavorable structural features—competitive primary production, small size, low per capita income, limited manufacturing capacity, weak financial sectors, poor transportation and communications infrastructure—make these ambitious models difficult to implement.

Fourth, African integration schemes have suffered from implementation lapses—including those due to weak governance. Some states could not cope with a loss of national sovereignty. Other factors include a lack

---

Box 7.8 Progress and Challenges for Africa's Subregional Groups

THE COMMON MARKET FOR EASTERN AND SOUTHERN Africa (COMESA) and the Southern African Development Community (SADC) both underwent significant institutional changes in the 1990s, with potential positive effects. South Africa joined the SADC, and agreement was reached on a SADC free trade area following ratification of the SADC Trade Protocol in 1998. Cooperation is under way on harmonizing financial infrastructure (including payments systems and accounting standards), standardizing and improving bank supervision, and improving management of water resources. In addition, South Africa—which accounts for more than 70 percent of Southern Africa's GDP—has signed a free trade agreement with the European Union, with profound implications for regional dynamics. Independent assessments indicate that the agreement will be largely beneficial to other SADC members.

COMESA has recently been focusing on moving toward a free trade area and supporting regional trade through a guarantee facility to help provide political risk cover. The existence of overlapping and competing groups—COMESA and SADC—is a lingering problem in East and Southern Africa, especially given the similarity of their agendas.

In the west, the Economic Community of West African States (ECOWAS) is the umbrella group for 16 countries. Within it are 10 francophone countries that belong to the CFA zone and have another subgroup—the West African Economic and Monetary Union (UEMOA). Despite the sharp division along linguistic lines, ECOWAS has helped keep the community together. Under its leadership, peace has been restored to Liberia and Sierra Leone. The ECOWAS travelers check—a step toward West African monetary union—was launched in July 1999.

The UEMOA has enjoyed significant achievements. Building on a convertible common currency (the CFA franc) and the relatively free movement of capital, a customs union—to be fully implemented in 2000—will help create a subregional economic space to attract investment.

The UEMOA faces challenges, however. The first is how to cope with the pressures unleashed by harmonized markets, including increased population movements, and revenue losses for some members, such as Burkina Faso. A second is not having the central bureaucracy become bloated and ineffective—the UEMOA includes a subregional court, subregional parliament, and other institutions, and the import duty to finance this is to be doubled from 0.5 to 1.0 percent. The third is to ensure sufficient flexibility to prevent the currency from again becoming pegged at an unsustainable level.

The key challenge in ECOWAS is to build bridges across the linguistic divide and fashion a viable subregional group. Ghana is surrounded by the UEMOA. Nigeria has two-thirds of the population and 55 percent of the GDP of ECOWAS countries. A regional integration arrangement in West Africa that leaves out Nigeria would be like leaving South Africa out of the SADC.

of adequate technical and management expertise, concerns about losing trade tax revenues, and concerns about equitable growth and polarized industrial transformation within the subregion.

The way forward. Given the political, institutional, and other problems that have hampered African integration, especially outside the CFA franc zone, alternative approaches are needed. One is to stress an outward orientation—or "open regionalism"—and a flexible design, based on cooperation between countries, to jointly implement specific projects. These can include transportation and communications infrastructure and investment regulation as well as trade policies (Oyejide, Ndulu, and Greenaway 1999; chapter 5).

Such an approach is not necessarily incompatible with deeper integration. It can provide greater flexibility and serve as a building block for eventual market integration once key constraints to intraregional trade, investment, and labor movements have been eliminated. McCarthy (1999) argues that since the focus is on specific issues, these are depoliticized and present less of a challenge to existing power structures. In time a culture of regional cooperation will develop, laying the foundation for market integration and the acceptance of the loss of sovereignty.

Indeed, since African economies are very small, both individually and as subgroups, the potential welfare gains from freer trade in Africa may be limited, at least in the short to medium term. This raises the issue of whether the principal focus of integration should be on promoting investment rather than intraregional free trade. Creating an economic space where investors can produce for regional as well as global markets may provide small African economies with better growth opportunities than simply removing barriers to trade among themselves.

The Cross-Border Initiative is an attempt to operationalize these principle (box 7.9). As an alternative to "integration by design," where countries are bound by treaty obligations, the Cross-Border Initiative is an example of "integration by emergence." Under the initiative faster reformers set the pace of integration within a framework of harmonized policies that accepts the principle of variable geometry (allowing different groups of countries to proceed at different speeds). Within the framework of a road map for tariff reform—a set of common targets for harmonizing trade policies, but without a treaty—participating countries have made good, if uneven, progress in removing barriers to trade among themselves, while also lowering barriers to trade with third parties.

An outward-oriented integration strategy may be the best approach

Box 7.9 The Cross-Border Initiative's "Integration by Emergence"

UNDER THE CROSS-BORDER INITIATIVE (CBI), launched in 1993, 14 countries in East and Southern Africa and the Indian Ocean have made progress on "integration by emergence." For example, the average trade openness rating of CBI countries—based on an International Monetary Fund methodology, with 0 being most open and 10 being least—improved from 8.3 in 1993–95 to 5.9 in 1998. (This compares with an average of 6.2 for all non-CBI African countries undergoing economic reform and 4.4 for the rest of the world excluding Africa.) Moreover, a few countries—Uganda, Zambia—have made considerable progress toward openness levels (rating of 2) in line with those of global good practice economies (Chile, Colombia, Singapore). Nevertheless, since this approach relies exclusively on peer pressure and example, without any formal treaty-based enforcement rules, the mechanism for locking in reforms may not be robust. And there may be complications arising from overlapping bilateral deals and complex rules of origin.

CBI countries have recently moved toward a more balanced approach, paying more attention to facilitating investment. For example, they have agreed to harmonize tariffs, regulations, and investment promotion policies. This approach combines tariff reform to lower the antiexport bias of trade policies with specific measures to remove barriers to cross-border investment. Specific actions on investment facilitation will be taken within a flexible framework of harmonization of policies, but without formal treaty obligations. The potential benefits of this approach would derive from attracting additional foreign investment—currently just 1.2 percent of GDP for participating countries—to produce for the regional market as well as for global markets, which offer still larger welfare gains.

Regional coordination offers African countries many benefits. It could provide a collective agency of restraint, helping to rationalize trade and investment policies and enhance their credibility. Beyond trade, regional cooperation could provide a multilateral lock-in mechanism for orchestrating convergence criteria on policies, regulations, and licensing. Recent proposals for trade areas with the European Union and the United States have been discussed in the context of the renegotiated Lomé Convention[4] and the Africa Growth and Opportunity Act.[5] Both arrangements call for broader, more reciprocal and participatory economic relationships. Africa stands to gain by developing a coordinated approach to the two initiatives, especially since both entail eligibility criteria for participating African countries. There will continue to be debates on how deep and how fast integration should proceed in Africa and in what areas. For example, in the long run it may be desirable for African countries to adopt a common currency or regional currency zones. But it is not clear how quickly these measures should be or could be implemented. And given Africa's marginalization in world trade, there might be a payoff if countries coordinated in subregional groups in multilateral negotiations at the World Trade Organization.

Africa and the world trade system. The World Trade Organization offers a multilateral forum for Africa to take advantage of a rules-based system for trade and development. Most African countries have acceded to the World Trade Organization, and the millennium round negotiations (which started in November 1999) will offer opportunities—and enormous challenges.

New structures of global governance can increase Africa's market access and clarify its rights in the international trading framework. But they also bring obligations, including giving up a degree of sovereignty over trade and investment. As a consequence of continued global liberalization, there will also be a continuing erosion of the preferences enjoyed by African countries. African countries will incur large financial costs as they create the institutions and implement the myriad standards demanded by the multilateral system. For some least developed countries, implementing World Trade Organization obligations would cost as much as an entire year's development budget. Finger and Schuler (1999, p. 1) note that WTO obligations reflect little awareness of development problems and little appreciation of the capacities of the least developed countries. In most cases standards have been developed with little input from the least developed countries, undermining their sense of ownership. More fundamentally, it is not clear that all of these standards are ideal for the least developed countries, and there is the ever-present danger that they will be used to protect markets.

What does this mean for Africa? African countries will need to pay more attention to multilateral negotiations and try to influence the outcomes. But only Nigeria and South Africa have six or more representatives at the World Trade Organization in Geneva, while about 20 African member countries have no representatives (World Bank 1999b). Multilateral institutions can offer technical assistance, including through the Integrated Framework for Trade and Development in the Least Developed Countries.[6] But a subregional pooling of expertise is essential: small, poor countries cannot go it alone.

Africa can use the multilateral system to achieve clearly defined goals. It can use the opportunity to lock in its reforms and so increase investor confidence. At the same time, it is important that African countries participate in setting the global agenda. They can partner with others to negotiate for the dismantling of restrictive trade practices that inhibit export diversification in poor countries. Three areas are important: agriculture (chapter 6), processed goods, and textiles and clothing. Free trade should work for the poor—as well as for the rich. The next opportunity must not be wasted.

World Trade Organization rule-making should be made compatible with the institutional, human capital, and infrastructure investments required for poor countries to benefit from the global trading system

Managing the Business Plan: The Role of the State

The state should manage structural transformation and help overcome market imperfections

Any serious plan for export diversification should include a strategy for structural economic transformation. Managing this must be the responsibility of the state. Still, nearly all development experiences suggest that even if the state delivers—providing stable macroeconomic policy, strong incentives, the rule of law, basic infrastructure, and the like—an adequate and diversified export response may not come quickly. Why? Because of market imperfections due to a variety of factors—such as incomplete or absent information on consumer tastes and producer needs in overseas markets, on the appropriate technology for producing competitive goods, and on the requirements for penetrating these markets.

The presence of market imperfections—and they abound in Africa—suggests an important role for the state in opening up the economy, either by directly subsidizing activities aimed at internalizing these externalities or by supporting creative institutional designs (such as exporter associations) to achieve the same goals.

Most African states lack the capacity to address these complex tasks. But such constraints will not just disappear. States have to develop the capacity to ease them as they pursue economic diversification. For example, a number of countries have offered matching grants to stimulate firms to acquire new technology and overcome critical thresholds, including information needed to comply with the standards of export markets. African firms cannot yet benefit from large agglomerations of skilled employees and the externalities these provide, so there is a case for subsidizing training. Another possible but debated area is whether to offer tax holidays. Many countries do so, competing with each other as well as with countries in other regions. But statutory tax rates in Africa are often high, and countries might benefit more from moving toward uniform and lower tax rates as tax bases are broadened. These and other selective measures should be approached with caution and should be continuously monitored to assess their effectiveness—in particular, that they do not simply subsidize activities that firms would do anyway. In addition, the experiences of other countries offer a useful guide.

Again, Chile provides a compelling case for a limited but important role for the state in export promotion. Chile and other Latin American countries are more relevant than Asia for Africa, because their endowments also include a rich natural resource base. As Chile makes clear, this does not necessarily inhibit development. In particular, abundant natural resources did not prevent industrialization—but industrialization was built on different foundations than in Asia. Chile's export promotion polices offer three useful lessons for Africa. First, well-managed temporary subsidies could prime the growth of nontraditional exports. Second, foreign direct investment is responsive to activities that open up new export possibilities or introduce new technologies. Finally, a growth strategy spearheaded by a few niche exports can pay handsome dividends (Agosin 1997).

Notes

1. Not all of these global standards—most of which are set by more developed countries—are helpful for Africa. Indeed, achieving these standards can be extremely costly for African countries (Finger and Schuler 1999). Moreover, across-the-board implementation of these global standards could limit trade between developing countries.

2. The Lagos Plan of Action (1980) was a declaration by African heads of states creating four regional groups (including one for North Africa) that would merge into an African Economic Union by 2000.

3. The political will to unite Africa politically and economically was recently put to the test in a September 1999 summit of the Organization of African Unity held in Libya. Some 43 heads of state and government attended the summit to work on a proposal for an African Union, tantamount to the United States, the former Soviet Union, or the European Union. The African Union will have a federal supreme court, a central bank, a monetary fund, an investment bank, and an elected legislature. The union will protect the continent on land, sea, and air and use the congress to help settle disputes between member states.

4. The European Union and ministers of the 71 African, Caribbean, and Pacific countries recently concluded negotiations on a new 20-year partnership agreement that replaces the Lomé IV Convention (which expired on 29 February 2000). The new agreement is based on three pillars—a political dimension, a new trade regime, and development cooperation—and will be signed in Fiji in May 2000. The agreement signaled a radical departure in relations between the European Union and African, Caribbean, and Pacific countries, toward broader and more reciprocal economic relations.

5. In 1999 the U.S. Congress approved the Africa Growth and Opportunity Act. This initiative is aimed at encouraging U.S. trade and investment in Africa by removing quotas and barriers for imports from African countries and establishing a U.S.-Africa free trade area. Political and economic conditions of the arrangement, however, suggest that some African countries may not be eligible to participate.

6. In particular, Elbadawi and Helleiner (forthcoming, p. 20) urge the World Bank to, "assist African members of the WTO to take full advantage of their rights therein and to defend themselves against the assaults of more powerful members." The Bank appears to be prepared to take on this role. In his address to the Seattle, Washington, meeting of the World Trade Organization in November 1999, World Bank President James Wolfensohn called for a "new trade agenda" that emphasizes the complementarities between World Trade Organization rule-making and the institutional, human capital, and infrastructure investments needed for poor countries to benefit from the global trading system.

CHAPTER 8

Reducing Aid Dependence and Debt and Strengthening Partnerships

I N AFRICA MORE THAN IN ANY OTHER REGION, ENGAGEMENT with the international community has come in the context of aid and debt. Africa enters the 21st century in the midst of intense debate on aid dependence and debt relief, two closely related issues. Past borrowing, accumulated into a huge stock of debt, discourages private investment and circumscribes the effectiveness of current and future aid. Relief from debt service payments, by releasing budget resources for other uses, is equivalent to an inflow of resources. It is unlikely that aid or debt relief can be effective without the other.

While debate continues on the best ways to deliver assistance and effect debt relief, there is little doubt that most African countries will continue to need significant aid to achieve the International Development Goals by 2015. As explained in chapter 1, simply preventing the number of poor people from increasing requires annual growth of 5 percent, while cutting the number of poor in half by 2015 will take growth of 7 percent or more. Especially given the decapitalization of Africa's economies, savings levels of 13 percent of GDP in the 1990s are far too low to support such growth rates. Reversing capital flight can bring additional resources and, especially when recovering from conflicts, some African economies have grown rapidly without high investment rates.

But in the long run, even with East Asian efficiency levels, investment of about 30 percent of GDP will be needed. From worldwide experience, private capital inflows of more than 5 percent of GDP are unlikely to be feasible or sustainable. Thus Africa faces a substantial savings gap. Aid cannot be phased out rapidly without high costs in terms of prolonged poverty. Falling aid, by requiring domestic savings to rise sharply, would prevent a rapid increase in consumption and slow the reduction in poverty (chapter 3). Africa also faces new challenges: macroeconomic and structural policies have

It is unlikely that aid or debt relief can be effective without the other

235

improved, but combating HIV/AIDS in a poor country will cost 1–2 percent of GDP (chapter 4).

Aid is no longer business as usual. Political support for aid is waning. Since 1990 foreign assistance from the United States has fallen 20 percent (in real terms) despite a $100 billion cut (in real terms) in the U.S. defense budget (Summers 2000). Relative to donor GDP, net disbursements of official development assistance have dropped almost 30 percent in real terms (O'Connell and Soludo forthcoming). The composition of aid flows is shifting from project assistance and structural adjustment loans toward humanitarian assistance and peacebuilding. And competition for aid has intensified, partly because transition economies in Eastern Europe are now also competing for aid.

Africa has been a loser in these trends. In the late 1980s it was envisaged that aid to Africa would grow in real terms. But net transfers per capita have fallen sharply, from $32 in 1990 to $19 in 1998 (figure 8.1). Why?

One factor may be Africa's lower strategic importance since the end of the Cold War—as evidenced by the very different global responses to conflicts in Kosovo and Sierra Leone. Another is donor fatigue, partly

Aid is no longer business as usual

Figure 8.1 Per Capita Transfers of Official Development Assistance to Africa, 1970–98

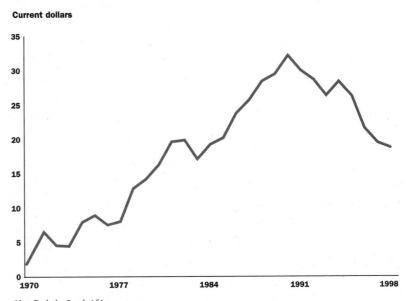

Current dollars

Note: Excludes South Africa.
Source: World Bank data.

explained by the belief that aid to Africa has done little to raise growth or reduce poverty. Indeed, despite large aid inflows (largely offset, however, by terms of trade losses; see chapter 1), Africa has grown slowly. Furthermore, aid—and the programs supported by aid—has not focused on the poor. A typical poor country receives net transfers of 9 percent of GDP through aid, but the poorest quintile of the population consumes only about 4 percent of GDP (chapter 2).

Many of the factors undermining aid effectiveness are amenable to reform. They include the support provided for "trusted allies" even when they pursue poor development policies, donor preferences on aid objectives and delivery mechanisms, and the effects of the debt over-hang. And donors and Africans alike are well aware of how a multi-plicity of aid processes and instruments have weakened accountability and ownership of development processes in Africa. The aid system is changing to address these problems. Paradoxically, however, aid to Africa is shrinking just as the features that have reduced its effectiveness are beginning to change.

Africa and its development partners need to work together for a more effective developmental aid regime—one that deconcentrates delivery systems, empowers local communities, and puts Africans in charge of their development programming, with development partners recogniz-ing and supporting Africa's leadership and responsibility. Intrusive micromanagement by a host of uncoordinated donors serves no one's interests. Rather, it weakens African bureaucratic capacity and account-ability and undermines aid effectiveness. Aid must not be seen as a sub-stitute for the productive energies of Africans.

While aid is moving in a new direction, its underlying principles—a comprehensive approach, strong ownership, selectivity, participation, partnership, decentralization—need further refinement. They need to become integrated with the sociopolitical processes of recipient countries. Work is needed to include aid flows in recipients' national budgets and financial management processes, to coordinate donor and country pro-cedures, to support decentralization, and to enhance debt relief. In some cases donors will have to adjust their procedures.

Aid also needs to support Africa's changing needs. Mechanisms need to be developed for regional aid delivery. Programs should not be con-fined to national borders—they should support economic integration, encouraging policy coordination and funding public goods such as vac-cines, regional transportation and communications infrastructure,

Aid to Africa is shrinking just as the features that have reduced its effectiveness are beginning to change

financial infrastructure for trade, and centers for developing critical skills, including in agricultural research (chapter 6). Aid should also focus on combating public bads such as multicountry conflict, infectious disease transmission, and drug trafficking.

Finally, even though aid cannot be phased out rapidly, an exit strategy is needed. This is not a matter of simply setting a timetable for phasing out aid. Rather, it requires a serious strategic partnership that enables Africa to outgrow aid dependence. Africans need to implement a "business plan" to reshape domestic regulations and institutions that deter domestic and foreign investment. For its part, the international community should open markets unconditionally to African exports, including those based on agriculture and processed primary products. This would be the clearest demonstration of a genuine commitment to Africa's long-term development—not dependency.

The Cold War left a legacy of ineffective aid, partly in the form of loans that have accumulated into large debt stocks

The Context and Profile of Aid

AID HAS GONE TO AFRICA FOR MANY PURPOSES—ONLY ONE OF which is development. Donors use aid to advance their values, their commercial interests, their cultural aspirations, and their diplomatic and political objectives. Aid flows reflect political pressures from groups in donor countries and bureaucratic imperatives from within their aid agencies, including pressures to spend all available aid funds within set budget cycles. The end of the Cold War diminished but did not eliminate the importance of diplomatic objectives for some governments. But the Cold War also left a legacy of ineffective aid, partly in the form of loans that have accumulated into large debt stocks.

Aid has also served development goals. Development aid has always sought to raise living standards and reduce poverty in poor countries. But concepts of how aid can help achieve those goals have shifted almost decade by decade (box 8.1).

African countries have been among the world's largest recipients of aid. Many receive net official development assistance equal to 10 percent of their GNP (at market exchange rates). In the early 1980s the top five African aid recipients were Sudan, Tanzania, Kenya, Somalia, and Zaire (now the Democratic Republic of Congo). All but one of these countries (Tanzania) played key roles in the Cold War politics of the United States

Box 8.1 Changing Thinking on Aid

SINCE THE END OF WORLD WAR II AID HAS SOUGHT to raise living standards and reduce poverty in poor countries. But concepts of how aid can achieve those goals have shifted considerably. During the 1950s and 1960s access to capital was considered crucial for investment and growth in poor countries. But private international capital was limited and disinclined to locate in poor countries. Thus public international capital was needed, preferably on highly concessional terms—that is, foreign aid. Aid needs were estimated on the basis of a target growth rate, the incremental capital-output ratio, and the funds available from domestic savings and international investment. Foreign exchange was seen as another constraint, so aid needs were also calculated using balance of payments gaps.

Ideas about aid shifted markedly in the 1970s. It came to be thought that growth did little to improve the lot of the poor—and may even worsen relative and absolute poverty. Thus aid was used more directly to help meet the basic needs of the poor, usually defined as basic health and education, rural roads, water, shelter, sanitation, and tools for increasing employment and income. Much of this aid was provided through complex development projects and focused on rural areas, on the assumption that most of the poor lived there.

In the 1970s surging oil prices and the rise and subsequent collapse of prices for other primary products—combined with extensive commercial borrowing—produced a severe debt and balance of payments crisis in many African countries. As governments sought debt relief and additional assistance to supplement their dwindling foreign exchange earnings, donor governments and international institutions began to condition their aid and debt relief on stabilization and economic adjustment programs. So, in the 1980s the focus of aid began to shift back to policies perceived to enhance growth—but unlike in the 1960s, the state was often seen as an obstacle to growth. In Africa aid became an incentive and source of finance for adjusting exchange rates, reducing fiscal deficits, reforming monetary policy, liberalizing trade, reducing price controls and subsidies, and shrinking the state's role in the economy.

In the 1990s development thinking shifted yet again. Development specialists began asking why investment and growth remained low even after economic reforms. The answer they came up with was the quality of governance. Where public institutions are weak, incompetent, or corrupt and where governments lack transparency or predictability, even the best reforms will not produce growth. A number of developed country governments came to identify democracy with good governance—and so pushed for political reforms as part of development. This phase coincided with the collapse of the socialist bloc and the spread of democracy through much of the developing world. In the mid-1990s some development experts and aid officials also began to argue that aid to civil society organizations—especially nongovernmental organizations working on human and civil rights—was important for development.

Several other shifts in development thinking occurred in the 1990s. There was a renewed emphasis on poverty reduction as a key purpose of aid. And there was increasing emphasis on addressing transnational problems. The discourse on aid and development has begun to incorporate these concerns by emphasizing environmental issues (such as global warming) and the spread of infectious disease. What is often not recognized is that a concern with global problems implies a shift from promoting growth and poverty reduction in the world's poor countries toward addressing problems wherever they occur.

A final shift evident at the end of the 1990s involved a growing emphasis on social justice and humanitarian assistance. The emphasis on gender equality, the importance of integrating ethnic minorities into society, and efforts to help the disabled and street children and to empower local communities arise as much from the strongly held values of groups supporting these programs as from the contribution such activities can make to development.

Source: Lancaster 1999.

and other major Western powers. By 1997 only one of these countries (Tanzania again) remained among the top five aid recipients; the others were Mozambique, Uganda, Madagascar, and Ethiopia. These latter countries had undertaken extensive political and economic reforms, and Ethiopia, Mozambique, and Uganda were recovering from long civil wars. Changes in the composition of the top recipients reflect the shifting considerations of donors—geopolitical strategic alliance is no longer the dominant factor.

Nongovernmental organizations have become increasing sources of aid to Africa

Since independence France has been the largest source of aid to Africa, primarily for its former colonies in West and Central Africa. Two multilateral institutions, the World Bank (through its soft loan window, the International Development Association) and the European Union, have periodically traded places as the second and third largest donors to Africa.

Aid flows to Africa have become less concentrated. In 1981–82 the five largest bilateral and multilateral aid sources (France, the World Bank, the European Union, Germany, the United States) provided three-quarters of net aid flows. By 1997 the five largest sources (the World Bank, France, the European Union, Germany, Japan) provided just over half of net aid flows. Nongovernmental organizations (NGOs) headquartered in developed countries have become increasing sources of aid to Africa, using resources from the citizens of their countries as well as their official aid agencies.

The purposes of aid are not broken down by region, but data published by the OECD's Development Assistance Committee show the worldwide breakdown. In 1997 technical assistance accounted for one-quarter of bilateral assistance, and the amount from multilateral sources is believed to be substantial. At some $4 billion a year, technical assistance has been one of the largest components of official development assistance to Africa. Quick-disbursing aid in support of economic reforms has averaged $3.1 billion a year excluding debt relief (World Bank 1998). The remaining aid has funded investment projects and other activities.

Aid to Africa is not only to governments. NGOs (indigenous and foreign) have proliferated in number and activities, and many donors channel their aid through them. In 1997 donors channeled 2 percent of their worldwide aid—nearly $1 billion—through NGOs. (These data do not include private funds raised and spent by NGOs). It would be surprising if this percentage were not higher in Africa given the growing reliance by the United States and other major aid donors on NGOs to implement their programs, especially for relief and reconstruction. The United States estimates that more than one-third of its development assistance worldwide is channeled through NGOs.

Influences on and Outcomes of Aid

D ESPITE CRITICISMS, AID HAS HAD MANY SUCCESSES IN AFRICA— controlling river blindness in West Africa, expanding family planning in Kenya and elsewhere, developing and disseminating better varieties of maize in Kenya and Zimbabwe and of rice in West Africa, developing and spreading oral rehydration treatment. These and other achievements have improved the lives of many Africans. Even in difficult environments, aid has funded many productive investment projects—roads, ports, public utilities and communication facilities, vaccination programs, the expansion of schools and health clinics.

Without increased balance of payments support in the 1980s, it is hard to imagine how Africa would have coped with huge terms of trade losses. In postwar countries such as Mozambique, generous aid has underpinned political reconciliation (chapter 2). Aid has also helped sustain essential reforms, including trade liberalization, that have adverse short-run effects on fiscal revenues. And donors, including international financial institutions, have been crucial for building capacity in certain institutions, notably central banks and ministries of finance.

Yet the perception of a disappointing record on growth and poverty reduction has prompted questions. Where did all the aid money go, and what has it bought? Why, despite high aid flows, was the income of the average African lower in 1997 than in 1970? Was this due only to exogenous factors, such as civil wars or terms of trade losses? A number of donors—the World Bank, U.S. Agency for International Development, U.K. Department for International Development, France, Sweden— assess the effectiveness of their aid by sector and region. These assessments often show less success in Africa in areas such as agricultural and rural development, development finance organizations, industrial projects, and especially projects (such as civil service reform) intended to strengthen African institutions. If aid had fully augmented national savings and high productivity was maintained, it would have raised per capita income in Zambia to levels comparable to those in OECD countries (Easterly 1997).

Despite criticisms, aid has had many successes in Africa

Aid has clearly not been the only factor at work. But why are outcomes so far from the possibilities?

Poor Selectivity

To be most efficient in reducing poverty, aid should be higher for countries with better policies and lower incomes

The domestic environment is a critical determinant of aid effectiveness. Some aspects of Africa's geography that have been held to impede development—its tropical location, variable (and in some cases low) rainfall, small share of population near the coast (Bloom and Sachs 1998)—also reduce the returns to aid. Poorly managed, extensive natural resources can also inhibit development, making governments less accountable to their people and spurring civil conflicts as groups vie to control resources (chapter 2). But geography and resources are not destiny. The remarkable economic progress made by Botswana—located in the tropics, landlocked with a small population, and endowed with abundant mineral resources, but with a demonstrated record of using aid well—shows that these factors are not insurmountable obstacles to development or to effective aid.

Policies can be even more important than physical factors. Collier and Dollar (1999) show that aid is more effective when it goes to countries with sound economic management—yet this criterion has had little influence on allocations. To be most efficient in reducing poverty, aid should be higher for countries with better policies and lower incomes. Instead, aid flows surge to countries with poor policies (figure 8.2), then are phased out prematurely as policies improve, even in poor countries. This approach greatly lowers the efficiency of assistance and its potential for increasing growth and reducing poverty.

Can aid encourage good policies? Much of the recent debate on aid effectiveness has been couched in polar terms: whether aid should be given before or after proven reforms. One World Bank study argues that there is little relationship between aid and policy reform (Burnside and Dollar 1997). Where there is a significant domestic constituency for economic reform or where donors can anticipate turning points in government policies, aid can encourage reform. But turning points are not always easy to recognize.

Further, donors have undermined potential incentives by providing aid even where conditions for its effectiveness are unfavorable. When aid is given to serve the political, military, and commercial interests of donors (or for humanitarian purposes), there is less chance that it will spur sound development policies.

Figure 8.2 Actual Aid, Poverty-Reducing Aid, and Policy Ratings

Percentage of GDP

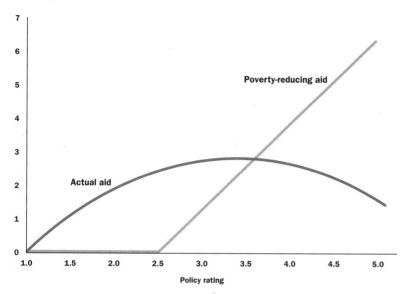

Note: Policy ratings are based on the World Bank's Country Policy and Institutional Assessments, which rank country policies from 1 (bad) to 6 (good).
Source: Collier and Dollar 1999.

Donor programs are fragmented and rarely negotiated with broad constituencies

Aid Delivery Mechanisms and Their Institutional Impacts

Donors loom large in Africa's small, aid-dependent countries, shaping development policies and identifying, designing, implementing, and evaluating projects. Donor dominance has several implications for the environment in which aid is implemented.

Weakened ownership of development policies and programs. A lot of aid comes with a lot of conditions attached. Even if donors' desired policies are appropriate—and the record confirms that good policies are needed for growth and poverty reduction—they are rarely negotiated with broad local consultation and so are widely seen by Africans as imposed. This creates what has been dubbed "choiceless democracy."

Compounding the problem, aid programs are highly fragmented. In the health sector alone the typical aid-receiving African country might have 30–40 donor and NGO initiatives, all with different priorities and procedures. To circumvent the weaknesses of African governments, donors often create project implementation units to ensure adequate accountability and rapid implementation. But in many cases these arrangements make matters worse, preventing integrated management of public spending and siphoning off talented civil servants (through high salaries) to work as project managers or consultants for donors.

The accounting standards and salary scales of the aid "economy" fragment budgets and programs and divert senior government officials from development challenges. Senior officials often spend more than half their time dealing with donors: seeking funds, negotiating, writing multiple reports, and managing successive rounds of debt relief.

Senior officials often spend more than half their time dealing with donors

Less accountability to Africans. Since at least the early 1990s, bilateral donors have offered support for democracy in Africa, while multilateral organizations have stressed broad participation in development programs. Aid is not the cause of weak institutions in Africa; institutions are no stronger in countries, such as Nigeria, where aid flows have been smaller. But when institutions are already weak, aid can make recipient governments less accountable to their people. With donors providing much development funding, there is less incentive to strengthen domestic accountability and economic governance for the use of resources (chapters 1 and 2). And with donors micromanaging aid, in many countries development activities are reduced to satisfying their demands.

Capacity building—and destruction. Despite massive technical assistance, aid programs have probably weakened capacity in Africa. Technical assistance has displaced local expertise and drawn away civil servants to administer aid-funded programs—precisely the opposite of the capacity-building intentions of donors and recipients. In some countries technical assistance accounts for 40 percent of aid, and much of the remaining aid is tied. But with large numbers of technical experts from donor countries in Africa—estimated by some at 100,000—a lot of technical assistance is also effectively tied, flowing back to donor countries with less long-run impact on the development of recipients' economies.

Reduced sustainability and transparency. Aid and its accompanying reforms have not been well marketed. As a result recipient countries have a limited understanding of what aid and its reforms intend to achieve and how they intend to achieve it. Aid agencies used to seek allies within African governments who were supportive of reforms (often ministers of finance and governors of central banks). But these allies were often limited in number and not always in office for the time needed to implement and consolidate reforms. Understanding the ends and means of aid-funded programs has therefore been a problem in Africa, especially where complicated reforms or technical assistance programs have been urged on governments by bilateral and multilateral aid agencies.

Stories of African officials not even having access to studies and data developed by multilateral institutions are common, so it is hardly surprising that such officials have invested little in the success of such programs. Neither have parliaments been adequately involved in discussions on aid and its applications—even though these usually have sizable budget impacts. But over the past 10 years considerable efforts have been made to strengthen consultative processes and to share data. (For example, the World Bank is making its databases available in electronic form.) And there appears to be better understanding and support for reforms than 10 or 20 years ago.

Funding difficulties and complexities have also weakened sustainability. Rather than fund balanced programs fully integrated with national budgets, donors have supported capital investments without adequate attention to the need for both counterpart funding and additional domestic resources to operate and maintain facilities. Without sufficient budget support, investments are likely to be ineffectively used and maintained—especially with debt service draining public budgets. Finally, the number and complexity of aid projects have sometimes overwhelmed African government agencies, leading to their collapse once aid ends. The integrated rural development projects of the 1970s and early 1980s required that multiple activities be managed and coordinated by a variety of government ministries—a challenge that would have taxed even the most efficient governments in developed countries.

Excessive country focus. Africa is the world's most fragmented region. It is demarcated by 165 borders into 48 countries—22 with less than 5 million people, 11 with less than 1 million. Small size imposes real constraints on development, and without economic cooperation and integration Africa will fall further behind the global frontier (Jaycox 1992, p. 66).

Yet with few exceptions, aid programs are confined to national economic spaces. African countries confront similar economic problems—and so need to support regional and international public goods (box 8.2). Regional public goods include regional infrastructure (roads, railways, ports, electric distribution and power-pooling systems), infectious disease control, centers of excellence for training, the underpinnings of regional markets and trade, and agricultural research and early warning systems for drought. A regional approach could lead to lower costs and faster

Recipient countries have a limited understanding of what aid and its reforms intend to achieve and how they intend to achieve it

245

growth than individual country efforts, while also encouraging policy coordination.

Excessive debt. High debt crowds out the effects of new aid in two ways (Elbadawi, Ndulu, and Ngung'u 1996). First, in stagnant economies rising debt service drains the fiscal resources needed for development. Even if total aid inflows exceed debt service outflows, most aid goes to projects: quick-disbursing nonproject assistance is less than debt service payments. As a result funds for recurrent spending shrink even as programs proliferate.

Second, a large stock of debt may signal taxes on future success and raises questions about the credibility and sustainability of announced reforms. High and fixed debt service obligations increase countries' leverage and raise uncertainty, especially if donor funding is decided on a short-term basis. In such circumstances investors wait until returns are high enough to cover their risk. Some have argued that debt relief encourages moral hazard. But sustaining large volumes of unserviceable debt does the same thing. It can pressure donors to continue funding countries despite weak development

High debt crowds out new aid

Box 8.2 Public Goods and Development Assistance

TWO PROPERTIES DISTINGUISH PUBLIC GOODS FROM other goods. There is no easy way to extract payment from those who use them—so they are nonexcludable. And one user's consumption does not diminish the benefits available to others—so their benefits are non-rivalrous. International public goods (or bads) generate benefits (or harms) that spill over national borders, either within a region or globally. "Public" does not necessarily imply that government must supply the good. Some (such as national defense) are indeed provided by the government. But others may be offered by the private sector or by both the private and public sectors.

International public goods differ from one another along at least three dimensions—the geographic range of benefit spillovers, the individual actions needed to supply the good, and the extent to which potential beneficiaries can be excluded. Each of these features has implications for schemes to address undersupply—and hence, for development assistance. In particular,

the different geographic extent of spillovers gives rise to the principle of subsidiarity, in which cross-border issues are dealt with at the relevant level of decentralization through available institutions.

Some global public goods—limiting global warming, curbing organized crime—are not especially relevant to Africa. But others—such as finding an effective vaccine against HIV/AIDS—are of special importance. The low income of many of those affected (or potentially infected) by HIV/AIDS has led to calls for donors to support private research by committing to purchase an effective vaccine, once developed, for distribution in Africa. Eliminating malaria is an example of a regional good, as are transit corridors, immunization programs, and peacekeeping forces. Policy coordination that widens the scope of markets and investments and increases efficiency can also be considered a regional public good.

Source: Kanbur, Sandler, and Morrisson 1999.

policies and reduce recipients' sense of accountability for outcomes. In such circumstances the impact of new aid—even if devoted to development—may not offset the negative effects of the debt stock.

Forging a New Strategic Partnership

H OW CAN AID BE MADE TO FOSTER DEVELOPMENT? SERIOUS rethinking is under way, and consensus is emerging that aid must change. The new approach must:

Consensus is emerging that aid must change and that it must focus on reducing poverty

- Clarify the purpose of aid in the post–Cold War era.
- Deconcentrate aid flows to bring delivery closer to recipients.
- Broaden aid beyond national boundaries to fund and encourage cross-border public goods.
- Take decisive action on the lingering debt burden.

There also seems to be broad consensus that the new approach to aid should be underpinned by four key principles:

- Being more selective in choosing aid recipients.
- Designing aid activities with the participation of potential beneficiaries and implementing them in partnership with other development organizations.
- Strengthening the capacity of recipients—whether central or local governments, private enterprises, or NGOs—charged with implementing programs.
- Restructuring aid delivery mechanisms to make recipients responsible for development—while recognizing the interest of donors that resources be used effectively.

What Purpose Should Aid Serve?

With the international community's endorsement of the International Development Goals for 2015, consensus seems to be emerging that aid should be targeted to poverty reduction. The World Bank and the International Monetary Fund (IMF) have found common ground, anchored on poverty reduction. In its Comprehensive Development

Framework, the Bank restates poverty reduction as its central mission (box 8.3). Similarly, the IMF has changed the name of its Enhanced Structural Adjustment Facility to the Poverty Reduction and Growth Facility.

Poverty reduction is not a new objective. But there are different emphases on how to achieve it. For some, the main avenue is through the resumption of growth—and this invokes a wide agenda. Others see poverty reduction through the lens of programs targeted to the poor, including community development projects. As described in previous chapters, however, Africa does not offer an either-or situation. Both channels are crucial for success.

Delivery must bring assistance closer to beneficiaries

Deconcentrating Delivery

To make aid more responsive to the needs of the poor, its delivery must be deconcentrated to local governments and communities (chapters 3 and

---

Box 8.3 The Comprehensive Development Framework and Poverty Reduction Strategies

INTRODUCED IN EARLY 1999 BY WORLD BANK President James Wolfensohn, the Comprehensive Development Framework (CDF) has gained wide acceptance within the development community as a guide for thinking on long-term development and poverty alleviation. The CDF calls for country ownership of a comprehensive, results-oriented development agenda integrating macroeconomic, structural, and social policies, developed with the broad participation of civil society. This approach is to be supported by donors on the basis of long-term, strategic, and coordinated partnerships.

In September 1999 the World Bank's Development Committee and the International Monetary Fund's Interim Committee linked debt relief and assistance programs more generally to the preparation of poverty reduction strategies by low-income countries. These strategies will be summarized in Poverty Reduction Strategy Papers (PRSPs) that will be presented to the Boards of the Bank and the IMF along with a staff assessment of the PRSP. The PRSP replaces the Policy

Framework Paper and will form the basis for the IMF's Poverty Reduction and Growth Facility, which replaces the Enhanced Structural Adjustment Facility. In low-income countries the PRSP will also provide the context for the World Bank's Country Assistance Strategy. The PRSP process is to be consistent with the principles of the CDF.

While the principles underlying the CDF and PRSP are widely accepted, countries vary in their readiness to implement them. Experience in some of the countries where the CDF has been piloted illustrates some of the tensions. Broadly based consultation can be take time to develop. When faced by the tight deadlines that often accompany donor processes, consultation and ownership may suffer. Another tension arises from the comprehensiveness of the approach. Despite the clear focus on poverty outcomes, it will be challenging to prioritize interventions. Finally, it is easier to improve country-driven donor coordination than to enhance selectivity among donors across activities in line with their comparative advantage.

4). At the same time, these entities need to be strengthened to improve their capacity to manage development programs. Transparent aid delivery systems and monitoring are essential to enable local communities to take charge and to prevent local elites from capturing limited resources. This approach does not, however, reduce the need for a capable central government—because managing decentralization and targeting will be a major challenge.

Moving beyond Boundaries

As noted, aid delivery mechanisms tend to focus on individual countries. Although this approach has been convenient for individual recipients and donors, the 21st century will see increasing cross-border activities in Africa and a growing need for policy coordination. Assistance should be delivered more widely to encourage this trend and to deliver regional public goods (see box 8.2), contain regional public "bads," and strengthen regional approaches for acquiring knowledge.

New technology holds huge potential for Africa, opening the way to a regionwide communications network (chapter 5). Regional capacity-building networks—such as the African Economic Research Consortium or the Council for the Development of Social Science Research in Africa—could offer models for extension to the sciences, engineering, and other critical areas. Just as current initiatives emphasize stakeholder participation in devising national programs, mechanisms need to be implemented to develop regional criteria on policies, programs, and aid delivery.

Cross-border trade facilitation is an important regional public good. Cross-border transactions are still hampered by Africa's weak institutions and inadequate support services. For example, it is difficult for an African construction company to compete with firms from OECD countries for competitively bid contracts in neighboring countries because of the high costs of obtaining a performance bond—if such bonds are even available to the African firm. The overhead costs of initiatives to facilitate cross-border trade are prohibitive for small African countries. Donors are assessing proposals for regional approaches, such as an Africa Guarantee Facility modeled after examples in Eastern Europe. But current mechanisms for regional assistance are weak.

Assistance should be delivered more widely to encourage cross-border activities and coordination

249

Enhancing Debt Relief

Aid will not be effective unless debt is reduced to sustainable levels

As noted, aid will not be effective unless debt is reduced to sustainable levels. The approach has proceeded in incremental steps, first with the Heavily Indebted Poor Countries (HIPC) initiative in 1996, then with the enhanced HIPC initiative in 1999 (box 8.4). The enhanced initiative is expected to provide deeper and faster relief and to help fight poverty. But the effectiveness of the enhanced initiative rests on adequate funding. And critics still question the adequacy and speed of relief, particularly when debt service is seen from a fiscal perspective (rather than relative to export revenues) and against the scale of social needs (Center for International Development 1999).

Box 8.4 The Enhanced Heavily Indebted Poor Countries Initiative

AFTER EXTENSIVE CONSULTATIONS WITH CREDITOR and debtor governments, NGOs, religious organizations, academics, and the general public, in September 1999 the World Bank and International Monetary Fund (IMF) announced a major expansion of the Heavily Indebted Poor Countries (HIPC) initiative. The 1996 initiative will be modified in two main ways. First, it will provide deeper, broader, and faster debt relief by:

- Qualifying countries for relief when the ratio of their net present value of debt to exports reaches 150 percent. Previously this ratio was 200–250 percent at the initiative's completion point.
- Commencing debt relief from the decision point, with irrevocable relief to be delivered at the completion point. Previously, relief from multilateral debt service began only at the completion point.
- Basing the length of the interim period on achieving key development actions rather than on a prespecified period.

Second, the enhanced initiative will link debt relief to poverty reduction programs by:

- Grounding debt relief—and indeed, all assistance from the Bank and IMF—on poverty strategies to be developed by each country through a consultative process and agreed in a new instrument, the Poverty Reduction Strategy Paper (see box 8.3).

- Clearly monitoring the use of the resources freed through debt relief—particularly how they are reflected in spending on key elements of the poverty reduction program, as well as the results of the program.

These changes are expected to double the amount of relief provided under the HIPC initiative. For countries covered by the Special Program of Assistance to Africa, this will total about $20 billion in net present value terms. This relief will be in addition to that provided by the Paris Club of official creditors. Moreover, the G–7 countries plan to cancel the debt owed on official development assistance loans by countries qualifying for HIPC relief.

The enhanced HIPC initiative is expected to lower debt service to the World Bank and IMF by about $1 billion in 2000–02. Depending on donor contributions to the HIPC Trust Fund, other multilateral institutions may also be able to increase debt relief.

One of the basic principles of the enhanced initiative is that the resources released should be in addition to the resources—including aid—now being provided. Because the enhanced initiative aims to expedite poverty reduction, recipient countries are expected to adjust macroeconomic policies to accommodate the resources freed by debt relief.

Source: World Bank 1999.

What Basis for Selectivity?

With the Cold War over, there are no longer compelling political or diplomatic reasons to channel large amounts of aid to corrupt governments (like that of Mobutu Sese Seko of the former Zaire). As a result donors have become more selective. Today almost 80 percent of quick-disbursing donor assistance to cofinance World Bank and IMF programs in Africa goes to good performers (OED 1998). And since 1996 World Bank adjustment lending has become more selective. But weaknesses remain in monitoring outcomes—and must be addressed if aid is to move away from detailed conditionality (World Bank 1998).

Aid donors and recipients may agree that selectivity is important for effective aid. But there is a long way to go before consensus is reached on how to implement such a strategy in Africa. The World Bank's Country Policy and Institutional Assessments rate a wide range of areas, including poverty reduction efforts, budget management, social and environmental policies, and structural and financial policies and institutions (chapter 1). But these assessments are confidential, so it is not clear how much consensus they reflect. If partnerships and transparency are to be institutionalized in the aid relationship, the Bank's assessments will need to become more open to public scrutiny, which requires that they be discussed with the recipient countries as well. This could encourage discussion between donors and recipients with the objective of reaching consensus on development priorities.

At a more general level, some actions are supported by a strong consensus, and donors can justify including these among their selectivity criteria. Examples might include enhancing the rule of law, promoting sound public auditing, and improving the delivery of human development services when cost-effective solutions are known. But in some areas there is legitimate controversy, such as policy toward the capital account. In these areas there is an argument for moving cautiously and learning by doing, so donors might agree to support different policies in different countries.

Greater transparency is needed in implementing selectivity

How to Implement Partnerships and Participation?

Each recipient and donor will likely have different views on the best ways to reduce poverty. Thus partnerships and dialogue are needed to build consensus and support coherent programs. Donors, governments, and NGOs must agree on the main goals of development, the barriers to their achievement, the priority actions for aid, and the strategies for applying aid (Lancaster 1999, p. 24). If goals and strategies were to derive from recipients' political and economic processes—rather than from donor demands—it would mark a sea change in the aid relationship, opening the way to more effective use and higher capacity for absorption. How can these principles be implemented?

There is a strong base on which to build. Aid agencies, including the World Bank, have worked with a variety of entities in developing countries, as well as with each other, to achieve development goals. In recent years civil society organizations and local governments have become involved in designing and implementing collaborative aid projects in Africa. The Bank's Comprehensive Development Framework, now being implemented in a number of countries, places external aid agencies and internal organizations in a broader context based on national consensus on development strategies (see box 8.3).

Donors will still need to decide how the concept of partnership translates into decisions on aid allocations—including to countries with views on development that differ from theirs. Donors might also consider adopting a code of conduct for their dealings with new democracies to ensure that civil society (including the press) and its representative institutions (particularly parliaments) are kept well informed and properly involved in aid programs and processes (chapter 2).

Confronting Capacity Constraints

Government capacity is key for development. Where governments are unable—or unwilling—to identify broad goals, adopt appropriate policies, implement processes and programs, and evaluate their operations in a transparent, predictable, and accountable manner, they are unlikely to be able to manage their economies or their aid effectively. For technical and political reasons, many African governments lack capacity.

Technical factors include inadequate expertise, poor professional development, weak evaluation and other systems, and disorderly and ineffective planning, budgeting, and programming. A number of initiatives have been launched to address these shortcomings, including the African Capacity Building Foundation, the Partnership for Capacity Building, training and technical assistance programs, and civil service reform programs. But a lot more of the large pool of technical assistance funding must be reallocated for Africa to develop, repatriate, and retain its own capacity.

Political factors—which reduce the demand for and supply of capacity—are harder to address. And it is not clear how well the new approach to aid can work where governance is weak. But many of the principles, including decentralizing service delivery to clients, can support a civic counterweight to government and help create a constituency for more effective and transparent management (chapter 2).

Common Pooling: An Ideal Approach?

At one end of the proposals for reforming aid is a common pool (box 8.5). Recipients would have complete ownership in the sense of having exclusive and final say on the development strategies that they followed. Donors would put unrestricted financing into a common pool to complement country resources, and the government would implement its strategies. Donors would not earmark funds for projects or programs, but would fund the common pool based on their assessment of the country's strategies and implementation.

Donor preferences might still shape development priorities, because countries would know what donors were willing to fund. But in an ideal form, a common pool would put an end to intrusive conditionality. Whether such an arrangement would satisfy donors is another matter. Donors need to respond to diverse constituencies and institutional requirements to show how—and how effectively—their funds are used.

Steps toward Better Aid

A number of African countries—Benin, Ghana, Tanzania, Uganda—have started to develop new aid relationships with donors, encouraging ownership and improving consultation and coordination. In addition, new instruments for delivering aid have been developed through the Special Program of Assistance (SPA), created in 1987 to increase quick-disbursing assistance in support of African reforms and coordinated by international financial institutions. One of the SPA's early successes was to foster the untying of quick-disbursing assistance. Over time its agenda has broadened to include the development and monitoring of sector programs, the implementation of guidance on public finance management,

Foreign technical assistance must be cut and reallocated for Africa to develop, repatriate, and retain its own capacity

253

and the specification of a fiscal framework for assessing aid flows and requirements. These efforts seek to bring aid flows—many of which do not flow through budget channels—into a unified system of public financial management that integrates donor support with national budgets and increases coherence between donor and national procedures for managing resources.

Sector programs incorporate fragmented donor support into a comprehensive sector strategy defined by the government, agreed by donors,

---

Box 8.5 The Common Pool Approach to Donor Coordination and Ownership

TODAY'S COUNTRY-FOCUSED SYSTEMS FOR DELIVERING aid must manage divergent views on development and poverty reduction while improving coordination, increasing ownership, and reducing aid dependence. The development community's response to this challenge has been partnerships. But partnerships are not a new idea for development—they have been suggested since the late 1960s.

What is needed is a more radical approach in which donors cede control to recipient governments, advancing their ideas on development through dialogues with the country and with each other rather than through specific programs and projects. A "common pool" approach to development assistance would build on current trends and experiences—but would push them much further. A recipient country would create its development strategies, programs, and projects, primarily in consultation with its people but also in dialogue with donors. It would then present its plans to donors, who would put unrestricted financing into a common pool. The common pool of development assistance, together with the government's resources, would then finance the overall development strategy.

Donors' financing would depend on their assessment of the country's strategies and programs and on the country's ability to implement them and monitor progress and spending. Donor views would be conveyed to the country and to other donors in the dialogue leading to financing decisions, but earmarking

of this or that donor's funds to this or that item would not be permitted.

This is an idealized setting, and many pragmatic and operational issues need to be settled. But the common pool approach builds on initiatives already under way, and it provides a direction for new initiatives. While increasing recipient ownership, it presents an institutional setting in which different views on development—and therefore different donors—can coexist and better coordinate. Donors could keep or develop a specialized focus. But this would not be in terms of financing projects and programs in specific sectors. Rather, it would be in the realm of providing specialized evaluations of country performance and programs, or providing specialized technical assistance—but only if requested by the country within the framework of the common pool.

Aid recipients following the common pool approach might experience a short-term drop in development assistance. But this drop could be planned for, the lower volumes would be used more effectively, and increased effectiveness would strengthen the argument for more assistance over the medium term. For donors, the common pool approach would greatly reduce the need for staff to develop, monitor, and evaluate projects. Although staff would still be needed to assess a country's program and to communicate with the government, the number of donor staff would likely decline.

Source: Kanbur, Sandler, and Morrison 1999.

---

and based on a sectorwide analysis and a consistent medium-term budget framework. Sector programs link sector spending with the overall macroeconomic framework and so improve public spending management, while the medium-term framework allows for longer-run planning for the capital and recurrent costs of new programs. Commitments under sector programs have risen rapidly to almost half of quick-disbursing assistance.

Nevertheless, limited capacity for program implementation has slowed disbursements under sector programs. Moreover, aid flows are rarely pooled under these programs and subjected to common financial management (preferably aligned with national budget procedures). This is partly because some donors face legal impediments to contributing to pooled funds. These impediments should be eased in cases where the financial management of pooled funds meets generally accepted standards, even if these differ from donor requirements.

Weak budget processes and financial management also impede aid pooling and other new approaches to aid. SPA guidance on public finance management is geared toward transforming the system for public expenditure reviews from one in which donors—notably the World Bank—provide assessments that are largely disconnected from the budget process, to a country-led approach in which the Bank and other donors advise and support the budget process and assess outcomes. This aim is to correct a number of problems: lack of ownership of public expenditure reviews by client countries, lack of integration with the budget cycle, recommendations that cannot be implemented or translated into a plan of action, and a focus on budget allocations rather than on spending management and outcomes. A number of countries have started to implement the guidance, with some success. Another effort to develop new aid relationships is a pilot project in Burkina Faso (box 8.6)

Commitments under sector programs have risen to almost half of quick-disbursing assistance

Away from Aid Dependence

DEVELOPMENT AID IS NOT A WELFARE ENTITLEMENT AND IS NO substitute for people's productive energies. Aid cannot be phased out rapidly, but plans should be made to free countries from high aid dependence. Such plans will not be credible, however, unless they are backed by comprehensive, realistic programs endorsed by

Box 8.6 Conditionality Revisited: A New Approach in Burkina Faso

AT THE INITIATIVE OF THE EUROPEAN UNION, THE Special Program of Assistance to Africa (SPA) is piloting a new approach in Burkina Faso that aims to enhance donor coordination, foster country ownership, and make aid flows less volatile. Burkina Faso had been receiving adjustment support since 1991, yet as late as 1997 only a small group in the Ministry of Finance was familiar with the reforms supported—even though these often affected other ministries. Disbursements were not conditioned on outcomes, so there was little monitoring of actual results. Yet a large number of donors multiplied demands on government for a variety of data and sometimes imposed conflicting conditions.

The government was asked to propose a matrix of outcome indicators for social sectors and performance indicators for budget management. Data were collected and analyzed between donor missions. The pilot generated some important lessons. Outcome indicators shift attention to results—surveys found that only a small part of budget allocations reached users, and the private sector complained of grave problems with the judicial system and governance. A results-based approach can also enhance ownership, although broadly based stakeholder involvement is not easy to achieve. Donor coordination confronted logistical difficulties but was appreciated by the government.

The pilot involves no actual assistance. Models for linking hypothetical disbursements to results will be simulated in 2000 and discussed with donors and the government.

Source: Emblad and Hervio 2000.

recipients and donors and anchored on an explicit ideology of making Africa economically competitive and reducing poverty.

Even within the current framework there is room for strategic partnerships that go beyond aid relationships. A one-size-fits-all approach will not work because African countries have very different starting points. Some have more poverty. Some have more human resources on which to build. Some—particularly those affected by conflict—have weaker institutions and capacity for development.

But whatever the country conditions, aid dependence cannot be reduced unless Africa begins to recover its lost share in world trade. Since the early 1970s Africa has lost trade equal to about 20 percent of GDP (chapter 1)—far more than it has received in aid. Part of this loss reflects declining terms of trade for many primary products. A larger part reflects the loss of traditional export shares and a failure to diversify exports into new, more dynamic sectors demanded by global markets. Trade policies are not the sole cause of Africa's slow export growth and diversification: many other factors affect growth, investment, and productivity more broadly (chapters 1, 7). But reforms have stabilized and even slightly increased Africa's world trade shares. In addition, exports have begun to diversify in a number of countries—particularly toward processed commodities, including agricultural products. To help shift African countries away from aid dependence, development partners must do all they can to accelerate these developments.

Protectionist policies in industrial countries have not been the main cause of Africa's declining trade share. But many impediments to open market access affect sectors where Africa can probably realize comparative advantage (chapters 6, 7). These include barriers to processed and temperate agricultural products and textiles and clothing, as well as large subsidies for agricultural products that compete with exports from Africa. Even moderately higher tariffs for, say, wood and leather products or textiles and clothing confer high protection on processing industries in industrial countries. And the threat of antidumping restrictions and other measures imposed to slow "disruptive" import growth—such as the restraint on clothing exports from Kenya to the United States—increases risk to potential investors. Africa must also cope with new requirements, including sanitary and phytosanitary standards, that were less restrictive when other exporters were establishing their footholds.

Thus there are many areas outside aid for forging a development pact with Africa. Emerging exporters should be granted full, tariff-free access to OECD markets for a wide range of exports, with exemptions from antidumping measures, countervailing duties, and other safeguards that create uncertainty about access. Such arrangements can be made compatible with World Trade Organization requirements by embedding them in a framework of reciprocity, where African countries and their industrial trading partners gradually move toward free trade arrangements, with a longer transition in Africa. This principle is included in the successor to the Lomé Convention negotiated in Fiji in January 2000 and underlies the Africa Trade and Opportunity Act being discussed in the United States (chapter 7).

Implementation of such proposals should not be piecemeal. Special efforts should be made to eliminate tariff peaks and high effective protection to processing industries, extending tariff cuts to all stages of production. Rules of origin will need to be generous so that they do not impede economic integration in Africa. Industrial countries should ensure that information is easily available on technical regulations, product standards, and sanitary and phytosanitary standards. A fund could be created to help new exporters test products and meet standards, including through changes in processing and marketing. And standards should

There are many areas outside aid for forging a development pact with Africa

be implemented in a way that minimizes costs, avoiding duplicative testing and excessive charges.

Because Africa's exports are so small, such measures would have minor costs for industrial countries. To be fully effective, they need to be implemented with other measures to sustain aid levels and improve aid processes—including to make better use of technical assistance to support capacity building in recipient countries. For the moment the goal must be "trade with aid" rather than "trade not aid." But fully opening markets to Africa sends an important signal that donors are genuinely committed to Africa's long-term development.

References

Chapter 1

Ablo, Emmanuel, and Ritva Reinikka. 1998. "Do Budgets Really Matter? Evidence from Public Spending on Education and Health in Uganda." Policy Research Working Paper 1926. World Bank, Washington, D.C.

Agenor, Pierre-Richard. 1998. "Stabilization Policies, Poverty and the Labor Market." International Monetary Fund, Research Department, and World Bank, Economic Development Institute. Washington, D.C.

Auty, Richard M. 1998. "Resource Abundance and Economic Development." Research for Action 44. United Nations University, World Institute for Development Economics Research, Helsinki.

Azam, Jean Paul, Augustin Fosu, and Njuguna Ndung'u. 1999: "Explaining Slow Growth in Africa." Background paper prepared for Africa in the 21st Century Project. World Bank, Washington, D.C.

Blackden, Mark, and Chitra Bhanu. 1999. *Gender, Growth, and Poverty Reduction: Special Program of Assistance for Africa, 1998 Status Report on Poverty in Sub-Saharan Africa.* World Bank Technical Paper 428. Washington, D.C.

Bloom, David E., and Jeffrey D. Sachs. 1998. "Geography, Demography and Economic Growth in Africa." *Brookings Papers on Economic Activity 2.* Washington, D.C.: Brookings Institution.

CBI (Cross-Border Initiative). 1999. "Cross-Border Initiative: Road Map for Investment Facilitation." Paper prepared for the Fourth Ministerial Conference, 25 March.

Collier, Paul. 1999. "On the Economic Consequences of Civil War." *Oxford Economic Papers* 51: 168–83.

Collier, Paul, and David Dollar. 1999. "Aid Allocation and Poverty Reduction." World Bank, Washington, D.C.

Collier, Paul, and Jan W. Gunning. 1998. "Explaining African Economic Performance." *Journal of Economic Literature* 37 (March): 64–111.

———. 1999. "Why Has Africa Grown Slowly?" *Journal of Economic Perspectives* 13 (3): 3–22.

Dabalen, Andrew. 1999. "Labor Markets in Sub-Saharan Africa: A Review." World Bank, Africa Region, Washington, D.C.

Demery, Lionel, and Micheal Walton. 1998. "Are Poverty Reduction and Other Twenty-first Century Social Goals Attainable?" World Bank, Washington, D.C.

Devarajan, Shanta, William Easterly, and Howard Pack. 1999. "Is Investment in Africa Too Low or Too High?" World Bank, Washington, D.C.

Dollar, David, and Craig Burnside. 1997. "Aid, Policies, and Growth." Policy Research Working Paper 1777. World Bank, Washington, D.C.

Easterly, William, and Ross Levine. 1997. "Africa's Growth Tragedy: Policies and Ethnic Divisions." *Quarterly Journal of Economics* 112: 1203–50.

Elbadawi, Ibrahim, and Francis Mwega. Forthcoming. "Can Africa's Saving Collapse Be Reverted?" *The World Bank Economic Review*.

Freedom House. Various years. *Freedom in the World: The Annual Survey of Political Rights & Civil Liberties*. New York.

Gelb, Alan H. 1988. *Oil Windfalls: Blessing or Curse?* New York: Oxford University Press.

Gelb, Alan H., and Robert Floyd. 1998. "The Challenge of Globalization for Africa." World Bank, Africa Region, Washington, D.C.

Guillaumont, Patrick, Sylvaine Guillaumont-Jeanneney, and Aristeme Varoudakis. 1999. "Economic Policy Reform and Growth Prospects in Emerging African Economies." Development Centre Technical Paper 145. Organisation for Economic Co-operation and Development, Paris.

Hamilton, Kirk, and Michael Clemens. 1999. "Genuine Savings Rates in Developing Countries." *The World Bank Economic Review* 13 (May): 333–56.

Hoeffler, Anke. 1999. "Augmented Solow Model and the African Growth Debate." Paper presented at the African Economic Research Consortium Workshop, Harvard University, 26–27 March, Cambridge, Mass.

IDA (International Development Association). 1998. *IDA Portfolio Review*. Washington, D.C.

IMF (International Monetary Fund). 1997. "The ESAF at Ten Years: Economic Adjustment and Reform in Low-Income Countries." Occasional Paper 156. Washington, D.C.

———. 1998. "External Evaluation of the Enhanced Structural Adjustment Facility: Report by a Group of Independent Experts." Washington, D.C.

Kostopoulos, Christos. 1999. "Progress in Public Expenditure Management in Africa: Evidence from World Bank Surveys." Africa Region Working Paper 1. World Bank, Washington, D.C.

Mkandawire, Thandika, and Charles Soludo. 1999. *Our Continent, Our Future*. Trenton, N.J.: Africa World Press.

Myrdal, Gunnar. 1968. *Asian Drama: An Inquiry into the Poverty of Nations*. New York: Twentieth Fund.

Ndulu, Benno J. 1986. "Governance and Economic Management." In Robert J. Berg and Jennifer Seymour Whitaker, eds., *Strategies for African Development*. Berkeley, Calif.: University of California Press.

OECD (Organisation for Economic Co-operation and Development). 1996. *Shaping the 21st Century: The Contribution of Development Co-operation*. Paris.

OED (Operations Evaluation Department). 1998a. *Annual Review of Development Effectiveness*. Washington, D.C.: World Bank.

———. 1998b. *The Special Program of Assistance for Africa (SPA): An Independent Evaluation*. Washington, D.C.: World Bank.

Ottaway, Marina. 1999. "Africa." *Foreign Policy* (spring): 13–24.

Reinikka, Ritva, and Jakob Svensson. 1998. "Investment Response to Structural Reforms and Remaining Constraints: Firm Survey Evidence From Uganda." World Bank, Africa Region, Washington, D.C.

Rodrik, Dani. 1998a. "Trade Policy and Economic Performance in Sub-Saharan Africa." NBER Working Paper 6562. National Bureau of Economic Research, Cambridge, Mass.

———. 1998b. "Where Did All the Growth Go? External Shocks, Social Conflict and Growth Collapses." Harvard University, Cambridge, Mass.

———. 1999. "Making Openness Work: The New Global Economy and the Developing Countries." Overseas Development Council, Washington, D.C.

Transparency International. 1998. "1998 Corruption Perceptions Index." Press release. Gottingen University, Germany.

UNCTAD (United Nations Conference on Trade and Development). 1998. *Trade and Development Report.* Geneva.

———. 1999. *Foreign Direct Investment in Africa: Performance and Potential.* Geneva.

UNDP (United Nations Development Programme). 1998. *Human Development Report 1998.* New York: Oxford University Press.

UNECA (United Nations Economic Commission for Africa). 1999. *Annual Report 1999.* Addis Ababa, Ethiopia.

Weder, Beatrice, Aymo Brunetti, and Gregory Kisunko. 1998. "Credibility of Rules and Economic Growth: Evidence from a Worldwide Survey of the Private Sector." *The World Bank Economic Review* 12 (3): 353–84.

Wood, Adrian, and Jorg Mayer. 1998. "Africa's Export Structure in a Comparative Perspective." United Nations Conference on Trade and Development, Geneva.

World Bank. 1989. *Africa's Adjustment and Growth in the 1980s.* Washington, D.C.

———. 1994. *Adjustment in Africa: Reforms, Results, and the Road Ahead.* A Policy Research Report. New York: Oxford University Press.

———. 1996. *A Continent in Transition: Sub-Saharan Africa in the Mid-1990s.* Washington, D.C.

———. 1997. *Confronting AIDS: Public Priorities in a Global Epidemic.* A Policy Research Report. New York: Oxford University Press.

———. 1998a. *Africa Can Compete! A Framework for World Bank Group Support for Private Sector Development in Sub-Saharan Africa.* Africa Region, Washington, D.C.

———. 1998b. *Global Economic Prospects and the Developing Countries.* Washington, D.C.

———. 1998c. "Higher Impact Adjustment Lending in Sub-Saharan Africa: An Update." Africa Region, Chief Economist's Office, Washington, D.C.

———. 1999a. *Intensifying Action Against HIV/AIDS in Africa: Responding to a Development Crisis.* Africa Region, Washington, D.C.

———. 1999b. *World Development Report 1998/99: Knowledge for Development.* New York: Oxford University Press.

Yeats, Alexander J. 1999. "Have Policy Reforms Influenced the Trade Performance of Sub-Saharan African Countries?" World Bank, Washington, D.C.

Chapter 2

Biggs, Tyler, Mayank Raturi, and Pradeep Srivastava. 1996. "Enforcement of Contracts in an African Credit Market: Working Capital and Finance in Kenyan Manufacturing." RPED Discussion Paper 71. World Bank, Washington, D.C.

Bratton, Michael, and Nicholas van de Walle. 1997. *Democratic Experiments in Africa.* New York: Cambridge University Press.

Chege, Michael. 1999. "Politics of Development: Institutions and Governance." Global Coalition for Africa, Washington, D.C.

Collier, Paul. 1994. "Demobilization and Insecurity: A Study in the Economics of the Transition from War to Peace." *Journal of International Development.*

————. 1998. "The Role of the State in Economic Development: Cross-regional Experiences." *Journal of African Economies* 7 (2): 38–76.

————. 1999. "The Challenge of Uganda Reconstruction, 1986–98." World Bank, Development Research Group, Washington, D.C.

Collier, Paul, and Hans Binswanger. 1999. "Ethnic Loyalties, State Formation and Conflict." Background paper prepared for Africa in the 21st Century Project. World Bank, Washington, D.C.

Collier, Paul, and Anke Hoeffler. 1998. "On Economic Causes of Civil War." *Oxford Economic Papers* 50: 563–73.

————. 1999. "Loot-Seeking and Justice-Seeking in Civil War." World Bank, Development Research Group, Washington, D.C.

Collier, Paul, and Sanjay Pradhan. 1998. "Economic Aspects of the Ugandan Transition to Peace." In H. B. Hansen and M. Twaddle, eds., *Developing Uganda.* London: James Curry.

Collier, Paul, Ibrahim Elbadawi, and Nicholas Sambanis. 2000a. "How Much War Will We See? Estimating the Likelihood and Amount of War in 161 Countries, 1960–1998." World Bank, Washington, D.C.

————. 2000b. "Why Are There So Many Civil Wars in Africa?" World Bank, Development Research Group, Washington, D.C.

Collier, Paul, Anke Hoeffler, and Catherine Pattillo. 1999. "Flight Capital As a Portfolio Choice." Policy Research Working Paper 2066. World Bank, Washington, D.C.

Collier, Paul, Anke Hoeffler, and Mans Soderbom. 1999. " On the Duration of Civil War and Post-War Peace." University of Oxford, Centre for the Study of African Economies, Oxford.

Doyle, Michael W., and Nicholas Sambanis. 1999. "Peacebuilding: A Theoretical and Quantitative Analysis." Working paper. Princeton University, Woodrow Wilson School of Public and International Affairs, Center of International Studies, Princeton, N.J.

Elbadawi, Ibrahim. 1999. "The Tragedy of the Civil War in the Sudan and Its Economic Consequences." In Karl Wohlmuth, ed., *Empowerment and Economic Development in Africa: African Development Perspectives Yearbook.* New Brunswick, N.J. and London: Transactions Publishers.

Gurr, Ted R., and Keith Jaggers. 1999. Polity 98 Project. *http://www.bsos.umd.edu/cidcm/polity/*

Johnson, R.W., and Lawrence Schlemmer, eds. 1996. *Launching Democracy in South Africa.* New Haven, Conn.: Yale University Press.

Lancaster, Carol. 1999. *Aid to Africa.* Chicago, Ill.: University of Chicago Press.

Legum, Colin. 1999. *Africa since Independence.* Bloomington: University of Indiana Press.

Lewis, W. Arthur. 1965. *Politics in West Africa.* Toronto: Oxford University Press.

Lijphart, Arend. 1977. *Democracy in Plural Societies: A Comparative Exploration.* New Haven, Conn.: Yale University Press.

Mamdani, Mahmood. 1996. *Citizen and Subject.* Princeton, N.J.: Princeton University Press.

Mkandawire, Thandika, and Charles Soludo. 1999. *Our Continent, Our Future.* Trenton, N.J.: Africa World Press.

Nohlen, Dieter, Michael Krennerich, and Bernard Thibaut. 1999. *Elections in Africa: A Data Handbook.* New York: Oxford University Press.

Rodrik, Dani. 1998. "Globalisation, Social Conflict and Economic Growth." *World Economy* 21: 143–58.

Sen, Amartya. 1994. "Economic Regress: Concepts and Features." In Michael Bruno and Boris Pleskovic, eds., *Proceedings of the World Bank Annual Conference on Development Economics 1993.* Washington, D.C.: World Bank.

Soyinka, Wole. 1999. *The Burden of Memory and the Muse of Forgiveness.* New York: Oxford University Press.

Tilly, Charles. 1993. *European Revolutions, 1492–1992.* Cambridge, Mass.: Blackwell.

Young, Crawford. 1994. *The African Colonial State in Comparative Perspective.* New Haven, Conn.: Yale University Press.

Zartman, I. William, ed. 1995. *Collapsed States: The Disintegration and Restoration of Legitimate Authority.* Boulder, Colo.: Lynne Reinner Publishers.

Chapter 3

Alesina, Alberto, and Dani Rodrik. 1994. "Distributive Politics and Economic Growth." *Quarterly Journal of Economics* 109 (2): 465–90.

Ali, A.G. Ali. 1999. "Inequality and Development in Africa: Issues for the 21st Century." Background paper prepared for Africa in the 21st Century Project. World Bank, Washington, D.C.

Ali, A.G. Ali, and Ibrahim Elbadawi. 1999. "Inequality and the Dynamics of Poverty and Growth." CID Working Paper 32. Harvard University, Center for International Development, Cambridge, Mass.

Appleton, Simon. 1999. "Education and Health at the Household Level in Sub-Saharan Africa." CID Working Paper 33. Harvard University, Center for International Development, Cambridge, Mass.

Castro-Leal, Florencia, Julia Dayton, Lionel Demery, and Kalpana Mehra. 1999. "Public Social Spending in Africa: Do the Poor Benefit?" *The World Bank Research Observer* 14 (February): 49–72.

Deininger, Klaus, and Lyn Squire. 1996. "A New Data Set Measuring Income Inequality." *The World Bank Economic Review* 10 (September): 565–91.

———. 1998. "New Ways of Looking at Old Issues: Inequality and Growth." *Journal of Development Economics* 57: 259–87.

Demery, Lionel. 1999. "Poverty in Africa: Capability, Opportunity and Security." Background paper prepared for Africa in the 21st Century Project. World Bank, Washington, D.C.

Demery, Lionel, and Micheael Walton. 1998. "Are Poverty Reduction and Other Twenty-first Century Social Goals Attainable?" World Bank, Washington, D.C.

Dercon, Stefan. 1998. "The Urban Labour Market during Structural Adjustment: Ethiopia 1990–1997." Working Paper WPS/98-9. University of Oxford, Centre for the Study of African Economies, Oxford.

Ghana Statistical Service. 1999. "Ghana Living Standards Survey." Accra.

Grootaert, Christiaan, Ravi Kanbur, and Gi-Taik Oh. 1997. "The Dynamics of Welfare Gains and Losses: An African Case Study." *Journal of Development Studies* 33 (5): 635–57.

Sahn, David E., Paul A. Dorosh, and Stephen D. Younger. 1999. "A Reply to De Maio, Stewart, and van der Hoeven." *World Development* 27 (3): 471–75.

World Bank. 1999a. *African Development Indicators 1998–99.* Washington, D.C.

———. 1999b. "Poverty Trends and Voices of the Poor." Poverty Reduction and Economic Management Network, Washington, D.C.

Chapter 4

Ainsworth, Martha. 1996. "The Impact of Women's Schooling on Fertility and Contraceptive Use: A Study of Fourteen Sub-Saharan Countries." *The World Bank Economic Review* 10 (January): 85–122.

Feachem, Richard, and Dean Jamison, eds. 1991. *Disease and Mortality in Sub-Saharan Africa.* Washington, D.C.: World Bank.

Fine, Jeffrey, Samuel Wangwe, Marcelina Chijoriga, Mick Foster, Richard Hooper, and Ibrahim Kaduma. 1999. "The Tanzania Education Sector Development Programme: Appraisal of Financial Planning and Management Review Team Final Report." African Economic Research Consortium, Nairobi, Kenya.

Frigenti, Laura, Alberto Hasth, and Rumana Haque. 1998. *Local Solutions to Regional Problems.* Washington, D.C.: World Bank.

Gallup, John L., and Jeffrey D. Sachs. 1998. "The Economic Burden of Malaria." Harvard University, Center for International Development, Cambridge, Mass.

Knight, John B., and R.H. Sabot. 1990. *Education, Productivity and Inequality: The East African Natural Experiment.* New York: Oxford University Press.

Leighton, C., and R. Foster. 1993. *Economic Impacts of Malaria in Kenya and Niger.* Bethesda, Md.: Abt Associates.

Mingat, Alain, and Bruno Suchaut. Forthcoming. "Une analyse economique comparative des systemes educatifs Africains." Universite de Bourgogne, Institut de Recherche sur l'Economie de l'Education, Dijon Cedex, France.

NRC (National Research Council). 1993. *Population Dynamics of Sub-Saharan Africa.* Washington, D.C.

OECD (Organisation for Economic Co-operation and Development). 1996. *Shaping the 21st Century: The Contribution of Development Co-operation.* Paris.

Peters, David H. 1999. *Health Expenditures, Services, and Outcomes in Africa.* Washington, D.C.: World Bank.

Psacharopoulos, George. 1994. "Returns to Investment in Education: A Global Update." *World Development* 22 (9): 1325–43.

SACMEQ (Southern Africa Consortium for Monitoring Educational Quality). 1998. "The Quality of Education: Some Policy Questions Based on a Survey." International Institute of Education Planning, Paris.

Shepard, D.S., M.B. Ettling, U. Brinkmann, and R. Sauerborn. 1991. "The Economic Cost of Malaria in Africa." *Tropical Medicine and Parasitology* 42 (3): 199–203.

Strauss, John. 2000. Personal communication. Michigan State University, Department of Economics, East Lansing, Mich.

Strauss, John, and Duncan Thomas. 1988. In Hollis Chenery and T.N. Srinivasan, eds., *Handbook of Development Economics.* vol. 3b. Amsterdam: North-Holland.

UN (United Nations). 1987. "Education and Fertility." In *Fertility Behaviour in the Context of Development: Evidence from the World Fertility Survey.* New York.

———. 1999. *World Population Prospects 1999.* New York.

UN ACC/SCN (United Nations Administrative Committee on Coordination/Sub-Committee on Nutrition). 1997. *Third Report on the World Nutrition Situation.* Geneva.

UNAIDS (Joint United Nations Programme on HIV/AIDS). 1998. *AIDS Epidemic Update: December 1998*. Geneva.

UNESCO (United Nations Educational, Scientific, and Cultural Organization). 1998. *World Education Report 1998*. Paris.

———. Various years. *Statistical Yearbook*. Paris.

UNHCR (United Nations High Commissioner on Refugees). 1998. "UNHCR by Numbers." *http://www.unhcr.ch/un&ref/numbers/table1.htm*

UNICEF (United Nations Children's Fund). 1996. *The Progress of Nations*. New York.

van der Gaag, Jacques, and Wim Vijverberg. 1987. "Wage Determinants in Côte d'Ivoire." Living Standards Measurement Study Working Paper 33. World Bank, Washington, D.C.

WHO (World Health Organization). 1999. *World Health Report 1999*. Geneva.

World Bank. 1994. *Better Health in Africa*. Washington, D.C.

———. 1995. *Priorities and Strategies for Education*. Washington, D.C.

———. 1997. *Health, Nutrition, and Population Sector Strategy*. Human Development Network. Washington, D.C.

———. 1999a. "Dynamic Risk Management and the Poor: Developing a Social Protection Strategy for Africa." Washington, D.C.

———. 1999b. *Intensifying Action Against HIV/AIDS in Africa: Responding to a Development Crisis*. Africa Region, Washington, D.C.

———. 1999c. "Knowledge and Finance for Education: Sector Assistance Strategy." Africa Region, Washington, D.C.

———. 1999d. "Population and the World Bank: Adapting to Change." Health, Nutrition, and Population Series. Human Development Network, Washington, D.C.

Chapter 5

Adam, Lishan. 1998. "The Dynamics of African Policy and Regulatory Environment in Information and Communications Sector." Paper presented at Commsphere Africa 1998, July.

Adam, Lishan, and Karima Bounemra Ben Soltane. 1999. "Information and Communication Technologies: A Boom or Hurdle to Africa?" Background paper prepared for Africa in the 21st Century Project. World Bank, Washington, D.C.

ADB (African Development Bank). 1999. *African Development Report 1999: Infrastructure Development in Africa*. New York: Oxford University Press.

Amjadi, Azita, and Alexander J. Yeats. 1995. "Have Transport Costs Contributed to the Relative Decline of African Exports?" Policy Research Working Paper 1559. World Bank, Washington, D.C.

Aryeetey, Ernest. 1997. "Rural Finance in Africa: Institutional Developments and Access for the Poor." In Michael Bruno and Boris Pleskovic, eds., *Annual World Bank Conference on Development Economics 1996*. Washington D.C.: World Bank.

Aryeetey, Ernest, and Lemma Senbet. 1999. "Essential Financial Market Reforms in Africa." Background paper prepared for Africa in the 21st Century Project. World Bank, Washington, D.C.

Aryeetey, Ernest, and W.F. Steel. 1992. "Incomplete Linkage between Formal and Informal Finance in Ghana." In W.F. Steel, ed., *Financial Deepening in Sub-Saharan Africa: Theory and Innovations*. Industry and Energy Department Working Paper, Industry Series Paper 62. Washington, D.C.: World Bank.

Ayogu, Melvin. 1999. "Addressing Infrastructure Constraints." Background paper prepared for Africa in the 21st Century Project. World Bank, Washington, D.C.

Barwell, Ian. 1996. *Transport and the Village: Findings from African Village-level Travel and Transport Surveys and Related Studies.* World Bank Discussion Paper 344. Washington, D.C.

Besley, Timothy. 1994. "Savings, Credit and Insurance." In Hollis Chenery and T.N. Srinivasan, eds., *Handbook of Development Economics.* Amsterdam: North-Holland.

Bloom, David E., and Jeffrey D. Sachs. 1998. "Geography, Demography and Economic Growth in Africa." *Brookings Papers on Economic Activity 2.* Washington, D.C.: Brookings Institution.

DBSA (Development Bank of Southern Africa). 1998. *Infrastructure: A Foundation for Development— Development Report 1998.* Midrand, South Africa.

Easterly, William, and Ross Levine. 1997. "Africa's Growth Tragedy: Policies and Ethnic Divisions." *Quarterly Journal of Economics* 112: 1203–50.

Gwilliam, Ken, and Zmarak Shalizi. 1999. "Road Funds, User Charges, and Taxes." *The World Bank Research Observer* 14 (2): 159–85.

Hanmer, Lucia, Graham Pyatt, Howard White, and Nicky Pouw. 1997. "Poverty in Sub-Saharan Africa: What Can We Learn from the World Bank's Poverty Assessments?" Institute of Social Studies, The Hague.

Jensen, Michael. 1999. "Policy Strategies for African Information and Communications Infrastructure." Paper presented at African Development Forum 1999. *http://www.un.org/depts/eca/adf*

Lee, K.S., and A. Anas. 1992. "Costs of Deficient Infrastructure: The Case of Nigerian Manufacturing." *Urban Studies* 29 (7): 1071–92.

Limão, Nuno, and Anthony Venables. 1999. "Infrastructure, Geographical Disadvantage and Transport Costs." Policy Research Working Paper 2257. World Bank, Washington, D.C.

Mariki, Wilberforce A. 1999. "African Competitiveness: Comparative Analysis of African Infrastructure." World Bank, Washington, D.C.

Mody, Ashoka, and Kamil Yilmaz. 1994. "Is There Persistence in the Growth of Manufactured Exports? Evidence from Newly Industrializing Countries." Policy Research Paper 1276. World Bank, Washington, D.C.

Nissanke, Machiko, and Ernest Aryeetey 1998. *Financial Integration and Development: Liberalization and Reform in Sub-Saharan Africa.* London and New York: Routledge.

Okigbo, Charles. 1999. *Communication and Poverty: The Challenge of Social Change in Africa.* Proceedings of the international conference on Connecting Knowledge in Communications, 14–17 April, Montreal, Canada.

Oshikoya, T.W., A. Jerome, M.N. Hussain, and K. Mlambo. 1999. "Closing the Infrastructure Deficit." Background paper prepared for Africa in the 21st Century Project. World Bank, Washington, D.C.

Popiel, P.A. 1994. *Financial Systems in Sub-Saharan Africa: A Comparative Study.* World Bank Discussion Paper 260. Washington, D.C.

Robinson, Marguerite S. Forthcoming. *The Microfinance Revolution: Sustainable Finance for the Poor.* World Bank.

Senbet, L.W. 1997. "The Development of Capital Markets in Africa: Challenges and Prospects." Paper presented at the sixth session of the Conference of African Ministers of Finance and the Meeting of Intergovernmental Group of Experts, 31 March–2 April, Addis Ababa, Ethiopia.

———. 1998. "Global Financial Crisis: Implications for Africa." Plenary synthesis. African Economic Research Consortium, Nairobi, Kenya.

Soyibo, Adedoyin. 1997. "The Informal Financial Sector in Nigeria: Characteristics and Relationship with the Formal Sector." *Development Policy Review* 15: 5–22.

Sparrow, F.T., and W.A. Masters. 1999. "Modelling Electricity Trade in Southern Africa 1999–2000." Purdue University, West Lafayette, Ind.

Struzak, Ryszard. 1997. "Spectrum Management for Wireless Services of the 21st Century." In *Global Communications Interactive 97*. London: Hanson Cooke.

Sylte, O. 1996. "Review of the Road Sector in Selected COMESA Countries (Eastern and Island)." United Nations Economic Commission for Africa and World Bank, Sub-Saharan Africa Transport Policy Program, Road Maintenance Initiative, Addis Ababa, Ethiopia, and Washington, D.C.

UNCTAD (United Nations Conference on Trade and Development). 1999. "African Transport Infrastructure, Trade and Competitiveness." Document TD/B/46/10. Geneva.

WEF and HIID (World Economic Forum and Harvard Institute for International Development). 1998. *The Africa Competitiveness Report 1998*. Geneva: World Economic Forum.

Weiss, J. 1998. "Infrastructure and Economic Development." Background paper prepared for the African Development Bank, Abidjan, Côte d'Ivoire.

Wilton, David. 1999. "Reducing the Cost of Government Finance in a Deregulated Market." Paper prepared for the World Bank Debt and Liquidity Management Workshop, Pretoria, South Africa.

World Bank. 1980. "Issues in Kenyan Agricultural Development." Annex 2 of *Kenya: Growth and Structural Change*. Washington, D.C.

———. 1993. *The East Asian Miracle: Economic Growth and Public Policy*. A Policy Research Report. New York: Oxford University Press

———. 1994a. *Adjustment in Africa: Reforms, Results, and the Road Ahead*. A Policy Research Report. New York: Oxford University Press.

———. 1994b. "Interest Rate Deregulation." Policy Review Note. Washington, D.C.

———. 1994c. *World Development Report 1994: Infrastructure for Development*. New York: Oxford University Press.

———. 1997. "Accelerating Malawi's Growth: Long-term Prospects and Transitional Problems." African Region, Washington, D.C.

———. 1999. *World Development Indicators 1999*. Washington, D.C.

Chapter 6

Adachi, T., and R.F. Townsend. 1998. "Overview of the 2KR Japanese Aid Program to Sub-Saharan Africa." World Bank, Washington, D.C.

Adelman, I. 1984. "Beyond Export-led Growth." *World Development* 12 (9): 937–49.

Ahmed, R., and N. Rustagi. 1987. "Marketing and Price Incentives in African and Asian Countries: A Comparison." In D. Elz, ed., *Agricultural Marketing Strategy and Price Policy*. Washington, D.C.: World Bank.

Anderson, J.R., and D.G. Dalrymple. 1999. "The World Bank, the Grant Program, and the CGIAR: A Retrospective Review." OED Working Paper 1. World Bank, Operations Evaluation Department, Washington, D.C.

Anderson, K. 1999. "Agriculture, Developing Countries, and the WTO Millennium Round." Revision of a paper presented at the World Bank conference on

Agriculture and the New Trade Agenda from a Development Perspective, World Trade Organization Secretariat, 1–2 October, Geneva.

Anderson, K., and A. Strutt. 1996. "On Measuring the Environmental Impact of Agricultural Trade Liberalization." In M.E. Bredahl, H. Ballenger, J.C. Dunmore, and T.L. Roe, eds., *Agriculture, Trade and the Environment: Discovering and Measuring the Critical Linkages.* Boulder, Colo.: Westview Press.

Anderson, K., B. Hoekman, and A. Strutt. 1999. "Agriculture and the WTO: Next Steps." Revision of a paper presented at the Second Annual Conference on Global Economic Analysis, 20–22 June, Helnaes, Denmark.

Anthony, K.R.M., B.F. Johnston, W.O. Jones, and V.C. Uchendu. 1979. *Agricultural Change in Tropical Africa.* Ithaca, N.Y.: Cornell University Press.

Aplers, E.A. 1977. "The East African Slave Trade." In Z.A. Konczacki and J.M. Konczacki, eds., *An Economic History of Tropical Africa: Volume One—The Pre-colonial Period.* Totowa, N.J.: Frank Cass.

Asea, P., and C. Reinhart. 1995. "Real Interest Differentials and the Real Exchange Rate: Evidence from Four African Countries." Paper presented at the African Economic Research Consortium Biannual Research Workshop, May, Nairobi, Kenya.

Badiane, O, F. Goletti, M. Kherallah, P. Berry, K. Govindan, P. Gruhn, and M. Mendoza. 1997. *Agricultural Input and Output Marketing Reforms in African Countries.* Washington, D.C.: International Food Policy Research Institute.

Bale, M., and E. Lutz. 1979. "The Effects of Trade Intervention on International Price Instability." *American Journal of Agricultural Economics* 61: 512–16.

Barrett, C.B. 1997. "Food Marketing Liberalization and Trader Entry: Evidence from Madagascar." *World Development* 25 (5): 763–77.

Binswanger, H.P. 1989. "The Policy Response of Agriculture." In S. Fischer and D. de Tray, eds., *Proceedings of the World Bank Annual Conference on Development Economics 1989.* Washington, D.C.: World Bank.

Binswanger, H.P., and K. Deininger. 1997. "Explaining Agricultural and Agrarian Policies in Developing Countries." *Journal of Economic Literature* 35: 1958–2005.

Binswanger, H.P., and E. Lutz. 2000. "Agriculture Trade Barriers, Trade Negotiations, and the Interests of Developing Countries." Paper presented at the Round Table for the United Nations Conference on Trade and Development, February, Bangkok.

Binswanger, H.P., K. Deininger, and G. Feder. 1993. "Power, Distortions, Revolt, and Reform in Agricultural Land Relations." Policy Research Working Paper 1164. World Bank, Washington, D.C.

Blackden, C.M., and C. Bhanu. 1999. *Gender, Growth, and Poverty Reduction: Special Program of Assistance for Africa, 1998 Status Report on Poverty in Sub-Saharan Africa.* World Bank Technical Paper 428. Washington, D.C.

Bloom, D., and J. Sachs. 1998. "Geography, Demography and Economic Growth in Africa." *Brookings Papers on Economic Activity* 2. Washington, D.C.: Brookings Institution.

Bond, M. 1983. "Agricultural Responses to Prices in Sub-Saharan Africa." *IMF Staff Papers* 30: 703–26.

Boserup, E. 1965. *The Conditions of Agricultural Growth: The Economics of Agrarian Change under Population Pressure.* New York: Aldine.

Brenner, R. 1977. "The Origins of Capitalist Development: A Critique of Neo-Smithian Marxism." *New Left Review* 14.

Bruce, J.W., and S.E. Migot-Adholla. 1994. *Searching for Land Tenure Security in Africa*. Dubuque, IA: Kendall Hunt.

Bruce, J.W., S.E. Migot-Adholla, and J. Atherton. 1994. "The Findings and Their Policy Implications: Institutional Adaptation or Replacement?" In J.W. Bruce and S.E. Migot-Adholla, eds., *Searching for Land Tenure Security in Africa*. Dubuque, IA: Kendall Hunt.

Brunetti, A., G. Kisunko, and B. Weder. 1997. "Institutional Obstacles to Doing Business: Region-by-Region Results from a Worldwide Survey of the Private Sector." Policy Research Working Paper 1759. World Bank, Washington, D.C.

————. 1998. "Credibility of Rules and Economic Growth: Evidence from a Worldwide Survey of the Private Sector." *The World Bank Economic Review* 12 (3): 353–84.

Brüntrup, M. 1997. *Agricultural Price Policy and Its Impact on Production, Income, Employment and the Adoption of Innovations: A Farming Systems-Based Analysis of Cotton Policy in Northern Benin*. Frankfurt, Germany: Peter Lang.

Byerlee, D., and P. Gregory. 1999. "Agricultural Biotechnology and Rural Development: Options for the World Bank." Biotechnology Task Force Discussion Paper. World Bank, Washington, D.C.

Cleaver, K. 1997. *Rural Development Strategies for Poverty Reduction and Environmental Protection in Sub-Saharan Africa*. Washington, D.C.: World Bank.

Cleaver, K., and G. Schreiber. 1994. *Reversing the Spiral: The Population, Agriculture and Environment Nexus in Sub-Saharan Africa*. Washington, D.C.: World Bank.

Coetzer, J.A.W., G.R. Thomson, and R.C. Tustin, eds., 1994. *Infectious Diseases of Livestock with Special Reference to Southern Africa*. Cape Town, South Africa: Oxford University Press.

Collier, P. 1998. "Comments on Bloom and Sachs." *Brookings Papers on Economic Activity 2*. Washington, D.C.: Brookings Institution.

Collier, P., and H.P. Binswanger. 1999. "State Reconstruction, Civil Wars and Ethnic Conflicts." Paper presented at the Can Africa Claim the 21st Century? conference, 6–10 July, Abidjan, Côte d'Ivoire.

Collier, P., and J.W. Gunning. 1997. "Explaining African Economic Performance." Working Paper 21. Oxford University, Centre for the Study of African Economies, United Kingdom.

Crosson, P., and J.R. Anderson. 1995. "Achieving a Sustainable Agricultural System in Sub-Saharan Africa." Building Blocks for Africa 2025 Paper 2. World Bank, Africa Region Technical Department and Environmentally Sustainable Development Division, Washington, D.C.

Curto, J.C. 1992. "Historical Demography and the Effects of the Slave Trade in Africa: An Analysis of the Major Quantitative Studies." CDAS Discussion Paper 77. McGill University, Montreal, Canada.

Delgado, C.L. 1992. "Why Domestic Food Prices Matter to Growth Strategies in Semi-Open West African Agriculture." *Journal of African Economies* (1) 3: 446–71.

————. 1996. "Agricultural Transformation: The Key to Broad-Based Growth and Poverty Alleviation in Africa." In B. Ndulu and N. van de Walle, eds., *Agenda for Africa's Economic Renewal*. New Brunswick, N.J.: Transaction Publishers.

————. 1998a. "Africa's Changing Agricultural Development Strategies: Past and Present Paradigm As a Guide to the Future." *The Brown Journal of World Affairs* 5 (1).

————. 1998b. "Sources of Growth in Small-holder Agriculture in Sub-Saharan Africa: The Role of Vertical Integration with Processors of High Value-added

Items." Paper presented at the Inter-Conference Symposium of the International Association of Agricultural Economists, 10–16 August, Badplaas, South Africa.

Delgado, C.L., and C.G. Ranade. 1987. "Technological Change and Agricultural Labor Use." In J.W. Mellor, C.L. Delgado, and M.J. Blackie, eds., *Accelerating Food Production in Sub-Saharan Africa*. Baltimore, Md.: The Johns Hopkins University Press.

Delgado, C.L., J. Hopkins, and V.A. Kelly. 1998. "Agricultural Growth Linkages in Sub-Saharan Africa." Research Report 107. International Food Policy Research Institute, Washington, D.C.

De Wilde, C. 1967. *Experiences with Agricultural Development in Tropical Africa*. vol. 1. Baltimore, Md.: The Johns Hopkins University Press.

Donovan, G. 1996. "Agriculture and Economic Reform in Sub-Saharan Africa." AFTES Working Paper 18. World Bank, Africa Region Technical Department, Washington, D.C.

Donovan, G., and F. Casey. 1998. *Soil Fertility Management in Sub-Saharan Africa*. World Bank Technical Paper 408. Washington, D.C.

Dorward, A., J. Kydd, and C. Poulton, eds. 1998. *Smallholder Cash Crop Production under Market Liberalization: A New Institutional Economics Perspective*. Oxon, U.K.: CABI International.

Drenge, H.E. 1990. "Erosion and Soil Productivity in Africa." *Journal of Soil and Water Conservation* 45 (4): 432–36.

Eicher, C.K. 1999. "Institutions and the African Farmer." Third Distinguished Economist Lecture. International Maize and Wheat Improvement Center, Mexico City.

Elamin, H., and E. Mak. 1997. "Adjustment Programs and Agricultural Incentives in Sudan: A Comparative Study." Research Paper 63. African Economic Research Consortium, Nairobi, Kenya.

Elbadawi, I. 1998. "Real Exchange Rate Policy and Non-Traditional Exports in Developing Countries." Research for Action 46. United Nations University, World Institute for Development Economics Research, Helsinki, Finland.

Evenson, R.E. Forthcoming. "Economic Impact Studies of Agricultural Research and Extension." In *Handbook of Agricultural Economics*.

Fage, J.D. 1977. "Slavery and the Slave Trade in the Context of West African History." In Z.A. Konczacki and J.M. Konczacki, eds., *An Economic History of Tropical Africa: Volume One—The Pre-colonial Period*. Totowa, N.J.: Frank Cass.

FAOSTAT (United Nations Food and Agriculture Organization Statistical Database). 2000. FAO Trade and Production Statistics. *http://apps.fao.org/default.htm*

Gardner, B. 1995. "Policy Reform in Agriculture: An Assessment of the Results of Eight Countries." University of Maryland, College Park.

Geering, W.A., P.L. Roeder, and T. Obi. 1999. "Manual on the Preparation of National Animal Disease Emergency Preparedness Plans." United Nations Food and Agriculture Organization, Rome. *http://www.fao.org/ag/aga/agah/empres/info/other/Manual1.pdf*

Gisselquist, D. 1994. "Import Barriers for Agricultural Inputs." United Nations Development Programme–World Bank Trade Expansion Program Occasional Paper 10. United Nations, New York.

Government of the Republic of Uganda 1998. "Towards a Sector Wide Approach: Developing a Framework for the Modernization of Agriculture in Uganda." Statement to the December 1998 Consultative Group Meeting. Kampala.

Harrison, P. 1987. *The Greening of Africa*. London: Paladin Grafton Books.

Hayami, Y., and J.P. Platteau. 1997. "Resource Endowments and Agricultural Development: Africa vs. Asia." *Serie Recherche (Belgium)* 192: 1–54. Facultes Universitaires Notre-Dame de la Paix, Namur, and Faculte des Sciences Economiiques et Sociales, Cashiers.

Herrmann, R. 1997. "Agricultural Policies, Macroeconomic Policies, and Producer Price Incentives in Developing Countries: Cross-country Results for Major Crops." *Journal of Developing Areas* 31: 203–20.

Hertel, T., K. Anderson, and J.F. Francois. 1999. "Agriculture and Non-agriculture Liberalization in the Millennium Round." Paper presented at the World Bank conference on Agriculture and the New Trade Agenda from a Development Perspective, World Trade Organization Secretariat, 1–2 October, Geneva.

Ingco, M., and R.F. Townsend. 1998. "Experience and Lessons from the Implementation of Uruguay Round Commitments: Policy Options and Challenges for African Countries." Paper presented at the International Workshop on Agricultural Policy of African Countries and Multilateral Trade Negotiations: Challenges and Options, 23–26 November, Harare, Zimbabwe.

Jaffee, S., and J. Morton. 1995. *Marketing Africa's High-Value Foods: Comparative Experiences of an Emergent Private Sector.* Dubuque, IA: Kendall Hunt.

Jayne, T.S., and S. Jones. 1997. "Food Marketing and Pricing Policy in Eastern and Southern Africa: A Survey." *World Development* 25 (9): 1505–27.

Jayne, T.S., M. Mukumbu, J. Duncan, J. Staatz, J. Howard, M. Lundberg, K. Aldridge, B. Nakaponda, J. Ferris, J. Keita, and K. Sanakoua. 1995. "Trends in Real Food Prices in Six-Sub-Saharan African Countries." Policy Synthesis 2. U.S. Agency for International Development, Bureau for Africa, Office of Sustainable Development, Washington, D.C. *http://www.aec.msu.edu/agecon/fs2/polsyn/no2.htm*

Josling, T. 1998. "Agricultural Trade Policy: Completing the Reform." Policy Analyses in International Economics 53. Institute for International Economics, Washington, D.C.

Kamarck, A.M. 1967. *The Economics of African Development.* New York: Praeger.

Karshenas, M. 1998. "Capital Accumulation and Agricultural Surplus in Sub-Saharan Africa and Asia." African Development in a Comparative Perspective Study 1. United Nations Conference on Trade and Development, Geneva.

Killick, T. 1990. "Structure, Development and Adaptation." Research Paper 2. African Economic Research Consortium, Nairobi, Kenya.

Kwanashie, M., I. Ajilima, and A. Garba. 1998. "The Nigerian Economy: Response of Agriculture to Adjustment Policies." Research Paper 78. African Economic Research Consortium, Nairobi, Kenya.

Larson, D., and Y. Mundlak. 1997. "On the Intersectoral Migration of Agricultural Labor." *Economic Development and Cultural Change* 45 (2): 295–319.

Lele, U., R.E. Christiansen, and K. Kadiresan. 1989. "Fertilizer Policy in Africa: Lessons from Development Programs and Adjustment Lending, 1970–1987." MADIA Discussion Paper 5. World Bank, Washington, D.C.

Lipton, M. 1977. *Why Poor People Stay Poor: Urban Bias in World Development.* London: Temple Smith.

———. 1987. "Agriculture and Central Physical Grid Infrastructure." In J.W. Mellor, C.L. Delgado, and M.J. Blackie, eds., *Accelerating Food Production in Sub-Saharan Africa.* Baltimore, Md.: The Johns Hopkins University Press..

———. 1993. "Urban Bias: Of Consequences, Classes and Causality." *Journal of Development Studies* 29: 229–58.

Manor, J. 1999. *The Political Economy of Democratic Decentralization.* A Directions in Development book. Washington, D.C.: World Bank.

McLean, K., G. Kerr, and M. Williams. 1998. "Decentralization and Rural Development: Characterizing Efforts of 19 Countries." Discussion note. World Bank, Washington, D.C.

Meerman, J. 1997. "Reforming Agriculture: The World Bank Goes to Market." World Bank, Operations Evaluation Department, Washington, D.C.

Meillassoux, C. 1981. *Maidens, Meals and Money: Capitalism and the Domestic Community.* New York: Cambridge University Press.

Migot-Adholla, S., P. Hazell, B. Blarel, and F. Place. 1991. "Indigenous Land Rights Systems in Sub-Saharan Africa: A Constraint on Productivity?" *The World Bank Economic Review* 5 (1): 155–57.

Morduch, J. 1999. "The Microfinance Promise." *Journal of Economic Literature* 37: 1569–1614.

Ng, F., and A. Yeats. 1996. "Open Economies Work Better! Did Africa's Protectionist Policies Cause Its Marginalization in World Trade?" Policy Research Working Paper 1636. World Bank, Washington D.C.

———. 1998. "Good Governance and Trade Policy: Are They the Keys to Africa's Global Integration and Growth?" Policy Research Working Paper 2038. World Bank, Washington D.C.

Nikolaus, G., R. Herrmann, and P. Günther. 1996. "Wie beeinflubt eine Spezialisierung der Entwicklungsländer auf Agrarexporte die Armutssituatation?" *Berichte über Landwirtschaft* 74: 298–326.

North, D. 1989. "Institutions and Economic Growth: A Historical Introduction." *World Development* 17 (9): 1319–32.

OAU (Organization of African Unity). 1996. "African Common Position on Food Security and Agricultural Development." Adopted by the Thirty-second Ordinary Session of the Assembly of Heads of State and Government, 8–10 July, Yaounde, Cameroon.

OECD (Organisation for Economic Co-operation and Development). 1997. "Agricultural Policy in OECD Countries: Measurement of Support and Background Information." Paris.

Oldeman, L.R. 1998. "Soil Degradation: A Threat to Food Security?" Report 98/01. International Soil Reference and Information Centre, Wageningen, The Netherlands.

Olomola, A.S. 1998. "Structural Adjustment and Public Expenditure on Agriculture in Nigeria." In T.B. Tshibaka, ed., *Structural Adjustment and Agriculture in West Africa.* Dakar, Senegal: CODESRIA.

Oyejide, T.A. 1986. "The Effects of Trade and Exchange Rate Policies on Agriculture in Nigeria." Research Report 55. International Food Policy Research Institute, Washington, D.C.

———. 1990. "Supply Response in the Context of Structural Adjustment in Sub-Saharan Africa." Research Paper 1. African Economic Research Consortium, Nairobi, Kenya.

Pardey, P.G., J. Roseboom, and N.M. Beintema. 1997. "Investments in African Agricultural Research." *World Development* 25 (3): 409–23.

Parker, A.N. 1995. "Decentralization: The Way Forward for Rural Development?" Policy Research Working Paper 1475. World Bank, Washington, D.C.

Place, F., and P. Hazell. 1993. "Productivity Effects of Indigenous Land Tenure Systems in Sub-Saharan Africa." *American Journal of Agricultural Economics* 75 (1): 10–19.

Pursell, G., and M. Diop. 1998. *Cotton Policies in Francophone Africa.* Washington, D.C.: World Bank.

Quisumbing, A., L.R. Brown, H.S. Feldstein, L. Haddad, and C. Peña. 1995. *Women: The Key to Food Security.* Washington, D.C.: International Food Policy Research Institute.

Reardon, T., K. Stamoulis, M.E. Cruz, A. Balisacan, J. Berdegue, and B. Banks. 1998. "The Importance and Nature of Rural Nonfarm Income in Developing Countries, with Policy Implications for Agriculturists." In *The State of Food and Agriculture.* Rome: United Nations Food and Agriculture Organization.

Rueschemeyer, D., E.H. Stephens, and J.D. Stephens. 1992. *Capitalist Development and Democracy.* Chicago, Ill.: University of Chicago Press.

Ruthenberg, H. 1980. *Farming Systems in the Tropics.* New York: Oxford University Press.

Saito, K. 1992. "Raising the Productivity of Women Farmers in Sub-Saharan Africa: Overview Report." World Bank, Population and Human Resources Department, Women in Development Division, Washington, D.C.

Saito, K., H. Mekonnen, and D. Spurling. 1994. *Raising the Productivity of Women Farmers in Sub-Saharan Africa.* World Bank Discussion Paper 230. Washington, D.C.

Scherr, S.J. 1999. "Soil Degradation: A Threat to Developing-Country Food Security by 2020?" Food, Agriculture and the Environment Discussion Paper 27. International Food Policy Research Institute, Washington D.C.

Schiff, M., and C. Montenegro. 1997. "Aggregate Agricultural Supply Response in Developing Countries: A Survey of Selected Issues." *Economic Development and Cultural Change* 45: 393–410.

Schiff, M., and A. Valdés. 1992. *The Plundering of Agriculture in Developing Countries.* Washington, D.C.: World Bank.

Sharma, N.P., T. Damhaug, E. Gilgan-Hunt, D. Grey, V. Okaru, and D. Rothberg. 1996. *African Water Resources: Challenges and Opportunities for Sustainable Development.* World Bank Technical Paper 331. Washington, D.C.

Strasberg, P.J., T.S. Jayne, T. Yamano, J. Nyoro, D. Karanja, and J. Strauss. 1999. "Effects of Agricultural Commercialization on Food Crop Input Use and Productivity in Kenya." Policy Synthesis 41. U.S. Agency for International Development, Bureau for Africa, Office of Sustainable Development, Washington, D.C.

Thirtle, C., D. Hadley, and R. Townsend. 1995. "Policy Induced Innovation in Sub-Saharan African Agriculture: A Multilateral Malmquist Productivity Index Approach." *Development Policy Review* 13 (4): 323–48.

Tilly, C. 1990. *Coercion, Capital, and European States, A.D. 990–1990.* Cambridge: Basil Blackwell.

Tobin, R. 1996. "Pest Management, the Environment, and Japanese Foreign Assistance." *Food Policy* 21 (2): 211–28.

Townsend, R.F. 1999. *Agricultural Incentives in Sub-Saharan Africa: Policy Challenges.* World Bank Technical Paper 444. Washington, D.C.

Tshibaka, T.B. 1986. "The Effects of Trade and Exchange Rate Policies on Agriculture in Zaire." Research Report 56. International Food Policy Research Institute, Washington, D.C.

———. 1997. "Effects of Domestic Economic Policies and External Factors on Export Prices and Their Implications for Output and Income in Cameroon." African Economic Research Consortium, Nairobi, Kenya.

Udry, C. 1998. "Comments on Bloom and Sachs." *Brookings Papers on Economic Activity 2.* Washington, D.C.: Brookings Institution.

UNAIDS (Joint United Nations Programme on HIV/AIDS). 1998. *AIDS Epidemic Update: December 1998.* Geneva.

UNCTAD (United Nations Conference on Trade and Development). 1998. *Trade and Development Report 1998.* Geneva.

Valdés, A., and J. Zietz. 1995. "Distortions in World Food Markets in the Wake of GATT: Evidence and Policy Implications." *World Development* 23 (6): 913–26.

Vogel, S.J., 1994. "Structural Changes in Agriculture: Production Linkages and Agricultural Demand-Led Industrialisation." *Oxford Economic Papers* 46: 136–56.

Vogel, S.W., and H. Heyne. 1996. "Rinderpest in South Africa—100 Years Ago." *Journal of the South African Veterinary Association* 67 (4): 164–70.

Voortman, R.L., B.G.J.S. Sonneveld, and M.A. Keyzer. 1998. "African Land Ecology: Opportunities and Constraints for Development." African Economic Research Consortium, Nairobi, Kenya.

Vyas, V.S., and D. Casley. 1988. "Stimulating Agricultural Growth and Rural Development in Sub-Saharan Africa." Policy Research Working Paper 15. World Bank, Washington, D.C.

World Bank. 1974. *Land Reform.* Development Series. Washington, D.C.

———. 1981. *Accelerated Development in Sub-Saharan Africa.* Washington, D.C.

———. 1994. *Adjustment in Africa: Reforms, Results, and the Road Ahead.* A Policy Research Report. Washington, D.C.

———. 1996. *Toward Environmentally Sustainable Development in Sub-Saharan Africa.* A Development in Practice book. Washington, D.C.

———. 1997a. *Rural Development: From Vision to Action.* A Sector Strategy Paper. Washington, D.C.

———. 1997b. *World Development Report: The State in A Changing World.* New York: Oxford University Press.

———. 1998. *Assessing Aid: What Works, What Doesn't, and Why.* A Policy Research Report. New York: Oxford University Press.

———. 1999a. *African Development Indicators 1999.* Washington, D.C.

———. 1999b. *Intensifying Action against HIV/AIDS in Africa: Responding to a Development Crisis.* Africa Region, Washington, D.C.

———. 1999c. *World Development Indicators 1999.* Washington, D.C.

Zwart, A., and D. Blandford. 1989. "Market Intervention and International Price Stability." *American Journal of Agricultural Economics* 71 (2): 379–86.

Chapter 7

Agosin, M. 1997. "Export Performance in Chile: Lessons for Africa." Working paper 144. World Institute for Development Economics Research, Helsinki, Finland. Forthcoming in G.K. Helleiner, ed., *Non-Traditional Exports in Sub-Saharan Africa: Issues and Experiences.*

Aron, J., and I. Elbadawi. Forthcoming. "Reflections on the South African Crisis of 1996 and Policy Consequences." In F. Mwega and N. Ndung'u, eds., *Macroeconomic Policies and Exchange Rate Management in African Economies,* San Francisco, Calif.: International Center for Economic Growth.

Biggs, T., M. Miller, C. Otto, and G. Tyler. 1996. *Africa Can Compete! Export Opportunities and Challenges for Garments and Home Products in the European Market.* World Bank Discussion Paper 300. Washington, D.C.

Bigsten, A., P. Collier, S. Dercon, M. Fafchamps, B. Gauthier, J. Gunning, R. Oostendorp, C. Pattillo, M. Soderbom, F. Teal, and A. Zeufack. 1998. "Exports of African Manufactures: Macro Policy and Firm

Behaviour." *Journal of International Development* 8 (1): 53–71.

Bloom, D., and J. Sachs. 1998. "Geography, Demography and Economic Growth in Africa." *Brookings Papers on Economic Activity 2*. Washington, D.C.: Brookings Institution.

Bourguignon, F. 1999. "Crime, Violence, and Inequitable Development." Paper presented at the Eleventh Annual World Bank Conference on Development Economics, April, Washington, D.C.

Collier, P. 1997. "Globalization: What Should Be the African Policy Response?" University of Oxford, Centre for the Study of African Economies, Oxford.

———. 1998. "Globalization: Implications for African Economic Management." World Bank, Washington, D.C.

Collier, P., and J.W. Gunning. 1999. "Explaining African Economic Performance." *Journal of Economic Literature* 37 (March): 64–111.

Collier, P., A. Hoeffler, and C. Pattillo. 1999. "Flight Capital As a Portfolio Choice." Policy Research Working Paper 2066. World Bank, Washington, D.C.

Easterly, W., M. Kremer, L. Pritchett, and L. Summers. 1993. "Good Policy or Good Luck? Country Growth Performance and Temporary Shocks." *Journal of Monetary Economics* 32: 459–83.

Elbadawi, I. 1998. "Real Exchange Rate Policy and Non-Traditional Exports in Developing Counties." Research for Action 46. World Institute for Development Economics Research, Helsinki, Finland. Forthcoming in G.K. Helleiner, ed., *Non-Traditional Exports in Sub-Saharan Africa: Issues and Experiences*.

———. 1999a. "Can Africa Export Manufactures? The Role of Endowments, Exchange Rates, and Transaction Costs." Policy Research Working Paper 2120. World Bank, Washington, D.C.

———. 1999b. "The Impact of Regional Trade/Monetary Schemes in Intra–sub-Saharan Africa Trade." In A. Oyejide, I. Elbadawi, and P. Collier, eds., *Regional Integration and Trade Liberalization in Sub-Saharan Africa*. London: Macmillan.

Elbadawi, I., and G.K. Helleiner. Forthcoming. "African Development in the Context of New World Trade and Financial Regimes: The Role of the WTO and Its Relationship to the World Bank and the IMF." In T.A. Oyejide, ed., *Africa and the New World Trading System*. London: Routledge.

Elbadawi, I., and B.J. Ndulu. 1996. "Long Run Development and Sustainable Growth in Sub-Saharan Africa." In M. Lundhal and B.J. Ndulu, eds., *New Directions in Development Economics*. London: Routledge.

Elbadawi, I., and C.C. Soludo. 1999. "Our Destiny in Our Hands: Achieving Manufactures Competitiveness Despite the Constraints of Geography in Africa." Background paper prepared for Africa in the 21st Century Project. World Bank, Washington DC

Finger, M.J., and P. Schuler. 1999. "Implementation of Uruguay Round Commitments: The Development Challenge." Policy Research Working Paper 2215. World Bank, Washington, D.C.

Guillamont, P., S. Guillamont-Jeanneney, and J.F. Brun. 1999. "How Instability Lowers African Economic Growth." *Journal of African Economies* 5 (1): 87–107.

Gunning, J.W. 1998. "Comments on 'Africa and the Global Economy.'" *Journal of African Economies* 7 (June): 162–65.

Helleiner, G.K. Forthcoming. *Non-Traditional Exports in Sub-Saharan Africa: Issues and Experiences*.

Hernandez, L., and K. Schmidt-Hebbel. 1999. "Capital Controls in Chile: Effective? Efficient? Endurable?" Paper presented at a World Bank workshop on Capital Flows, Financial Crises, and Policies, 15–16 April, Washington, D.C.

Kasekende, L., N. Ng'eno, and N Lipumba. 1999. "Regional Integration and Economic Liberalization in Eastern and Southern Africa." In A. Oyejide, I. Elbadawi, and S. Yeo, eds., *Regional Integration and Trade Liberalization in Sub-Saharan Africa*. vol. 3. London: Macmillan.

McCarthy, C. 1999. "Regional Integration in Sub-Saharan Africa: Past, Present and Future." In A. Oyejide, B. Ndulu, and D. Greenaway, eds., *Regional Integration and Trade Liberalization in Sub-Saharan Africa*. vol. 4. London: Macmillan.

Mengistae, T., and C. Pattillo. 1999. "Foreign Trade and Productivity in Africa." Background paper prepared for Africa in the 21st Century Project. World Bank, Washington, D.C.

Mistry, P.S. 1995. *Multilateral Development Banks: An Assessment of Their Financial Structures, Policies and Practices*. The Hague: FONDAD.

Njinkeu, D. 2000. "Introductory Notes to the ECA/APIC Electronic Round Table." United Nations Economic Commission for Africa, Addis Ababa, Ethiopia.

Oyejide, A. 1999. "Trade Liberalisation and Regional Integration in a Globalising World Economy." Background paper prepared for Africa in the 21st Century Project. World Bank, Washington, D.C.

Oyejide A., I. Elbadawi, and P. Collier, eds. 1999. *Regional Integration and Trade Liberalization in Sub-Sahara Africa*. vol. 1. London: Macmillan.

Oyejide A., I. Elbadawi, and S. Yeo, eds. 1999. *Regional Integration and Trade Liberalization in Sub-Saharan Africa*. vol. 3. London: Macmillan.

Oyejide, A., B. Ndulu, and D. Greenaway, eds. 1999. *Regional Integration and Trade Liberalization in Sub-Saharan Africa*. vol. 4. London: Macmillan.

Oyejide A., B. Ndulu, and J. Gunning, eds. 1999. *Regional Integration and Trade Liberalization in Sub-Saharan Africa*. vol. 2. London: Macmillan.

Rodrik, D. 1994. "Getting Interventions Right: How South Korea and Taiwan Grew Rich." NBER Working Paper 4964. National Bureau for Economic Research, Cambridge, Mass.

———. 1995. "Trade Strategy, Exports and Investment: Another Look at East Asia." Discussion paper. Institute of Policy Reform, Washington D.C.

———. 1996. "Understanding Economic Policy Reform." *Journal of Economic Literature* 34 (March): 9–41.

———. 1997. "Trade Policy and Economic Performance in Sub-Saharan Africa." Paper prepared for the Division of International Cooperation of the Ministry for Foreign Affairs, Sweden.

Soludo, C.C. 1998a. "Africa: Industrialization Strategy in the Context of Globalization." In E. Iqbal and M.S. Khan, eds., *Trade Reforms and Regional Integration in Africa*. Washington, D.C.: International Monetary Fund.

———. 1998b. "Trade Policy Reforms and Supply Responses in Africa." Discussion paper 6. United Nations Conference on Trade and Development, Geneva.

———. 1999. "Human Capital Development and Endogenization of Geography As Framework for Africa's Competitiveness." Paper presented at the Forum on the Future Competitiveness of African Economies, 3–5 March, Dakar.

UNIDO (United Nations Industrial Development Organization). 1996. *The Globalization of Industry: Implications for Developing Countries beyond 2000*. Vienna.

Williamson, J. 1995. "Exchange Rate Policy and Development Strategy." Paper presented at the research workshop of the African Economic Research Consortium, 2–8 December, Johannesburg, South Africa.

———. 1997. "The Washington Consensus Revisited." In L. Emmerij, ed., *Economic and Social Development in the XXI Century.* Baltimore, Md.: The Johns Hopkins University Press.

Wood, A. 1997. "Openness and Wage Inequality in Developing Countries: The Latin American Challenge to East Asian Conventional Wisdom." *The World Bank Economic Review* 11: 33–57.

Wood, A., and K. Berge. 1997. "Exporting Manufactures: Human Resources, Natural Resources and Trade Policy." *Journal of Development Studies* 34: 35–59.

Wood, A., and J. Mayer. 1998. "Africa's Export Structure in a Comparative Perspective." United Nations Conference on Trade and Development, Geneva.

World Bank. 1998. "Africa Can Compete! A Framework for World Bank Group Support for Private Sector Development in Sub-Saharan Africa." Africa Region, Private Sector Finance Group, Washington, D.C.

———. 1999a. "A Strategy for Exchange Rate Management in Malawi." Africa Region, Washington, D.C.

———. 1999b. *World Development Report 1999/2000: Entering the 21st Century.* New York: Oxford University Press.

Chapter 8

Bethelemy, J.C., and A. Vourc'h. 1994. *Debt Relief and Growth.* Paris: Organisation for Economic Co-operation and Development.

Bloom, D.E., and J.D. Sachs. 1998. "Geography, Demography and Economic Growth in Africa." *Brookings Papers on Economic Activity 2.* Washington, D.C.: Brookings Institution.

Burnside, C., and D. Dollar. 1997. "Aid, Policies, and Growth." Policy Research Working Paper 1777. World Bank, Washington, D.C.

Center for International Development. 1999. "Implementing Debt Relief for the HIPCs." Harvard University, Cambridge, Mass.

Collier, P., and D. Dollar. 1999. "Aid Allocation and Poverty Reduction." Policy Research Working Paper 2041. World Bank, Washington, D.C.

Dornbusch, R. 1991. "Policies to Move from Stabilization to Growth." In by S. Fischer, D. de Tray, and S. Shah, eds., *Proceedings of the World Bank Annual Conference on Development Economics 1990.* Washington, D.C.: World Bank.

Easterly, W. 1997. "The Ghosts of Financing Gap: How the Harrod-Domar Growth Model Still Haunts Development Economics." Policy Research Working Paper 1807. World Bank, Washington, D.C.

Elbadawi, I.A. 1996. "Consolidating Macroeconomic Stabilization and Restoring Growth in Africa." In B. Ndulu and N. van de Walle, eds., *Policy Perspectives on African Development Strategies.* Washington, D.C.: Overseas Development Council.

Elbadawi, I.A., B.J. Ndulu, and N. Ndung'u. 1996. "Debt Overhang and Economic Growth in Sub-Saharan Africa." In Z. Iqbal and R. Kanbur, eds., *External Finance for Low-Income Countries.* Washington, D.C.: International Monetary Fund.

Emblad, S., and G. Hervio. 2000. "Conditionality Revisited: A New Approach in Burkina Faso." PREMnote 35. World Bank, Development Economics Vice Presidency and Policy Reduction and Economic Management Network, Washington, D.C.

Jaycox, E. 1992. *The Challenges of African Development.* Washington, D.C.: World Bank.

Kanbur, R., T. Sandler, and K.M. Morrisson. 1999. *The Future of Development Assistance: Common Pools and International Public Goods.* Overseas Development Council Policy Essay 25. Baltimore, Md.: The Johns Hopkins University Press.

Lancaster, C. 1999. "Foreign Aid in Africa: Challenges and Opportunities in the XXIst Century." Background paper prepared for the Africa in the 21st Century project. World Bank, Washington, D.C.

Mkandawire, T., and C. Soludo. 1999. *Our Continent, Our Future: African Perspectives on Structural Adjustment.* Trenton, N.J.: Africa World Press.

O'Connell, S., and C. Soludo. Forthcoming. "Aid Intensity in Africa." *World Development.*

OED (Operations Evaluation Department). 1998. *The Special Program of Assistance for Africa (SPA): An Independent Evaluation.* Washington, D.C.: World Bank.

Sachs, J. 1996. "Growth in Africa: It Can be Done." *The Economist,* 29 June.

Serven, L. 1996. "Irreversibility, Uncertainty and Private Investment: Analytical Issues and Some Lessons for Africa." Paper presented at the African Economic Research Consortium research workshop, May, Nairobi, Kenya.

Soludo, C.C. 1998a. "Africa: Economic Performance and Policy Stance Indices." Discussion paper ESPD/98/02.

United Nations Economic Commission for Africa, Addis Ababa, Ethiopia.

————. 1998b. "Africa: Industrialization Strategy in the Context of Globalization." In Z. Iqbal and M.S. Khan, eds., *Trade Reform and Regional Integration in Africa.* Washington, D.C.: International Monetary Fund.

————. 1999a. "Human Capital Development and Endogenization of Geography As Framework for Africa's Competitiveness."

————. 1999b. "Towards A Regional Approach to Africa's Infrastructure Crisis." Research report. United Nations Conference on Trade and Development, Geneva.

Summers, Lawrence H. 2000. "A New Framework for Multilateral Development Policy." Remarks to the Council on Foreign Relations, 20 March, New York.

World Bank. 1998. "Higher Impact Adjustment Lending in Sub-Saharan Africa: An Update." Africa Region, Chief Economist's Office, Washington, D.C.

————. 1999. "Special Program of Assistance—Phase Five: Towards New Aid Relationships." Washington, D.C.